The Wineland Millennium

Páll Bergþórsson

THE WINELAND MILLENNIUM

Saga and Evidence

Mál og menning
Reykjavík 2000

All citations are translated by Anna Yates except citations from the following:

P. 56 and pp. 183–184 King's Mirror. Translated by Laurence M. Larson. American-Scandinavian Foundation 1917.

P. 134 Sturlunga Saga. Translated by Julia McGrew. Twayne Publishers 1970–1974

Pp. 116–117 Book of Icelanders / Book of Settlements, in The North Atlantic Saga. Translated by Gwyn Jones. Oxford University Press 1986.

P. 141 Saga of the People of Vatnsdal. Translated by Andrew Wawn. The Complete Sagas of Icelanders. Leifur Eiríksson Publishing 1997.

P. 152 and p. 161 Grágás. Translated by Andrew Dennis, Peter Foote, Richard Perkins. University of Manitoba Press 1980.

Eirik the Red's Saga and The Saga of the Greenlanders are translated by Keneva Kunz.

This book is published with support from the Millennium Commission of Iceland

Cover design: Erlingur Páll Ingvarsson
Maps: Jean-Pierre Biard
Layout: Mál og menning
Printing: Prentsmiðjan Oddi hf.

ISBN 9979-3-2035-4

Table of Contents

FOREWORD

by

The President of Iceland
Ólafur Ragnar Grímsson

The Icelanders have neither palaces nor triumphal arches dating from the early settlement, no monuments paying tribute to vanished times. Our national treasures are medieval manuscripts, worn thin by the hands of generations which have sought strength and entertainment from reading the noble texts.

Medieval Icelandic literature has a wealth of themes and forms. Its greatest achievement is the Sagas of Icelanders, accounts set in the early days of the settlement. They portray people's lives and fates so masterfully that the sagas rank with the leading works of world literature.

The Sagas of Icelanders have been the foundation of Icelandic culture, forged the nation's identity and inspired people to bold deeds in times of adversity. In an enchanting way they also mark the start of the recorded history of North America, through the accounts given in the Vínland Sagas – the Saga of Eirik the Red and the Saga of the Greenlanders – which recount the extraordinary navigational achievements of Leif Eiriksson the Lucky, Thorfinn Karlsefni and Gudrid Thorbjarnardottir: the first European attempts to establish a settlement in the vast new continent of America.

Páll Bergþórsson brilliantly applies his knowledge and experience from extensive studies of climatology, oceanic currents and the natural environment to draw well-argued conclusions from these ancient texts, thereby shedding light on the sailings and discoveries of Icelandic seafarers a thousand years ago.

The publication of Páll Bergþórsson's remarkable studies in English is a welcome initiative, giving the international academic community and interested readers the opportunity to discuss and judge them at first hand.

I sincerely hope that this book will form an important part of the extensive dialogue now taking place about the collective heritage of the Icelanders and the people of North America, a heritage which preserves one of the greatest achievements of navigation and discovery in the history of humankind.

INTRODUCTION

> After that they saw the sun and could take their bearings. Hoisting the sail, they sailed for the rest of the day [*dægur*] before sighting land. They speculated among themselves as to what land this would be.

In these simple words, an Icelandic saga tells of that extraordinary event that took place a thousand years ago in the history of geographical knowledge, when the Icelander Bjarni Herjolfsson set eyes on the continent of North America – the first known European to do so. His discovery was to pave the way for Leif Eiriksson – Leif the Lucky – to set foot on the unknown continent, probably at the place where the lovely city of Québec now stands, on the shores of the St. Lawrence River in Canada. He named the country *Vínland* (Wineland). Like Jacques Cartier five hundred years later, he found vines, grapes and excellent timber, as well as other prized resources. Leif later built "large houses" where he spent the winter, waiting for favourable conditions to sail home to Greenland in the spring. This was probably at L'Anse aux Meadows in Newfoundland. Leif was the son of another great explorer, Eirik the Red, who was the first Nordic settler in Greenland; he came from Breidafjord in western Iceland, according to the historian Ari the Wise, who was born half a century after the Wineland voyages, in AD 1067.

It was another important event, that served to confirm the essential truth of the Wineland sagas, when the famous Norwegian writer Helge Ingstad found the ruins of Leif's Camp at L'Anse aux Meadows at the northernmost tip of Newfoundland in 1961.

After Leif's expedition, other Wineland journeys followed. Leif's brother Thorvald explored the southern shore of the Gulf of St. Lawrence, and Icelander Thorfinn Karlsefni travelled farther down the east coast of North America. He spent about three years on the

Bay of Fundy in Canada, where his son Snorri was born, and also lived for a time by a lake he called Hop (Icelandic *hóp* = lagoon). There are many indications that the lagoon in question was the site of the present huge harbour at New York in the USA. Here Thorfinn found mild weather and valuable resources, such as grapes, wild rice, winter flounder, and a variety of game animals, but he was compelled to return to Iceland, as he was not prepared for ongoing strife with the aboriginal inhabitants, the Native Americans. They had vast manpower, and their weapons were only slightly less sophisticated than those of the Nordic settlers. This was before the days of the firearms, which were to play a crucial role in the European conquest of America five hundred years later.

This is a brief summary of the conclusions drawn in this volume, based on a variety of sources, old and new, in such fields as archaeology, geography, meteorology, navigation, anthropology, botany and zoology. Like most other important historical events, this discovery was not an isolated phenomenon. With the exception of a handful of Irish monks, Iceland was an unpopulated country when seafarers from the Nordic countries, most of them Norwegian, initiated the migration of a whole nation to the island around 870 AD. The settlement of Iceland was completed by the founding in 930 AD of the Althing, the oldest parliament in the world. The settlement of a new country required courage and initiative, but above all skills and navigational knowledge. The settlement of Greenland and Wineland, about a hundred years later, was a logical consequence of this initiative. But we would have only the haziest knowledge of these events had it not been for the literary culture of the Icelandic people, that reached its zenith in the Sagas of Icelanders. These sagas tell of Icelanders in the early centuries of the nation's history, and most are set in Iceland. The sagas number about 40 in total; the oldest surviving manuscripts of them date mainly from the 14th and 15th century, although the originals must have been written at a considerably earlier date. The Sagas of Icelanders are Iceland's major contribution to world literature, but none bears an author's name. Unique in medieval literature, the sagas are based both upon oral traditions and upon the methods of history writing taught in ecclesiastical schools. One of the best-known of the sagas is *Njáls saga* (the Saga of Njal). The sagas are also linked to other branches of medieval literature, which were important in their own fields, written as history or as practical reference books. Examples of these are for instance *Landnámabók* (The Book of Settlements), a detailed account of the settlement of Iceland, and *Grágás*, the most extensive Nordic legal code from the middle ages. Icelandic literature also included various other writings, both prose and poetry, with Icelandic or foreign themes; among them are most of the Nordic Sagas of Kings, an important field of Nordic medieval literature, which reached its peak in *Heimskringla*, the masterpiece of Snorri Sturluson (1178–1241).

The Wineland journeys are described primarily in two sagas, *Eiríks saga rauða* (Eirik the Red's Saga) and *Grænlendinga saga* (the Saga of the Greenlanders). Both sagas appear in full in this volume (pp. 235–276), and some readers may prefer to read the sagas first, before continuing to read the arguments of the book.

The saga translations which appear here are by Keneva Kunz. They are republished here by kind permission of Leifur Eiríksson Publishing and of Penguin Books. The translations appear here as originally published, but omitting footnotes. In order to maintain consistency with the saga translations, Icelandic personal names and placenames have been slightly modified in this book, substituting th for þ and d for ð, omitting all accents over letters, and omitting endings. The name *Leifur* thus appears as Leif, *Guðríður* as Gudrid, etc. For readers who are interested in knowing the full Icelandic form of names, these appear in the index (pp. 285–300). In the saga translations, the placename *Vínland* has been rendered Vinland, but in the main text of the book the present author prefers to use the self-explanatory "Wineland," which is consistent with "Iceland" and "Greenland."

Not surprisingly, in stories that date back a thousand years, there are many points and concepts in the sagas which are subject to different interpretations, and which have given rise to considerable controversy. In some cases, the present author's interpretation is not entirely the same as that of the translator. Words such as *dægur*, *eyktarstaður* and *húsasnotra* will be discussed in the relevant chapters of the book. Where such debatable words occur in the saga text, the Icelandic word has been added, italicised in parenthesis e.g. "day [*dægur*]" to clarify the point.

Much has been said and written about the Wineland sagas. Attempts have been made to chart the routes of the Wineland travellers, and to ascertain where Wineland was.

But interpretations have been highly variable, to the point that they provide more confusion than guidance. Many readers of the sagas have inferred from this that it is pointless to try to use the sagas in this way, but the present writer does not regard the case as hopeless. In recent times, various evidence has appeared that requires attention.

By a detailed scrutiny of the Wineland sagas and writings about them, the present author has developed a hypothesis regarding the routes of the Wineland voyagers and most of the places they visited on their journeys. But these proposals should be seen only as an initial theory on the solution to the Wineland puzzle. This must be followed up by field work, which may reveal misinterpretations that must be revised and corrected. On the other hand, such field work should also confirm that some of the places are correctly identified. This can then be used as the basis of further study.

Pursuing this method, the author made field trips to Nova Scotia, New Brunswick and the cities of Québec and New York. This book includes some of the research carried out on these journeys. Hopefully, this work will contribute to a more definite identification of the location of Wineland in the future.

The discovery of Wineland, and Nordic exploration in the New World, are among the most remarkable events in the history of exploration. The state of textual studies of the Wineland Sagas is excellent, but the same cannot be said of topographical studies. Topographical investigations have yielded wildly differing conclusions, and the contributions of the last few decades have not rectified this. And much remains to be done.

WHERE DID THEY GO?

The journey of Bjarni Herjolfsson

The first journey to the New World was made by Bjarni Herjolfsson, according to Chapter 1 of the Saga of the Greenlanders: he
sailed from Eyrar (now Eyrarbakki) in Iceland, and missed Greenland. Some people have cast doubt on the story, but there seems to
be no particular reason to do so. However, the extent of his journey
has sometimes been exaggerated, by the assumption that Bjarni
travelled to *Vínland* or Wineland (as far as Leif the Lucky's later
journey), though without going ashore. Even if he did not travel so
far, his achievement must be regarded as a remarkable one.

*In the spring of 1997, the author of this book visited the child-
hood home of Bjarni Herjolfsson at Eyrarbakki. Bjarni's father,
Herjolf, lived on the farm of Drepstokk. In the great Basendar
flood of 1799 the farm became uninhabitable, but overgrown
ruins of the farmhouse can still be seen adjacent to the river estuary (photo page i). These ruins are a conserved site. The hill
on which the farmhouse stood commands extensive and pictur-
esque views.*

Bjarni was a seafarer, whose accidental voyage of discovery began
when he returned to Iceland to find that his father had departed to
settle in Greenland. Bjarni decided to follow him, although he had
never before sailed in the Greenland Sea.

When Bjarni set off from Eyrar, it must be assumed that he had
been given some information on the sea route to Greenland, and
where along its shores to look for settlement. It is even possible
that his father, Herjolf, had left a message for him on where he
planned to settle. This was particularly necessary in view of the

fact that the Greenland settlements were generally located by fjords, or even at the head of the fjord, and were thus not easily seen from out at sea.

Medieval descriptions of sailing routes indicate that the route regarded as safest to Greenland was "Eirik's route," i.e. west-wards from the Snæfellsnes peninsula on Iceland's west coast, then southward and around the south of Greenland. Bjarni may have intended to take this route, but it is more likely that he headed directly west from Eyrar: he may well have been setting off rather late in the season, as his actions later in the journey indicate. But it makes little difference whether he set off straight from Eyrar or not. An attempt will be made here to trace his route, and to imagine how he may have reasoned when faced with the prob-lems he encountered.

They first sailed "for three days, until the land had disappeared below the horizon. Then the wind dropped and they were beset by winds from the north and fog; for many days [*dægur*] they did not know where they were sailing." (A *dægur* is a night or a day, a pe-riod of 12 hours, and will here be termed a half-day). It is not un-likely that they had waited for a favourable (easterly) wind direc-tion, when they set off to sea. There would have been a low pressure area south of the Greenland Sea, which would have sent warm and rather humid air to the north on the eastern side of the low, and then westwards to the north of the low-pressure area. When this air reached westwards as far as the edge of the cold Arc-tic current that flows southward along the east coast of Greenland, the cooling from the sea would have led to fog forming, so that the seafarers could not see the sky. They found themselves in trouble (weather map p. xiii)

At this point they had little choice but to assume that the wind was still easterly, and to set the sail accordingly. It is also possible that they based their actions on their experience from the ocean journey between Iceland and Norway, which will be discussed be-low. In that region it is a useful rule of thumb that in foggy condi-tions the wind will be southerly, as it is blowing over ever-cooling seas, so the humidity condenses. Working on this principle, it would have seemed reasonable for Bjarni to steer to port, to avoid the ship drifting northwards in what he believed was a southerly

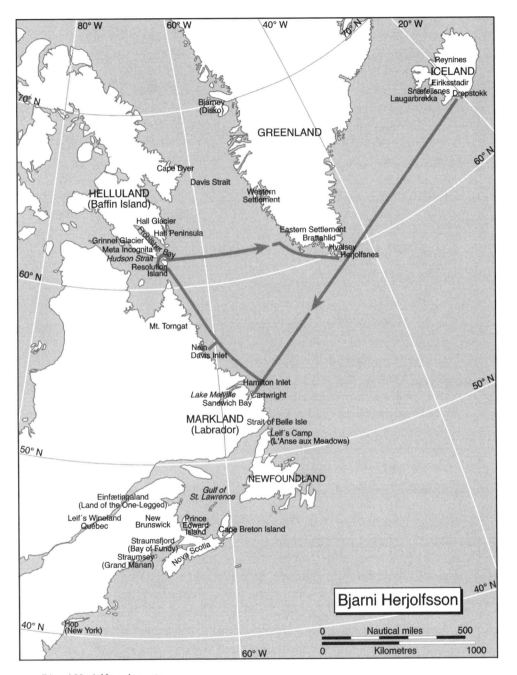

Bjarni Herjolfsson's route.

fog. But the travellers were venturing into a new area of the Greenland Sea, where none of them had been before, and weather patterns are different here. It may be regarded as a rule that an easterly wind on the Greenland Sea will swing around to northerly as it approaches Greenland, as the high glaciers force the winds to blow along the coast. This change in wind direction probably took place at about the time the fog was formed. Instead of turning to port, in fact, the seafarers ought to have done the exact opposite, turning to starboard in order not to sail past the southernmost point of Greenland. This sealed their fate: they missed Greenland, and headed southwest, or perhaps even south, across the ocean, for as long as they could not see the sky, even if the fog lifted. They may perhaps have corrected their course to some extent during their many days at sea, turning to the right, as they must have noticed the nights growing darker, indicating that they were headed southwards.

Some may object that the saga states that the travellers found themselves in a northerly wind. If they had correctly identified the wind direction at once, they might never have gone off course. It was probably only later that they realised that the wind must have been northerly after the fog came down.

The distance to the place in southern Labrador that is closest to South Greenland can be estimated as being about 1,200 nautical miles from Eyrar, about 15 half-days' sailing from Eyrar. The distance normally sailed in a half-day, 75–80 nautical miles, is discussed below (see p. 144). Bjarni may be assumed to have passed a short distance south of Greenland, so it is unlikely that his journey was much faster than this, unless the wind was particularly favourable. But it is not unlikely that these 15 half-days would have sufficed to bring them close to the coast of Labrador.

At this point they saw the sun and were able to take bearings. The sun would have been higher in the sky than in the south of Greenland, according to the descriptions they had been given, and the nights much darker than when they set off. Hence it is likely that the North Star, Polaris, was visible during the night, and clearly lying lower in the sky. This would indicate that they had travelled far to the south. This could have been measured by means of an astrolabe, discussed below (see p. 176). But in spite of these clues, they must have regarded it as possible that they had not yet travelled far enough west to reach Greenland. They may also have been aware of birds or whales, indicating that land was nearby. So their initial decision, to sail on westwards, was quite reasonable.

After sailing for a half-day they saw land, and Bjarni decided to sail inshore. But the land was flat and wooded, and thus clearly not Greenland, where there were said to be great glaciers. The description fits the land south of Hamilton Inlet, such as Sandwich Bay, Labrador. Today the village of Cartwright, with quite a good anchorage, stands at the mouth of the inlet, on the 54th parallel. The land is fairly low-lying, at least in comparison with their expectations of Greenland, which must have been the crucial question for Bjarni.

Captain Cartwright, after whom the village is named, sailed into the mouth of Sandwich Bay in the summer of 1775, and gave a memorable description of the place.[1] On the journey northwards along the coast of Labrador, the land was very barren and cold, with abundant sea ice and snow in early July. But as soon as the ship arrived at Cartwright, the environment was transformed. They almost seemed to be in the Tropics: "The hills were of moderate height, completely covered with spruces, larches, firs and birch, and the shores were bordered round with verdant grass. The water, too, instead of pans of ice, was mottled over with ducks and drakes. The sun was extremely hot, and zephyrus played upon us with tropical warmth." This abrupt change from the outer headlands to the land in the inlets is attributable to the cold Labrador Stream off the coast. Inland, where the effect of the Labrador Stream ceases, the sun can warm the land as it does at similar latitudes in northern England or southern Denmark.

If the distances Bjarni was to sail northwards are accepted as reliable, his first landfall in the west cannot have been much farther south than Sandwich Bay. It is worth noting that this means he was never anywhere near Wineland, and indeed the saga never says that he was. Although he is said to have reached first one land, then another, and a third, it need not be assumed that they were all separated by ocean or straits, any more than Scotland is separate from England, for instance.

But Bjarni must have suspected that they had reached an unknown land, much farther south, and probably farther west, than Greenland. He did not go ashore, presumably not wishing to lose any time. In addition, he may not have wanted to risk a confrontation with natives, whom he could have seen from afar, as there were probably Inuit communities in this region.

Now they had to rely on the guidance of the elevation of the North Star and of the sun, and also the fact that nights were much darker than they would have expected in Greenland. It would thus seem reasonable to sail northwards until the nights were as short as they were at Eyrarbakki, and until the elevation of the sun at midday was the same – or perhaps rather lower, as summer was almost over. It is quite possible that Bjarni had an astrolabe or other instrument to measure the elevation of the sun, as mentioned before.

Bjarni decided to sail away from land initially, but probably remaining close enough to see land from time to time. No doubt remaining within sight of land was a matter of importance on unfamiliar routes, but it makes sense to keep away from coastal skerries and headlands. Summer clouds over land build up along the coast by day, visible from a distance of 50 nautical miles or more, while elongated mountain clouds created by offshore winds may also provide a clue to the presence of land (see photo p. xiii).

When they had sailed for two half-days Bjarni felt it was time to check the coast to the west. On the headlands of the coast, little will have been visible other than naked rock, barren due to the icy cold of the Labrador Stream; just within the mouth of the bay, the land looked quite different. They sailed inshore, and saw that it was flat and wooded.

This could be at Davis Inlet, or farther north near the Inuit village of Nain, founded by missionaries in 1770, north of the 56th parallel.[2] Conditions for sailing inshore are, however, far better at Davis Inlet than at Nain, where there are skerries offshore. Both these places have abundant forests, which stretch north to the 58th parallel. The land here is lower-lying than farther north, but it would be an exaggeration to call it flat.

In order to sail from Sandwich Bay to Davis Inlet in two half-days they would have to sail at a speed of 7–8 knots, which is en-

Photograph from William Hovgaard's book of Davis Inlet, where Bjarni Herjolfsson may have sailed close to the shore after a passage of two half-days north along the Labrador coast. The slopes are wooded.

tirely believable. One cannot expect great accuracy in measurement of time, and two half-days could well have meant two-and-a-half, and three could mean three-and-a-half, in which case the sailing speed might be lower.

The Saga of the Greenlanders states that the wind had dropped when Bjarni intended to sail on after the second landfall, and that his men wished to go ashore. This is a convincing description of the weather in southwesterly winds and clear conditions in this area, as near the mouths of bays there is a tendency for onshore sea breezes to counteract the southwesterly wind that otherwise prevailed.

But Bjarni was convinced that this was not Greenland, and flatly refused to go ashore. They travelled on for three half-days, catching a southwesterly wind as they moved off shore. The wind al-

At the mouth of Frobisher Bay on Baffin Island, black slabs of rock may be seen among lighter rocks. The explorer Frobisher was interested in them because he thought they contained gold. These could be the slabs seen by Thorfinn Karlsefni's company, and which gave Helluland (Stone-slab land) its name. From D.D. Hogarth et al.

lowed Bjarni to sail north, or rather northwest, and it was also an advantage that the wind was blowing off the land, as this generally provides much better sailing conditions than in an ocean wind.

They then turned once again towards land, and found a land that was high and mountainous with a glacier and offered "nothing of use," so that it could not be Greenland. When they saw glaciers on their way northwards along the coast of the unknown land, there can hardly be any doubt that they were close to Baffin Island. There are, admittedly, patches of snow on the slopes of Mt. Torngat in the north of Labrador, but no actual ice caps. They sailed along the shore and saw that it was an island, which means that it cannot have been Labrador. This may have been Resolution Island, which has an area of about 1000 km², just south of Baffin Island. There are in fact no glaciers, but heavy snow in the mountains that lasts through the summer. Northwest of the island is Grinnel Glacier on the Meta Incognita Peninsula on Baffin Island, covering an area of 130 km². On the Hall Peninsula a little farther north is the Hall Glacier, with an area of 490 km².[3]

In order to reach Resolution Island from Davis Inlet or Nain in three half-days, a speed of 7–9 knots would have to be maintained after reaching the open sea. This is a high speed, but is quite possible in the helpful southwesterly breeze, which would have been very useful on a Viking ship, in spite of blowing almost across their route. Since the wind was blowing off shore, the sea would be calmer than under similar conditions out on the ocean.

An attempt has been made here to trace the route sailed by Bjarni Herjolfsson along the eastern coast of Labrador and north to Baffin Island, which were probably the lands later named Markland and Helluland. A photograph from Frobisher Bay on Baffin Island (p. 20) confirms that the land was barren and "offered nothing of use." The picture also shows flat chunks of black rock that might well have been called "slabs," as recounted in the Eirik the Red's Saga – so large that two men could lie foot-to-foot across them – and after which the land was later named. This will be discussed in the section on the journey of Thorfinn Karlsefni (see p. 57).

By now they must have realised that the elevation of the sun was almost the same as at Eyrar, and the nights nearly as bright. So the decision to head east to Greenland from Resolution Island was logical. They sailed on a stiff southwesterly breeze, heading eastwards on the assumption that Greenland must be ahead of them. The speed of the ship must have been high as the wind rose, to the point that Bjarni restrained his men from sailing too fast. After four half-days they saw the high mountains and glaciers of Greenland. From the southernmost point of Baffin Island to Greenland is 380 nautical miles by the shortest route. But if they headed directly east, ensuring that the elevation of the sun remained unchanged, they would have to sail 440 nautical miles, maintaining a speed of nine knots for four half-days. This was quite possible in a *knörr*, the Vikings' freight vessel, on the fairly strong southwesterly breeze. This would have brought them to land only 70–100 nautical miles north of the Eastern Settlement (near modern Narssarsuaq).

It is in fact unlikely that they reached Greenland exactly at Herjolfsnes, where Bjarni's father had settled, as the saga may seem to imply. This would have necessitated following a course rather south of east. This would have been unwise, and it is improbable that Bjarni would have been willing to risk missing Greenland again. But now they had arrived; all they had to do was sail southwards, and watch out for the landmarks of the Eastern Settlement as they had been described. They caught sight of a headland, where a boat had been beached. This was Herjolfsnes, which bore the name of Bjarni's father, Herjolf. The seafarer's achievement was a great one; stoicism, good sense and the mariner's expertise had triumphed over the unfamiliar and terrifying ocean, and the caprices of the weather. Bjarni gave up the seafaring life, and in due time took over his father's farm. Thus ends one of the most detailed and convincing descriptions of a sea journey in all of saga literature.

After Bjarni's journey

At the beginning of chapter 2 of the Saga of the Greenlanders, Bjarni Herjolfsson is said to have sailed to Norway and met Earl Eirik, in flat contradiction to the previous sentence, which states that he gave up seafaring. This is said to have led to great discussion on exploration, and Leif Eiriksson then began to plan his journey of exploration. As if to imply that this were dependent upon Earl Eirik in Norway being kept informed!

Opinions on this are mixed. Olafur Halldorsson suggested in his doctoral thesis, *Grænland í miðaldaritum* (Greenland in Medieval Writings) that this strange sentence may be attributable to copyist Jon Thordarson misreading the text of the Saga of the Greenlanders when he copied it into the Flatey Book.[4] Dr. Halldorsson believes that the name of Eirik the Red is unlikely to have been written in full in the source manuscript; if it was abbreviated *E.r.*, with the *r* extending below the line, in the original manuscript, the copyist may have read *E.r* as *E.j*, interpreting it as *Eiríkur jarl* and not *Eiríkur rauði*. In keeping with this, Jon Thordarson felt he should add a few words on Bjarni's journey to Norway.

It has sometimes been suggested that the reference to Earl Eirik means that Bjarni did not tell of his journey to the New World until many years after it happened. If Halldorsson's theory, that Earl Eirik plays no part in the story, is correct, this would remove any reason to believe this interpretation. It also supports the statement in the previous sentence, that Bjarni gave up seafaring. But the question of when Bjarni travelled to Greenland remains unanswered. It seems likely that the subsequent journeys of Leif and his brother Thorvald were made around the time that Greenland was converted to Christianity, as Thorvald is buried by Christian rites at Krossanes, as mentioned below. This was probably shortly after Bjarni Herjolfsson's discovery of new lands. Thus Bjarni can hardly have gone to Greenland earlier than shortly before AD 1000, and not, as many have assumed, immediately after Eirik the Red, who emigrated around AD 985. Olafur Halldorsson regards this as likely.

Also, if it is assumed that Bjarni went to Greenland at about the same time as Eirik the Red, in 985 AD or shortly afterwards, but did not tell of the journey until Earl Eirik Hakonarson had come to power in Norway in AD 1000, one might expect some resentment of this 14- or 15-year silence on the subject. But there is no such hint in the saga; Bjarni is only criticised for his lack of curiosity about the lands he saw, without exploring them further. It would also be highly unlikely that Bjarni and his crew could all have kept quiet about this remarkable journey for so long, even if they had some mysterious reason for doing so. It made sense, on the contrary, for Bjarni to make his arrival known without delay; he was a merchant, and would want to spread news of the goods he had brought, and not least to inform the lord of the manor at Brattahlid, Eirik the Red.

This example demonstrates the importance that one word, or even one letter, may have: *r* or *j*. Hence it is not surprising that manuscripts may become garbled in one copy after another over the centuries, not to mention the garbling of sagas in their oral form before that. This is to be expected, and little can be done about it; but one must not fall into the trap of dismissing the historical value of the whole saga due to such faults.

There is no reason to doubt that the story of Bjarni Herjolfsson's voyage to the New World has some basis in reality, and that it led to subsequent explorations.[5] But the account gives no real reason to suppose that Bjarni travelled farther than Labrador. Had he done so, he would not have been able to sail north to Helluland in a period of five half-days. So he probably never saw the land of wine, let alone stepped ashore and found the grapes for himself. It may therefore be true, as stated in Eirik the Red's Saga, that Leif chanced upon land where he had not expected any to be found, with fields of self-sown wheat and vines – whether Leif found Wineland after losing his way at sea on his way from Norway, or on a journey to Wineland. Thus the discrepancy between the Saga of the Greenlanders and Eirik the Red's Saga need not be as great as has sometimes been maintained. According to the Saga of the Greenlanders, Bjarni was the first European discoverer of the New World, and Leif simply followed up with a journey of exploration, while according to Eirik the Red's Saga, Leif himself was blown off course and came across new lands. Instead of arguing about the likelihood of the respective versions, it should be possible to reach a compromise, that Bjarni Herjolfsson found North America, while Leif found Wineland. But whoever made it, the discovery of the New World could be expected to take place some day by chance, by seafarers missing Greenland and sailing on westwards. Was Columbus not on his way to India when he ran across the Caribbean islands? That famous explorer probably never set foot on the American continent, any more than Bjarni Herjolfsson, although he dropped anchor in a South American river estuary.

Leif the Lucky

Many people have been sceptical about the background to Leif Eiriksson's journey to Wineland; was he a missionary travelling on behalf of King Olaf Tryggvason, who blundered across Wineland, as stated in Eirik the Red's Saga, or did he deliberately set off for Wineland from Greenland, as the Saga of the Greenlanders states, or both? Leif's journey is described in detail in the Saga of the Greenlanders, and it seems reasonable to follow this, rather than the brief account in Eirik the Red's Saga. Leif appears to have sailed into the Gulf of St. Lawrence, where Bjarni had not entered, and then sailed across the Gulf in two half-days. After this he travelled west along the south coast of the bay, probably to Québec, taking a different route from that later followed by Thorfinn Karlsefni. This is where Leif's main landing-place in Wineland ought to be.

Let us consider Leif's itinerary as recounted in the Saga of the Greenlanders, and the topography described there. There is no

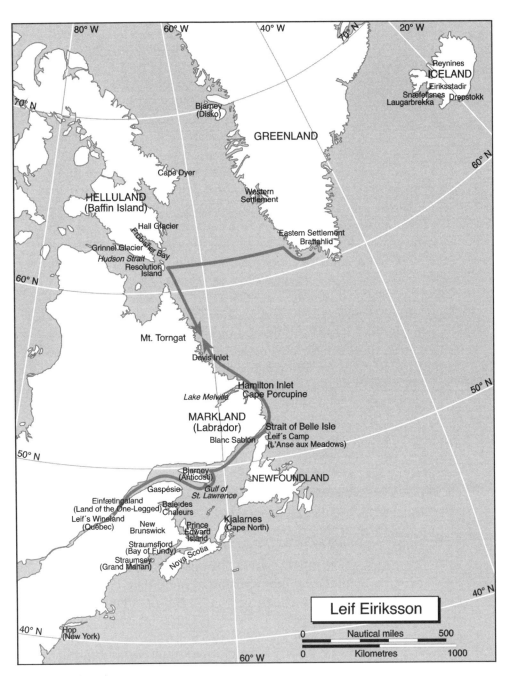

Leif Eiriksson's route.

mention of a journey to Norway, or of Leif being a missionary to Greenland. Leif appears to have made his journey shortly after Bjarni had found the New World, following lively discussion of exploration. It may even have been the year after Bjarni's historic journey. On the other hand, it is not unlikely that he used his newly-acquired ship to travel to Norway as recounted in Eirik the Red's Saga. But in the Saga of the Greenlanders, which deals almost exclusively with journeys to Wineland, travelling to Norway may not have been regarded as particularly interesting, as such journeys were commonplace. Chapter 2 of the saga states:

> Leif, the son of Eirik the Red of Brattahlid, sought out Bjarni and purchased his ship. He hired himself a crew numbering thirty-five men altogether.

On arrival at Helluland, it is stated that this was the land Bjarni saw last. Thus one may deduce that Leif sailed the same route from Greenland as Bjarni had followed on the last leg of his journey, from Baffin Island and Resolution Island. Probably he sailed north of the Eastern Settlement for about one half-day, then followed a line of latitude westwards until he saw the glaciers of Baffin Island. It cannot be guaranteed that he followed this route, but this is of limited importance for what follows. But Leif appears to have been determined to do better than Bjarni:

> They sailed up to the shore and cast anchor, put out a boat and rowed ashore. There they found no grass, but large glaciers covered the highlands, and the land was like a single flat slab of rock from the glaciers to the sea. This land seemed to them of little use.
>   Leif then spoke: 'As far as this land is concerned it can't be said of us as of Bjarni, that we did not set foot on shore. I am now going to name this land and call it Helluland (Stone-slab land).'

The name of Helluland is here explained differently from the account in Eirik's saga; this will be discussed further with regard to Thorfinn Karlsefni's journey of exploration.

After this no more mention is made of Bjarni Herjolfsson in the account of Leif's journey. There is thus no reason to suppose, as some have done, that the two lands called Markland and Wineland by Leif are the same as those seen by Bjarni. Leif now sailed from Helluland, probably across the Hudson Strait:

They then returned to their ship, put out to sea and found a second land.

Once more they sailed close to the shore and cast anchor, put out a boat and went ashore. This land was flat and forested, sloping gently seaward, and they came across many beaches of white sand.

Leif then spoke: 'This land will be named for what it has to offer and called Markland (Forest Land).'

On their departure from Helluland, they must have crossed the Hudson Strait; beyond it was Markland. The northernmost part of it is admittedly without forests, but the name Markland (Forest Land) may be justified by the fact that woods covered much of the region. The brief description gives no clue as to how long they sailed along the coast of Markland. But they travelled widely. When they saw the woods after which the land is named, they had sailed about 250 kilometres south along the coast. There are extensive white sands south of Cape Porcupine. *Blanc Sablon* (White Sand) is also the name of a place reached after passing through the Strait of Belle Isle between Labrador and Newfoundland.[6] For this reason, and also in view of the later part of the story, it seems reasonable to deduce that they sailed along the shore of Labrador and into the Gulf of St. Lawrence, and some distance along its northern shore. It is not until this point that a journey of two half-days on a northeasterly breeze would take them to a new land, south of the Gulf of St. Lawrence, as chapter 2 of the saga states:

They then returned to the ship without delay.

After this they sailed out to sea and spent two days [*dægur*] at sea with a northeasterly wind before they saw land. They sailed towards it and came to an island, which lay to the north of the land, where they went ashore. In the fine weather they found dew on the grass, that they collected in their hands and drank, and thought they had never tasted anything as sweet.

This may be interpreted as a southwest-bound journey across the Gulf of St. Lawrence from Markland. The island may conceivably be Anticosti, which is probably the island called Bjarney (Bear Island) in Eirik's saga. We now refer to a map on p. 65.

If Leif sailed southwest along the coast of Labrador about 15–20 nautical miles offshore, he might have spotted the island of Anticosti, then travelled on south of its easternmost point, which is about 60 nautical miles from Labrador. According to sailing guides, a tolerable anchorage exists at the easternmost point of the south coast, in a little bay that bears the name of Cybele, the goddess of wild nature. In northeasterly winds, this would provide safe haven. Inland from Cybele Bay is a faunal reserve, three or four kilometres square, where Leif may have gone ashore, looked around in the fine weather and tasted sweet dew. If he then sailed on westwards along the south coast of the island, about 15–20 nautical miles offshore, he could have noticed Cape Gaspé (Gaspésie), a headland 210 metres high, which is about 100 nautical miles from the easternmost point of Anticosti. This is thus equivalent to a total of a journey of two half-days, 160 nautical miles, across the Gulf of St. Lawrence, first southward to Anticosti, then westward in a favourable northeasterly wind. For the travellers to remain constantly in sight of land, visibility would have to be 20–25 nautical miles; this is common during off-shore winds, when weather conditions are dry and bright. Clouds that often form over landmasses and islands would have made them easier to see. From this point the obvious course would be to sail on between Anticosti and Cape Gaspé, "between the island and the headland that stretched out northwards from the land," as the saga says.

This is entirely consistent with the account given in the Saga of the Greenlanders. The hypothesis has been put forward that the island where Leif landed was Prince Edward Island. This would not be consistent with the distance sailed, as Prince Edward Island would be a passage of three or four half-days from Markland (Labrador). But a far stronger argument against this hypothesis is that it would require Leif to sail before the wind a long distance out to sea, without knowing whether land lay ahead. This would have been unwise in the extreme for the first European navigator in that region, and quite unlike Leif, who appears to have been a wise and cautious explorer. The passage of two half-days described here, from Labrador to the south coast of the Gulf of St. Lawrence, via an island, is the only possible route that remains entirely within sight of land, which must have been regarded as highly desirable by mariners.

It seems to me probable that Thorfinn Karlsefni too called at Cybele Bay, which he named Bjarney (Bear Island), as will be discussed below. He would have known of the place from Leif, and his travelling companions from Greenland would also have known the way. Further arguments will be adduced below in support of the theory that Leif sailed beyond Gaspésie; these include, for instance, the natural resources of the St. Lawrence valley and Thorfinn Karlsefni's journey in search of Thorhall the Huntsman, which took him almost as far as Québec.

But is the story of the dew not exaggerated or imaginary? Not necessarily. There is a phenomenon known as honeydew, a sweet substance that forms on leaves on which aphids or other insects feed. This can form in such copious quantities in hot dry weather that it falls to the earth in large amounts. Honeydew is said to form mostly on linden trees, rose bushes and maple. This could be the bushy mountain maple which grows as far north as Newfoundland and Anticosti. Rain or dew after honeydew has formed could clearly lead to the dew under the tree becoming sweet to taste. Kristleifur Thorsteinsson of Husafell is familiar with honeydew, and says he has known it to be found on grass.[7] Forester Asgeir Svanbergsson and timber expert Haraldur Agustsson have also seen this phenomenon in Reykjavik.[8] On the leaves of a hibiscus in the home of the present author, drops sometimes form which become light-coloured specks with a sweet taste. But the best-known honeydew is from the shrub *Tamarix mannifera* in the Sinai desert, according to a recent Biblical commentary. The syrup forms small white grains which the Bible likens to coriander seed, that taste like honeycake. This bread of heaven was called *manna*, and this is the derivation of the Latin name of the shrub, *mannifera*. Honeydew thus appears to play a part in more than one journey to a Promised Land: Leif Eiriksson's expedition to Wineland, and the Israelites' journey through the wilderness, led by Moses.

It was not surprising that Leif's followers were enchanted by their experience on this beautiful morning, and one can imagine them exchanging delighted glances as they tasted the dew in the fine weather, captivated by the charms of this new and untouched world that had been waiting for them since time immemorial. They continue:

> Afterwards they returned to their ship and sailed into the sound which lay between the island and the headland that stretched out northwards from the land. They rounded the headland and steered westward. Here there were extensive shallows at low tide and their ship was soon stranded, and the sea looked far away to those aboard ship.
>
> Their curiosity to see the land was so great that they could not be bothered to wait for the tide to come in and float their stranded ship, and they ran aground where a river flowed into the sea from a lake. When the incoming tide floated the

Battures de Beauport, Québec. Leif's route.

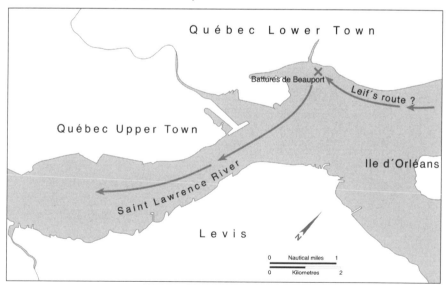

ship again, they took the boat and rowed to the ship and moved it up into the river and from there into the lake, where they cast anchor. They carried their sleeping-sacks ashore and built booths. Later they decided to spend the winter there and built large houses.

There was no lack of salmon both in the lake and in the river, and this salmon was larger than they had ever seen before.

There is no doubt here that Leif sailed westwards. The Gaspé Peninsula was probably the headland that stretched out northwards from the land and the island was probably Anticosti. The strait between them is called the Détroit d'Honguedo (in sailing directions, the Gaspé Passage). Farther on they would enter the St. Lawrence river. This was probably in the lake, 2–3 km wide, that the St. Lawrence may be said to flow through before it passes through a narrow mouth by Québec. Hence it would be natural for Leif and his men to regard the river beyond Québec as a lake. The name Québec is a Native American word meaning "the place where the river narrows." Sea charts show that offshore from Québec are shallows, as the story indicates.[9] If one assumes that Leif sailed between the Gaspé Peninsula and Anticosti, the conditions described in the saga can hardly be found until the travellers reach Québec.

Let us now consider whether the conditions at Québec city are consistent with the quotation from the Saga of the Greenlanders, above.

According to navigational guides, at the western bank of the St. Lawrence, 2–3 kilometres from the central part of Québec, are extensive shallows called Battures de Beauport. The river bottom is slate, covered with silt. This slate bottom extends over much of an inlet about two kilometres across, and it stretches as much as one-and-a half kilometres (seven cables) from the shore. Ships sailing up the river are warned of these shallows, as when the tidal current flows up the river on the western shore, it tends to carry onto the shallows, due to the effects of local eddies formed in these conditions. But unlike modern seamen Leif and his company had no sailing guide, and so they could not have been on their guard. They must have been close to the shore when their ship ran aground, as the sea was a long way out at low tide, and they could not resist jumping overboard and going ashore in a boat. But as soon as the ship floated up on the rising tide, they moved it upriver, probably on the St. Lawrence, and into what they called a lake. The river is a kilometre across at its narrowest point in this region, where it flows past the oldest district of the lovely city of Québec. A short distance upstream from the narrows, however, the river is over two kilometres across, so it would not be unreasonable to call it a "lake" or "lagoon"; the St. Lawrence is the largest river in North America that flows into the Atlantic. Tidal influence on the river is considerable, but due to the effects of the river's own flow, the falling tide lasts much longer than the rising tide, and flows much faster, especially through the narrows. In spite of being a tidal river, the water of the St. Lawrence is fresh in this region; those who were used to reading the signs of nature would have noticed at once that this indicated that a river was flowing through, and a river of no small size.

The account of the salmon is also believable. In olden times salmon migrated up the St. Lawrence; salmon abounded as far up as Lake Ontario, 600 km above Québec, and also migrated up most of the tributaries of the St. Lawrence.[10] At the season when Leif and his company were probably in the region, the salmon is likely to have kept mostly to the tributaries, but it is not unlikely to have been found also in the St. Lawrence proper.[11] The statement in the saga that the salmon was very large is also consistent with the rule that salmon are larger, the farther they are from the sea. This is believed to relate to the fact that a salmon requires great strength and stamina to swim upstream for a long distance, and so salmon are generally two or three years old before they set off up-river to spawn.[12]

While this does not constitute proof of where Leif made his camp, one could hardly expect to find a place more consistent with the description of the saga than at Québec.

The suggestion has been put forward that Leif's Camp may have been farther east on the southern shore of the St. Lawrence, in Miramachi Bay on the east of the Gaspé Peninsula. It has also been maintained that Miramachi could be Hop, where Thorfinn Karlsefni subsequently settled; this will be discussed below. I feel that

The childhood home of Bjarni Herjolfsson was at Drepstokk, Eyrarbakki in south Iceland. Due to erosion by the Ölfusa river and the sea, the farm had to be moved to this hilltop at some time before 1700, after which it was abandoned. The surroundings are barren sand. The ruins are a protected site. Photo Pall Bergthorsson.

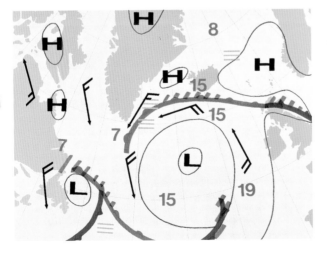

This weather map from 13 August 1997 shows similar weather conditions to those that probably prevailed when Bjarni Herjolfsson sailed to Greenland. A humid, mild easterly forms fog over the cold ocean currents at the west of the Greenland Sea. The wind direction changes suddenly to northerly due to the proximity of land, and the ship is carried southwards.

In the footsteps of Eirik the Red and his family in the summer of 1997. Archaeologists Gudmundur Olafsson and Ragnheidur Traustadottir have excavated a long hearth from the early period of habitation at Eirik the Red's farmstead, Eiriksstadir in Haukadalur. Photo Helgi Bjarnason.

The reconstruction of Eirik the Red's farmstead at Eiriksstadir in Haukadalur was completed in in the year 2000. Photo Stefan Örn Stefansson.

The lighthouse on Cape North, which the author believes was the Kjalarnes of the Wineland sagas, where Thorvald Eiríksson had the fragments of his broken keel raised up. Photo Baldur Palsson.

Wild rice grows, among other places, throughout the St. Lawrence valley and east across New Brunswick, and is also found in Nova Scotia. The author believes that the "self-sown wheat" of Eirik the Red's saga was wild rice. Photograph taken near Amherst. Photo Baldur Palsson.

iii

Aerial photo of Kelly's Point (Krossanes) at Big Bras d'Or on the east of Cape Breton Island. The author believes that the topography resembles the location of Thorvald Eiriksson's death, described in the Saga of the Greenlanders. Photo Nova Scotia Geomatic Centre.

Moose. Native Americans made boats of moose hide. Photo Art Wolfe/The Image Bank.

iv

this location is not at all consistent either with the description of Thorfinn's journey, or of Leif's passage across the St. Lawrence. The account of the lake and the river is not consistent with Miramachi Bay. Inland from the bay, admittedly, wild grapes are said to grow, but vegetation maps of the region show neither wild rice nor the butternut tree; the fact that both of these were found by the Wineland explorers must be regarded as proven. All these plants, on the other hand, are found in the present day in the vicinity of Québec city. This will be discussed in detail below (p. 208), along with other natural local phenomena.

This brings us to the part of the saga account that is neither consistent with Québec, nor with Miramachi Bay, or anywhere else on the St. Lawrence. This requires special scrutiny and possibly rectification. The saga says:

> It seemed to them the land was so good that livestock would need no fodder during the winter. The temperature never dropped below freezing, and the grass only withered very slightly.

This does not apply to any part of the Gulf of St. Lawrence: in December, January and February, temperatures average 5–10°C below freezing, with fairly abundant precipitation, which naturally falls mostly as snow.[13] The Gulf largely freezes over. This raises the question: why does the saga say the winters were so mild? I feel a likely explanation is that, before the sagas were recorded in writing, the information about mild weather conditions at Thorfinn Karlsefni's settlement at Hop became confused with the accounts of Leif's journey. This may have been because both Leif and Thorfinn were reputed to have found the same exotic plants: grapes and self-sown wheat. Hence the conclusion may have been drawn that weather conditions were similar in both places, not only in summer, but also in winter. Thorfinn's journey, which took him much farther south, and the mild winters at Hop, could thus explain this misleading statement on the mild winters in Leif's Wineland.

It is also worth scrutinising the precise wording of the passage, that it *seemed* to Leif's men that the livestock would require no win-

ter fodder. Could this not indicate that they never spent a winter in
the land of wild vines, and simply drew a false conclusion about
winter conditions, because of the warmth of the summer? Summer
conditions at Québec are similar to those in England or Ireland, for
instance, where winters are generally free of frost and snow, so
that sheep can normally stay out at pasture all winter, and the
grass does not wither. The voyagers might have known of this
from those who had travelled to these countries. Leif, however,
had no reason for concern about livestock, as he had not taken any
on his journey. Thus conditions for sheep in the winter were never
tested, wherever Leif's Camp was located.

Where could they have spent the winter other than in the St.
Lawrence valley? It seems to me likely that they would have sailed
out through the Gulf of St. Lawrence and made camp there, perhaps on the Strait of Belle Isle, in order to cover some of the distance home to Greenland before the winter, and to be ready to sail
when the sea ice melted off Labrador. They are unlikely to have
travelled farther that autumn, when the nights were growing dark
and weather conditions deteriorating. They would have chosen a
place to camp where they had access to timber and other building
materials, and where they could stock up on fish and other supplies for the winter months.

In this context, the ruins of Icelandic-type turf houses, found at
L'Anse aux Meadows in Newfoundland, should be mentioned.
Birgitta Wallace believes that this is where Leif built his houses,
which he subsequently loaned to other travellers to Wineland, but
refused to give them. No vines could have been found there, due
to the cold climate. There is no navigable river, and conditions are
in other respects quite different from those described in the Saga of
the Greenlanders. Nor have any traces been found of the temporary camp that is supposed to have been built initially.

But various factors support Birgitta Wallace's view that Leif's
Camp was in Newfoundland, and the Wineland sagas must not be
interpreted too literally. It is possible to imagine that Leif's Camp
was originally built as temporary accommodation, as the saga indicates, in what is now the St. Lawrence valley; the explorers must
have required some shelter while they gathered grapes, timber,

and other commodities. But it may be imagined that they did not build Leif's large houses here, as they intended to sail home to Greenland. Once they reached the northernmost point of New-foundland, they would have realised that they could not sail further that autumn due to the dark nights, weather conditions and sea ice. So they settled down to spend the winter. They would have had the whole of October to build the houses, as this month is generally free of frost; they may have built one or more houses that autumn. These would be the large houses called Leif's Camp in the Saga of the Greenlanders.

But why should Leif have decided against spending the winter in the St. Lawrence valley? Apart from the fact that he probably wanted to travel part of the way home before the spring, he may also have been thinking of safety. It is not unlikely that he saw Native Americans in the St. Lawrence valley that summer, although this is not mentioned, since he thought it necessary to keep half his men at the camp at all times. The saga tells that Leif had good eye-sight, and was observant, since it was he who spotted the shipwrecked travellers on a reef and rescued them. So it is not unlikely that when he sailed through the Strait of Belle Isle between New-foundland and Labrador, on his way from Greenland, he noticed that there were no signs of habitation on the Newfoundland side. This could be a good place to wait for spring. Birgitta Wallace maintains that at this time there were neither Native Americans nor Inuits on the northernmost point of Newfoundland.

This is speculation, of course, but little would have to be added to the saga for this to be correct. This places the ruins in New-foundland in a logical context of the Wineland sagas. It is less likely that large houses were built in Québec, and others later at L'Anse aux Meadows. We know for sure that these were large and well-constructed buildings, thanks to Helge Ingstad's discovery.[14]

The interesting observation made by Leif and his men, that in midwinter the sun reached *dagmálastaður* and *eyktarstaður*, will be discussed in the chapter on navigation in the Viking Age (see p. 161); it will be demonstrated that this observation is applicable to L'Anse aux Meadows, as accurately as one could ask. Yet another clue that this is where Leif built his large houses.

Vines

Later in this book, the discovery by the explorer Cartier of vines in 1535 by the St. Lawrence River and on the Île d'Orléans will be discussed (see p. 214). These were probably riverbank grapes, which are still present today. Although in this fastidious age in matters of food and drink, riverbank grapes are not regarded as fit for human consumption nor for use in wine-making, it is not unlikely that Leif's men enjoyed them, when Tyrkir, a companion of Leif's from childhood, had found the vines. The account seems to imply that Tyrkir was inebriated when he returned, as chapter four states:

> Leif soon realized that the companion of his childhood was pleased about something ... For a long time Tyrkir only spoke in German, with his eyes darting in all directions and his face contorted. The others understood nothing of what he was saying.

Some people feel that Tyrkir's tipsiness after finding the grapes illustrates the narrator's ignorance. But it is not impossible that his reaction was due to his anticipation of drinking wine, and memories relating to past enjoyment of wines – especially his joy at bringing good news to his friend and master, Leif. The description of Tyrkir under the influence could also be quite true, if related to another occasion, after wine had been made.

There are also doubts about the reliability of the account of cutting vines for the ship:

> 'We'll divide our time between two tasks, taking one day for one task and one day for the other, picking grapes or cutting vines and felling the trees to make a load for my ship.'

This need not, however, be wrong. The vine species found in the region, *Vitis riparia*, climbs up tall trees, such as the sugar maple, as discussed below. The grapes could be gathered by cutting the trees down one day, and picking the grapes the following day. This would be a reasonable procedure.

Another suggestion, that makes less sense, is the theory proposed by some, that the vines were so strong and flexible that branches of vine, 6–18 mm in diameter, could be used as substitutes for the spruce roots which were used to lash the hull of ships to the cross-beams, and for other purposes.[15] These lashings had to be renewed frequently – a total of 100 to 150 metres of fibres on each occasion.[16] An unused bundle of such spruce roots was found at the L'Anse aux Meadows site, as will be mentioned below. It is possible that the vines could be used for weaving baskets. The Greenlanders knew this craft; at the "Farm beneath the Sand" in the Western Settlement in Greenland, remnants of wicker baskets have been found.[17] The vines could thus have been a trading commodity. This theory is, however, rather far-fetched and unnecessary.

But it need not be wrong that Leif kept the grapes through the winter and transported them to Greenland in the ship's boat, provided that the grapes were dried in the autumn to make raisins. Raisins had been known since the days of King David in Israel three thousand years ago. A letter from Bishop Arni of Bergen written in 1308 to Bishop Thord of Greenland says that several gifts are being sent with the letter, including one barrel of grapes. The letter also informs the recipient of the death of King Eirik, known as "the priest-hater," nine years before.[18] Communications, then, must have been few and far between. Poul Nørlund maintains that these "grapes" must have been raisins, and this may be assumed to apply also to the grapes with which Leif filled his boat. Bishop Arni also clearly knew that the Greenlanders would enjoy this treat.

It has been maintained that the Wineland travellers were unlikely to have known how to make wine. But very simple methods can be sufficient. Babcock points out that the *Historie of Travaile in Virginia* states that in modern times 20 gallons of wine have been made simply by crushing grapes by hand.[19] After being left to stand for five or six days, the wine was strong and alcoholic. Adam of Bremen also states specifically that the grapes of Wineland have been used to make excellent wine.[20] Gathorne-Hardy suggests that Tyrkir may have made such an experiment before long – perhaps even concealing the liquor until he could taste it after a few days, after which he came merrily to meet the search party.[21]

*Camille Rousseau has written a large guide to the flora of Qué-
bec, including wild rice, riverbank grapes and butternut
trees.[22] All these species are found in many places in the St.
Lawrence valley. My son Baldur and I saw an example of this
when we visited a member of staff of the Botanical Collection of
Laval University, Claude Roy, and his family.[23] It was a delightful evening, with a full moon, and Jupiter bright in the
southern sky. There was still a touch of red in the sky, and bon-
fires were lit in some gardens. The river was calm and powerful, though far more polluted than in Leif's day. M. Claude Roy
and his wife were warm and welcoming, and their young
daughter made a drawing of Baldur – wearing angel's wings.
The first thing we saw in their garden was riverbank grapes,
which were beginning to darken, though not fully ripe (28 August 1996). Mme. Roy said that she knew of the grapes being
used for wine. In the shallows by the riverbank grew wild rice,
and Claude promised to dry and send us some. And as we said
our farewells, he asked Baldur to reach up into a tree for some
butternuts. They were not fully ripe, green and sticky, but of
full size. Back home in Iceland they achieved their true colour,
shape and firmness. Then he pointed across the river to what
had been a Native American village. There, and in other places,
the Wineland travellers could have built a camp on dry and
treeless land. We will never forget these resources of Wineland
that we saw that August evening.*

Thorvald Eiriksson

The background to Thorvald's journey is given in the third chapter
of the Saga of the Greenlanders:

> There was great discussion of Leif 's Vinland voyage and his
> brother Thorvald felt they had not explored enough of the
> land.

In the following we should note that the intention was to explore
Wineland. Chapter four says:

In consultation with his brother Leif, Thorvald now prepared for this journey with thirty companions. They made their ship ready and put to sea, and nothing is told of their journey until they came to Vinland, to Leif 's camp, where they laid up their ship and settled in for the winter, fishing for their food.

Whether Leif's Camp was near Québec, or at L'Anse aux Meadows, as suggested above, it may seem strange that they could catch fish for food, in the harsh winter frosts. This objection is, however, without foundation. Leif could have told the sceptics that all through September and October, and into November, temperatures are generally above freezing, giving plenty of time to build up stores of dried fish, and perhaps other seafood, which would last through the cold months until spring. At L'Anse aux Meadows some whale bones and seal bones have been found, and one fish bone; the soil is very acid, so conditions for preservation of bones are poor. Bark containers, sewn together with spruce roots, may have been used, Birgitta Wallace believes, as covers for net stones. Nearby was a small pile of stones about the size of an egg or a fist. These may have been weights for fishing.[24] And there was plenty of firewood to heat the houses. There was abundant driftwood, for instance, at L'Anse aux Meadows. They then began their exploration, and the topographical descriptions in chapter four should give more of a clue to where Wineland may have been.

That spring Thorvald said they should make their ship ready and several men were to take the ship's boat and go to the west of the land and explore there during the summer. They thought the land fine and well forested, with white beaches and only a short distance between the forest and the sea. There were many islands and wide stretches of shallow sea.

Nowhere did they see signs of men or animals. On one of the westerly islands they did find a wooden grain cover, but discovered no other work by human hands and headed back, returning to Leif 's camp in the autumn.

The phrase *fyrir vestan landið* (the west of the land) appears to mean here "the western part of the land." The description of the country could apply to the region from Québec east to the Gaspé Peninsula, perhaps to Prince Edward Island and the north coast of Nova Scotia. The distance between forest and sea may be said to be short throughout the region; at least it was so before modern man began to fell the forests. According to seamen's guides, it appears that sandy shores are found mostly on the east of the Gaspé Peninsula, especially the Baie des Chaleurs.[25] There are many islands, both at the landward end of the Gulf of St. Lawrence, where the Île d'Orléans is the largest, and east of the peninsula. There are many shallows, and in some areas there is chalk; there and in various other places the sands may be white. When it is stated that they returned to Leif's Camp in the autumn, it may be assumed that they travelled a considerable distance from western Wineland, which they were exploring. This may be consistent with Leif's Camp having been in Newfoundland.

The only indication of self-sown wheat in the Saga of the Greenlanders is a wooden grain cover or "helmet" (*kornhjálmur*) found by Thorvald Eiriksson's men on the western part of the island. This may well be the Île d'Orleans, in the inner reaches of the Gulf of St. Lawrence. This cannot have been cultivated grain, such as maize, since they found no other signs of human habitation. But the grain was probably gathered for food, most likely by Native Americans, and the cover protected it from birds. This brings us to wild rice or "self-sown wheat."

In later centuries Jesuits said that the Native Americans gathered wild rice in chests of bark. The grain cover could be a chest of this kind. But there are other possibilities. Latter-day maize containers used by the Native Americans were described as follows:[26]

> When thoroughly dry it [maize] was usually stored in caches, although it was sometimes placed in wooden receptacles about three feet high, made by cutting hollow logs into sections.

The shape of the object is not clearly stated, but it may well have resembled a "helmet," with the split wood in vertical strips: a wooden receptacle for storing grain. It could, of course, equally well have been used for wild rice. Maize does not grow this far north.

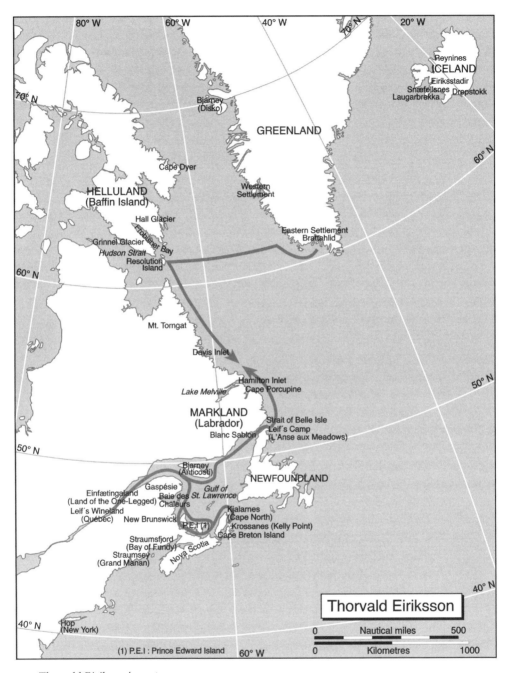

Thorvald Eiriksson's route.

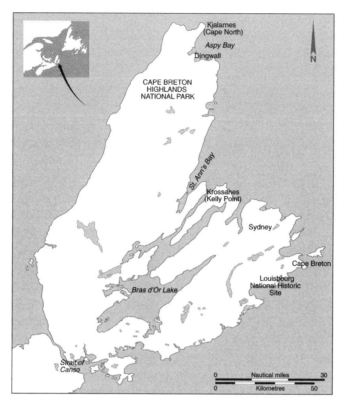

Kjalarnes
(Cape North)

Aspy Bay

Dingwall

CAPE BRETON
HIGHLANDS
NATIONAL PARK

St. Ann's Bay

Krossanes
(Kelly Point)

Sydney

Cape Breton

Louisbourg
National Historic
Site

Bras d'Or Lake

Strait of
Canso

Nautical miles   30

Kilometres   50

*Cape Breton
Island*

Exploration farther east the following year is described in chapter 4:

> The second summer Thorvald explored the country to the east on the large ship, going north around the land [*hið nyrðra fyrir landið*]. They ran into stormy weather around one head-land, and they were driven ashore, smashing the keel of the ship. They stayed there a long time, repairing their ship. Thorvald then said to his companions, 'I want us to raise the broken keel up on this point and call it Kjalarnes (Keel point).' This they did.

The Icelandic words *hið nyrðra fyrir landið* entail that they travelled along the north coast. It would appear logical to interpret this as meaning that they explored eastern Wineland, following their ex-ploration of the previous year. There are various indications later in the story that Kjalarnes was Cape North, at the north of Cape Breton Island. At a small headland, Money Point, where a lighthouse now stands, the coast turns abruptly to the south.[27] Cape North is about 300 metres high: off the shore violent squalls are common, according to sailing directions. From time to time a dangerous tidal race also occurs, which is hazardous for ships. The outflow of the Gulf of St. Lawrence meets another ocean current that sometimes flows northward along the coast of Cape Breton Island. This current is due to a prevailing northeasterly wind raising the water level in the Bras d'Or Lake; when the wind drops, the water flows out of the lake into the sea. Eirik's saga has another account of a ship running into trouble, when Thorhall the Huntsman went north of Kjalarnes and tried to beat to the west. They met opposing winds, that carried them out to sea. Both of the Wineland sagas seem to be in agreement about the violent weather conditions at "Keel Point."

At nine in the morning of Sunday 18 August 1996, we got a motor boat to take us from the village of St. Lawrence out beyond Money Point, in fine weather and calm seas. This is the northern outpost of Nova Scotia. Our steersman was a cheerful seaman, Henry Burton, with his young son. Henry takes people out whale watching, and also invites them to try sea angling.

Money Point had in former times a lighthouse-keeper and foghorn; the old lighthouse is now in a museum in Ottawa, and the lighthouse is automated. As we expected, we did not see the oldest landmark, the broken keel of Thorvald Eiriksson's ship from a thousand years ago. The description in Eirik's Saga fits well: "wild and desolate woodland." The coast is mostly steep, an almost continuous series of light-coloured screes and cliffs below wooded slopes. The area was deserted, although two horses were grazing near the lighthouse. Henry recognised them, and called out to them by name, but they ignored him and carried on grazing. Offshore from the lighthouse are shallows, and we sailed around them. Although in many places it seems possible to sail close inshore, in some cases, we felt that

> *we were squeezing through dangerously narrow straits be-*
> *tween land and rock pillars where cormorants perched and*
> *spread their wings. We saw two rusty ships' hulls on the shore;*
> *one was a Norwegian vessel,* Carita, *that sank two decades*
> *ago, and waits to be obliterated by time. Weather conditions at*
> *sea when it foundered may have been similar to those experi-*
> *enced by Thorvald Eiriksson.*

In order to carry out repairs on the vessel, Thorvald's men would have required the right conditions. These seem to exist at Aspy Bay, just south of the headland. In the village of Dingwall is a good harbour, sheltered in all wind directions, although it may be impossible to sail in or out of the harbour mouth in high easterly winds. It is also possible that they eased the vessel into one of the lagoons beyond an 8-kilometre-long sandy reef: North, Middle and South Lagoon. The sandy reefs are pinkish-yellow; the seaward side is barren, while the inland side has considerable scrub growth. No doubt in the woods nearby it was possible to find large trees for repairing the ship. It was natural for them, as explorers, to raise the broken keel as a sign for seafarers, up on Kjalarnes itself, where Thorfinn's men later found a ship's keel on their journey. The Saga of the Greenlanders and Eirik the Red's Saga are consistent here, although one saga attributes the naming of the place to Thorvald and the other to Thorfinn.

Thorvald then continued his expedition, and dark deeds were performed:

> They then left to sail to the east of the country and entered the mouths of the next fjords until they reached a cape stretching out seawards. It was covered with forest. After they secured their ship in a sheltered cove and put out gangways to the land, Thorvald and all his companions went ashore.
>
> He then spoke: 'This is an attractive spot, and here I would like to build my farm.' As they headed back to the ship they saw three hillocks on the beach inland from the cape. Upon coming closer they saw they were three hide-covered boats, with three men under each of them. They divided their forces

and managed to capture all of them except one, who escaped with his boat. They killed the other eight and went back to the cape. On surveying the area they saw a number of hillocks further up the fjord, and assumed them to be settlements.

The obvious interpretation is that they sailed from Kjalarnes southwards along the east coast of Cape Breton Island. The next noticeable "fjords" or bays along this route are St. Ann's Bay and Big Bras d'Or; the latter is in fact a strait between the sea and the large saltwater lake, Bras d'Or Lake, in the centre of the island. The mountainous headland between the bays, Kelly's Mountains, is about 20 km long.

It is interesting that the natives lie beneath their skin boats. Inuits do not do this: the kayak is too small, while the umiak, the larger women's boat, is too heavy for one man to carry. But in the 16th century, Jacques Cartier wrote that the Native Americans had no dwellings other than under their boats, which they turned over before lying down on the ground.[28]

It is unlikely, however, that the Native Americans of the saga had no dwellings but their boats. The reference to "hillocks" farther up the fjord provides a clue that they may have lived in wigwams – dome-shaped houses made of poles lashed together at the top and covered with bark or mats, leaving a hole for smoke to escape. These are very different from the homes of the Inuit, which were largely underground, as indicated in the account of Thorfinn Karlsefni's journey, discussed below.

After Thorvald's men had mercilessly slaughtered eight men who lay beneath their skin boats on the beach, while a ninth escaped, natives approached them in boats, and attacked with their bows and arrows. After the battle, Thorvald said:

'I have been wounded under my arm,' he said. 'An arrow flew between the edge of the ship and the shield into my armpit. Here is the arrow, and this wound will cause my death. I now advise you to prepare for your return journey as quickly as possible, but take me to that cape I thought was such a good farm site. Perhaps the words I spoke will prove true enough and I will dwell there awhile. You will bury me there and mark my grave with crosses at the head and foot, and call the spot Krossanes (Cross point) after that.'

On 18 August 1996, Baldur and I decided to try to find, on the headland between St. Ann's Bay and Big Bras d'Or, the landscape where the natives were slain and where Thorvald died. We crossed St. Ann's Bay by a great sand reef, and then by ferry. We tried to drive from Englishtown out to the shore on the western side of the headland between the fjords, but the road soon became impassable. It was clear that nobody would regard this side as a good farm site, and the map shows no lowland along the shore. So we crossed the headland, where a good gravel road led all the way to Cape Dauphin on the outermost point of the headland. There we saw nothing that resembled the description in the Saga of the Greenlanders – no headland, moorage or sands – and this was something of a disappointment. We met a couple who had retired to the island. The woman grew up on a farm nearby, where there had been three cows; farms of similar size could have existed farther down the coast. We turned southwards again. The strip of low-lying land along the coast grew wider as we travelled farther south; its total area is approximately 5 km² about 15–50 metres above sea level. The lowlands come to an end at their widest point, about six kilometres inland from Cape Dauphin. According to information from the Nova Scotia Cartographic Institute in Amherst, the soil in this hilly lowland area is quite suitable for farming if the forests are cleared, although only a little of the land has been cultivated, partly because it is so remote. In some places the soil is stony, but this could be used for grazing. The land is, however, best suited for arboriculture, and there were clear signs of this. We then proceeded to the town of Sydney, where we stayed at a pleasant old hotel, the Hotel St. Paul.

It was not until the following morning that we realised that the cape at the southern end of the lowland area west of Big Bras d'Or could have been Krossanes. We drove straight back to take a better look. As we approached New Campbellton, we stopped at a sandy beach 10–30 metres wide between the road and the sea; from here we had a good view of the lowland area leading to the wooded headland about 500 metres away, across an attractive bay, Kelly's Cove. Boats could easily be landed at this beach (see aerial photograph p. iv). The cove is an excellent moorage; east of the cove is a marina that serves the little village of New Campbellton. The road runs along a causeway across the bay; on the lake within the causeway was a man in a boat. The road then turns outwards along the bay, out to the cape and along the coast to the north.

On the cape is a narrow strip of land below the road, which appears undisturbed. Would it be worthwhile for archaeologists to examine this place? It commands good views both across the bay and inland along the length of the inlet. "Here I would like to build my farm," said Thorvald. There would have been a beautiful view, and this would make an ideal place for a grave barrow, as archaeologist Dr. Kristjan Eldjarn described them: "a dry and attractive place, near a farm, yet outside the field area, preferably not very low-lying, often on a river bank."[29] Although Thorvald is said to have been buried by Christian rites, with crosses at head and foot, it is not unlikely that these recent converts would be influenced by heathen notions of suitable burial places. Today, the headland is a Christian stronghold, as a Bible School is located there. Young people were playing games on a neat field where the forest has been cleared. So the name Krossanes (Cross Point) is fitting once more.

From the Icelandic settlers' point of view, the woods would have been a disadvantage, as they would want to grow grass and find pasture for their livestock. But there is hardly a part of Nova Scotia that is not wooded, and Thorvald must have been prepared to accept this. And by felling or burning the trees, the lowland area north of the headland would have provided land for several farms. The headland and the cove beyond are only about 6 kilometres inland from the mouth of Big Bras d'Or. Conditions for fishing are therefore favourable, and it is likely that Thorvald Eiriksson would have borne this in mind.

The place also fits well with the background to the story: Keel

Point on the northeast point of Cape Breton Island, and the mouths of fjords which were nearby when they continued their journey. On their travels no doubt they first sailed into the mouth of St. Ann's Bay. If the location of the story were there, it would have been natural for the saga to mention only this bay. But this is not done, and therefore it may be deduced that the location is to be found at Big Bras d'Or, as our search indicated. And since they sailed into the mouths of bays and to the headland, it seems clear that the cape is not at the end of the peninsula between the bays, but along the edge of one of the bays.

Was this the Krossanes of the Saga of the Greenlanders? This is a question that may never be answered, but if it is so, the description in the saga fits the real topography extraordinarily well: good land for farming on a peninsula between the mouths of two bays, a wooded cape with a beautiful view, a suitable burial place for Thorvald nearby, good moorage, and an adjacent beach which can easily fit the account of the natives' boats and wigwams. And in addition, none of the other details of the story conflict with this being the place.

Thorvald's crew now returned to their companions, and loaded up with grapes and vines before returning to Greenland the following spring, to tell their news. They must have gathered the grapes in the autumn, and kept them through the winter at Leif's Camp, presumably in the form of raisins.

It is interesting that Thorvald preferred to make his home in a place other than Leif's Camp, which was admittedly an excellent place for spending the winter, in order to make an early return to Greenland in the spring. It was also an ideal base camp for making expeditions to gather various commodities from Wineland. But the annual mean temperature was lower than at any Icelandic farm, with frequent sea ice. However, on the east coast of Nova Scotia, where Krossanes appears to have been, the summers are warmer than anywhere in Iceland (or Greenland). There are forests of hardwood, and grass grows well where the forest is cleared and the soil is suitable; conditions for freshwater and sea fishing are also good. Furthermore, it is tempting to infer that by this expedition Thorvald pointed the way for Thorfinn Karlsefni's journey to Straumsfjord and Hop in the next Wineland expedition.

Thorstein Eiriksson's search for Wineland

The Saga of the Greenlanders states that Eirik the Red died the winter after Leif's return from Wineland, while according to Eirik the Red's Saga he lived longer. During Thorvald's expedition to Wineland, his brother Thorstein had married Gudrid Thorbjarnardottir. He planned to head to Wineland, but never reached it, as they were carried off course at sea and did not know where they went. They landed at Lysufjord in the Western Settlement on Greenland's west coast, and Thorstein died there that winter, along with many of his men.

Thorstein Eiriksson could hardly have wandered off course in this way if he had travelled as far north up Greenland's coast as Thorfinn was to do later – as will be discussed below (see p. 53). From there, it would have been a journey of only two half-days across to Helluland; it would have been possible to wait for favourable weather for such a brief voyage. So it is likely that Thorstein took a route similar to that of Bjarni, Leif and Thorvald; a journey of about four half-days across to the southernmost point of Helluland. He may even have intended to take a short cut, steering southwest straight from Eiriksfjord, then found himself in bad weather, with tragic consequences. It is not unlikely that this experience would have encouraged Thorfinn Karlsefni and Gudrid to take the less hazardous route across the strait to Helluland. Ill-fated though Thorstein's journey was, it provides an interesting footnote: the bodies of Thorstein's men who had died of the pestilence were taken to Eiriksfjord for burial. Olafur Halldorsson says:[30]

> In 1961 the remains of the church of Thjodhild [Eirik the Red's Christian wife] were found. The church and graveyard were subsequently excavated and carefully studied. At the south wall of the church a grave was found containing a jumble of bones, later revealed to be the bones of 12 men and a child aged 12–14. These men were 1.77m tall on average, while the

average height of males buried in the churchyard was 1.71m. Could this be Thorstein Eiriksson and his crew, whom he had selected for their size and strength? This hypothesis is not entirely random: the grave is situated at the southern wall of the graveyard. This indicates, in the first place, that those buried there were of high rank, and in the second place that the church must have been practically new, as there was space for burial at the south wall.

Regarding Olafur Halldorsson's hypothesis, archaeologist Kristjan Eldjarn, later president of Iceland, commented:[31]

> ... if this should be the reality behind the story, the conformity with the tall men in the mass grave is so spectacular that one cannot help feeling that everything fits neatly together. But one should, as always, keep an open mind.

The journey of Thorfinn Karlsefni

Let us take a look at chapter 8 of Eirik the Red's Saga, when Thorfinn Karlsefni's journey to Wineland is in preparation:

> That winter there was much merrymaking in Brattahlid; many board games were played, there was storytelling and plenty of other entertainment to brighten the life of the household. There were great discussions that winter in Brattahlid of Snorri and Karlsefni setting sail for Vinland, and people talked at length about it. In the end Snorri and Karlsefni made their vessel ready, intending to sail in search of Vinland that summer. Bjarni and Thorhall decided to accompany them on the voyage, taking their own ship and their companions who had sailed with them on the voyage out.
>
> A man named Thorvard was married to Freydis, who was an illegitimate daughter of Eirik the Red. He went with them, along with Thorvald, Eirik's son, and Thorhall who was called the Huntsman. For years he had accompanied Eirik on hunting trips in the summers, and was entrusted with many tasks. Thorhall was a large man, dark and coarse-featured; he

was getting on in years and difficult to handle. He was a silent man, who was not generally given to conversation, devious and yet insulting in his speech, and who usually did his best to make trouble. He had paid scant heed to the faith since it had come to Greenland. Thorhall was not popular with most people but he had long been in Eirik's confidence. He was among those on the ship with Thorvald and Thorvard, as he had a wide knowledge of the uninhabited regions. They had the ship which Thorbjorn had brought to Greenland and set sail with Karlsefni and his group. Most of the men aboard were from Greenland. The crews of the three ships made a hundred plus forty men.

Thorfinn's expedition is said to comprise three ships, with one hundred and forty men aboard. This has generally been interpreted to mean the "great hundred" i.e. 10x12 = 120, making the total number 160. This is, however, dubious, as chapter 11 of the saga states that "ten tens" of men remained at Straumsfjord while "four tens" sailed south to Hop, i.e. a total of 140. This is also a more credible figure in view of the fact that the three vessels had to carry, not only the crews, but also livestock and other goods taken on the journey. Admittedly, Thorhall the Huntsman is said to have gone north past Kjalarnes with nine men, and they may not have been included in the 100 left at Straumsfjord. The number of people involved in the expedition, though not entirely clear, may have been 140, 150 or 160. This may seem a large number. But Thorfinn's ship was probably a large one; the Saga of the Greenlanders says that sixty men and five women were aboard.

From the sagas one may infer that Thorfinn found out all he could about previous Wineland journeys during his winter at Brattahlid. He was accompanied by Thorhall the Huntsman, who had often hunted with Eirik the Red during the summers; so he was probably familiar with the northern reaches. It is not improbable that they had some idea in advance of the most favourable route to the New World, as the discussion at Brattahlid implies.

Thorfinn can hardly have set off from Brattahlid until early August, due to the sea ice off Labrador. Manuscript AM557 of Eirik the Red's Saga (*Skálholtsbók*) says:

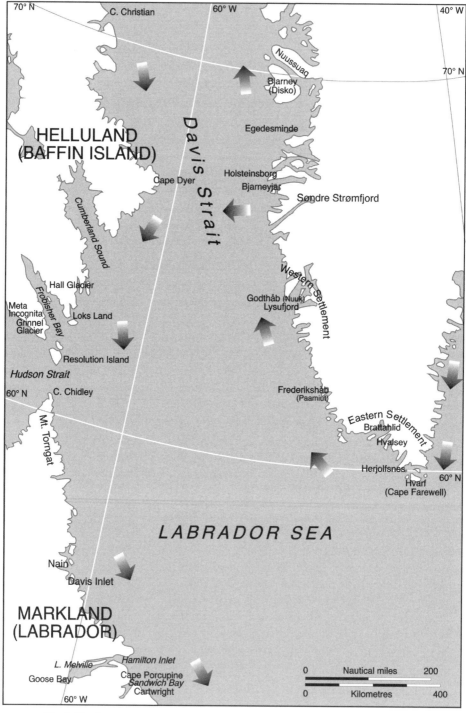

Davis Strait.

> They sailed along the coast to the Western Settlement, and then to the Bear Islands [Bjarneyjar].

The question is, where were the Bjarneyjar? In the fjord south of Holsteinsborg, on Greenland's west coast, are three sizeable islands. The smallest, Manitsorssuaq, is 15 km², while the largest is 150 km². These may well be the Bjarneyjar, directly east of Cape Dyer on Baffin Island, where the strait is at its narrowest. The version in *Hauksbók*, on the contrary, says that they sailed from Bjarney (Bear Island), which is generally believed to be the island now called Disko, about 200 km north of Holsteinsborg.[32] But the narrative of *Skálholtsbók* (chapter 8) gains credibility from the fact that the Bjarneyjar (Bear Islands) are mentioned twice, clearly in the plural, while *Hauksbók* mentions Bjarney (Bear Island) only once, and rather illegibly at that.

In addition, Hauk Erlendsson, the main copyist of the manuscript, penned this chapter himself; and he is known to have had more of a tendency to edit and embroider than other copyists of the manuscript.

If they set off from Disko, Cape Dyer on Baffin Island would have been about three half-days away. The shortest distance to Cape Dyer is, however, from Holsteinsborg or nearby, a distance of about 178 nautical miles, or a journey of about two half-days, as stated in the saga.

At this point, the coast of Greenland may be said to bend a little to the right, when sailing from the south; the land, in other words, reaches a little farther west at this point than it does to the north and south. One may imagine that the travellers picked a good moorage to wait for favourable conditions for this important sea journey. Holsteinsborg has a good natural harbour, and the islands to the south ought also to provide shelter from the ocean waves. Modern maps show various hunting sites on the islands. So this may have been one of the places used by the hunters sent north from the Eastern Settlement during the summer, who included Thorhall the Huntsman, one of Thorfinn's company. Hunters probably established some kind of camp on the islands; these may have been booths with turf and stone walls, roofed with canvas when occupied, similar to those used as temporary residences at the summer parliamentary assemblies at Thingvellir in Iceland. It would also have been important to have facilities for cooking onshore, as lighting a fire aboard ship was to be avoided at all costs.

In this context it is interesting to consider *Grönlandia vetus, chorographia á afgömlu kveri,* a short passage of the Greenland chronicle, quoted by Arngrim Jonsson the Learned (1568–1648) in his book *Gronlandia.*[33] It says:

> From the Western Settlement to Lysufjord is six days' rowing, thence six days' rowing to Karlbudir, thence three days' rowing to Bjarney [Bear Island].

Olafur Halldorsson believes that this should read "Eastern" not "Western" settlement, as Lysufjord was in the Western Settlement. He also believes that the Karlbudir camp was in the wilderness north of the Western Settlement (Lysufjord). According to Norwegian sources, a day's rowing was half the distance of 12 hours' sailing, or 35–40 nautical miles.[34] This is quite reasonable, on the assumption that seafarers rowed along the coast only in daylight, although the speed of most rowing vessels was nearly three knots (three nautical miles per hour). Six days' rowing would thus be nearly 240 nautical miles, which is not far from being the distance between the Eastern and Western Settlements (Lysufjord), and also the distance between the Western Settlement and Holsteinsborg. And the three-day journey north to Disko is about half this distance on the map. This all fits together, and is a certain indication that Karlbudir was near Holsteinsborg, and also that Bjarney (Bear Island) was Disko. According to this, Karlbudir would have been an ideal place to wait for a favourable breeze to Helluland; it is likeley to have had good moorage, and probably a camp ashore, either at Holsteinsborg or on the islands to the south (Bjarneyjar?).

But there are other possibilities regarding this place. Probably Thorhall the Huntsman had spent long periods there hunting in the summer, and made exploratory forays. It was known at that time, after the journeys of Bjarni, Leif and Thorvald, that there was land to the west. The distance across the Davis Strait is only about 178 nautical miles, approximately as far as from the West Fjords of Iceland to Greenland. It is said that sometimes, from the middle of

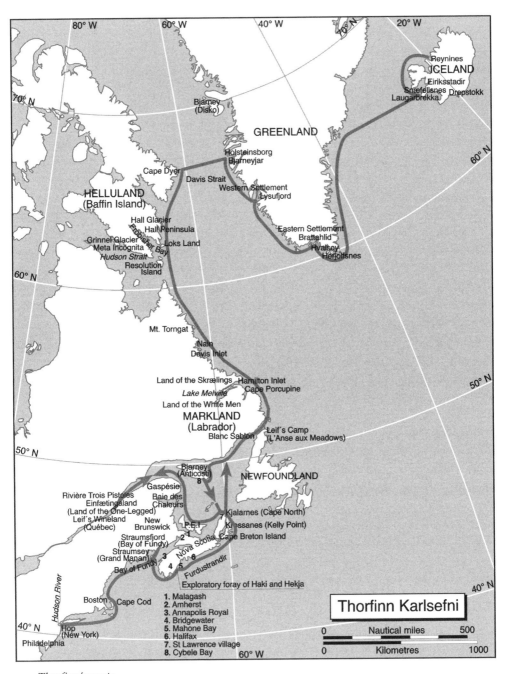

Thorfinn's route.

the Greenland Sea, both Greenland and Iceland can be seen. In the vicinity of Greenland, mirages are commonly experienced, as refraction makes islands and mountains visible that would normally be below the horizon.[35] Snæfellsjökull glacier, which stands 1,446 metres high, has been seen from the sea at a distance of up to 500 kilometres (270 nautical miles); it was seen by Captain John Bartlett on the *Effie M. Morrisey* on 17 July 1939, when conditions were conducive to mirages.[36] This was one of the warmest summers ever experienced in Iceland; mirages are especially likely when warm air comes into contact with relatively cold sea. Over Baffin Island, in addition, there would probably be quite high banks of cumulus clouds, formed over the hot, bare rock and mountains. This bank of clouds along the coast would be visible from a far greater distance than the land itself, and it is probable that experienced seafarers knew and used this clue. Over mountains and glaciers beyond the shoreline there would sometimes be high banks of streamlined (lenticular) mountain clouds which would be visible from afar (see picture p. xiii). The probability is thus great that the existence of this land west of Holsteinsborg had rapidly been discovered by the Greenlanders.

From this it may be inferred that when there was a northerly wind and clear sky at Bjarneyjar (Karlbudir?), which looked likely to hold for at least a day, Thorfinn set a westerly course and sailed off. In this context, we may consider the statement of *Konungsskuggsjá* (the King's Mirror) that small seas

> … have no great perils and one may risk crossing them at almost any time; for one has to make sure of fair winds to last a day [*dægur*] or two only, which is not difficult for men who are weatherwise.[37]

In addition, the sun does not set at night in these regions in the summer, when Thorfinn was presumably travelling. A sidewind was favourable for Viking ships, as mentioned above, provided it was not too strong a breeze. The northerly wind would have had the advantage in this case that it would have been easy to turn and sail back if necessary, with the wind to port. In the Davis Strait, winds are generally either northerly or southerly, funnelled between the adjacent lands and mountains, as happens elsewhere, for instance in the Denmark Strait between Iceland and Greenland. The story continues in chapter 8 of Eirik's Saga, economically told:

> They sailed along the coast to the western settlement, then to the Bear islands and from there with a northerly wind. After two days [dægur] at sea they sighted land and rowed over in boats to explore it. There they found many flat slabs of stone, so large that two men could lie foot-to-foot across them. There were many foxes there. They gave the land the name Helluland (Stone-slab land).
>
> After that they sailed with a northerly wind for two days [dægur], and again sighted land, with large forests and many animals. An island lay to the south-east, off the coast, where they discovered a bear, and they called it Bjarney (Bear Island), and the forested land itself Markland.

Once they have arrived at Helluland, it is interesting to consider where the description might fit.

In 1994, a book was published on Martin Frobisher's travels to Baffin Island in 1576–1581.[38] Frobisher appears to have kept mostly close to the mouth of Frobisher Bay; his original plan was to find the supposed Northwest Passage to India and China. He came across a mineral he was convinced contained gold, and transported 1,000 tons of it back to Europe. The rock, which he called "black ore," is black in colour, harder than glass, and with three times the density of water. It contains a large amount of hornblende, and it is believed to have been formed from magma deep beneath the earth's crust. It formed hardened intrusions about 1,900 million years ago, in the Proterozoic era. These rock layers were then lifted up, and subsequently exposed by weathering. The rock was then eroded by glaciers, which carried off lumps of the black rock, and dispersed them over the lighter-coloured surrounding rock. These rocks are often in the form of blocks or slabs, with vertical striations (see photograph on page 20). The largest of the slabs weighs at least nine tons, and measures 1–3 metres each way; so it is not unreasonable to say that two men might "lie foot-to-foot across them." Because of the dark colour, the rocks are very noticeable. To Frobisher's disappointment, the rock turned out to contain even less gold than ordinary rock.

But while Frobisher's "black ore" turned out less precious than he had hoped, it may be said to be valuable in another way; it lends credibility to the Saga of Eirik, since it undeniably appears to fit the description of the large slabs from which Helluland drew its name, as recounted in chapter 8 of the saga.

There is nothing to contradict the statement that there were many foxes in Helluland, since the Arctic fox is found all over Arctic Canada. The foxes of Helluland are thus no help in deciding whether Helluland was Baffin Island or Labrador. But if Helluland was northern Labrador, it would have taken more than two half-days to sail there from Greenland. And if Markland were southern Labrador, which was wooded, there would have been no sea passage between Helluland and Markland. Hence it is more likely that Helluland was Baffin Island.

Eirik's Saga goes on to mention a sea journey of two half-days, presumably across the open sea of the Hudson Strait, until they reached Markland (which would thus be Labrador). On the map this is a distance of about one-and-a-half half-days, assuming a speed of 78 nautical miles per half-day – departing from Loks Land, around the Hall Peninsula, and passing Resolution Island, probably remaining within sight of land the whole time. While the woods (*mörk*) from which the name Markland is derived, do not begin until some 135 nautical miles south of the northernmost point of Labrador, this does not mean that the whole land might not be named for the woods – just as Iceland is only partly icy, and Greenland only partly green.

As mentioned above, the assumption is made here that the explorers had some information on the topography before they set off; otherwise it would have been extremely rash to set off for Wineland with the intention of settling. According to both of the Wineland sagas, Leif had already sailed to Wineland by this time, and here it has been argued that he travelled westwards along the Gulf of St. Lawrence and on to Québec. But it is reasonable to assert that the true Wineland was not the northernmost point of Newfoundland, which is a harsher environment than most Icelandic rural areas. The saga indicates, on the contrary, that Thorfinn believed the best prospects for settlement were farther south than the Gulf of St. Lawrence. This was a natural continuation of Thorvald Eiriksson's exploration of this region. But clearly opinion was divided on this matter. As will emerge later, this disagreement had important consequences.

The next spring, Thorhall the Huntsman wanted to travel westward along the Gulf of St. Lawrence. A good landmark on this route was the island of Anticosti. It would have been ideal for Thorfinn to be guided there by Thorhall, after which he intended to head southwards along the eastern side of the land, following Thorvald Eiriksson's route. Here the assumption is made that they followed the coast of Markland until they reached Anticosti, called Bjarney (Bear Island) in the saga. A long section of the coast north of this lies northeast-southwest, and hence the saga's statement that Bjarney lay "to the south-east, off the coast" would make sense. Black bears are found on Anticosti, and the Native Americans called it "the land where bears are hunted." It is about 8,000 km^2 in area, and wooded. The journey from the northernmost point of Markland to Bjarney (Bear Island) could hardly have taken less than 12 half-days, if no delays occurred. It is probable that Thorfinn chose the same landing-place as Leif on Bjarney, at Cybele Bay at the eastern end of the southern coast.

Across the Gulf of St. Lawrence
After arrival at Bjarney (Bear Island), here identified as Anticosti, chapter 8 of Eirik's Saga continues:

After another two days [*dægur*] passed they again sighted land and approached the shore where a peninsula jutted out. They sailed upwind along the coast, keeping the land on the starboard. The country was wild with a long shoreline and sand flats. They rowed ashore in boats and, discovering the keel of a ship there, named this point Kjalarnes (Keel point). They also gave the beaches the name Furdustrandir (Wonder beaches) for their surprising length.

This is best understood as meaning that they sailed across the Gulf of St. Lawrence from Bjarney (Anticosti) and arrived at Kjalarnes. It is highly likely that they knew of the ship's keel that had been raised up there during Thorvald's expedition. A passage across the Gulf of St. Lawrence, out of sight of land, could be based on the knowledge acquired in Thorvald's Wineland expedition. This is an important link between the Saga of the Greenlanders and Eirik the Red's Saga.

The *Hauksbók* version of the saga gives another account of the journey from Markland. This section was written down by Hauk himself, who shortened the account radically. There is no mention of a journey of two half-days. Instead Thorfinn sails "south along the land a long time, and they reached a headland with the land lying to starboard."

Copyist Hauk is known to have taken a fairly free hand with the ancient text, and so this version must be counted as rather spurious. But many people have based their theories on this version, concluding, for instance, that Kjalarnes was Cape Porcupine way up north in Labrador. This makes it far more difficult to picture a credible setting for the rest of the saga, than if one assumed that Kjalarnes was Cape North, south of the Gulf of St. Lawrence.

North, then south

It is time to pause in our narrative and consider the journey so far. Why did they first sail such a long way north up the coast of Greenland, instead of heading directly west, or even southwest, from Greenland? There were ample reasons for this. In the first place, the plan appears to have been to call at the Western Settlement before departure, and from there they did not have to travel much farther north. In the second place, it is important to keep journeys across open sea to a minimum, rather than risking being carried off course or being caught in storms at sea. It has also been pointed out that it is better for the ship's cargo, men and animals, to sail the shortest distance across open sea. It is usually safe to risk sailing across small seas, says the *King's Mirror*, as quoted above.

This is quite consistent with experience of popular weather predictions; it is often possible to deduce from the clouds and wind what the weather will be like for 12 hours or longer. But on a journey of many days directly from Eiriksfjord to Labrador, storms may blow up, that cannot be foreseen before departure. And this longer route was not as slow as it might appear, due to favourable currents and winds. Thorfinn Karlsefni was a good seafarer, says the saga, and so he probably knew that in these northerly latitudes westerly winds grow stronger and more frequent as one travels farther south, so that it was best to avoid headwinds and storms southwest of Greenland. Probably this was precisely the error made by Thorstein Eiriksson when his ship was carried off course on the way to Wineland. This disastrous event would have taught Thorfinn Karlsefni to stick to coastal routes. He would also have been familiar with the coastal currents, which could be used to advantage. In the northern hemisphere, coastal currents flow so that land is on the starboard side when the ship follows the current, i.e. northwards along the west coast of Greenland, southwards along the coast of Labrador. He may or may not have known that the wind has a tendency to follow the direction of the coastal current, although irregularly. This may be explained to the modern reader as being due to the fact that atmospheric pressure is generally rather lower over sea than over land, especially cold land, and winds always blow anticlockwise around low-pressure areas, such as the low normally located between Greenland and Labrador, although this is scarcely visible on charts of average atmospheric pressure. To the east of this indistinct low, southerly winds are relatively frequent, while northerly winds are more common to the west, along by Labrador. This provides favourable conditions for the journey to America.

Taking all the factors into account, Thorfinn Karlsefni's route, north along the Greenland coast, across the Davis Strait, and south along the Labrador coast, may be regarded as a sensible one, that did credit to a "merchant of good repute."

Three journeys of two half-days
When Eirik's Saga describes Thorfinn's journey along the Greenland coast and that of America, the precise length of the journey is never stated; only vague indications are given ("they sailed for a long time"). But when it comes to the journey from Bjarneyjar (Bear Islands) to Helluland, the saga says they were out at sea for

two half-days, and the same applies to the passage from Helluland to Markland, and again from there to Kjalarnes. The duration of the journey is thus only specified when it is across open sea; such journeys were also hazardous, involving dangers that seafarers did their best to avoid. On a coastal journey of exploration, no doubt the crew often went ashore, or lay at anchor overnight, so the actual duration of the journey would be less obvious, while at open sea the journey was continuous, at least while the summer nights remained light.

The interpretation placed upon these descriptions of journeys is crucial to an estimate of how far Thorfinn and his company could have gone that first summer. Some people have interpreted the journey of three times two half-days as meaning that the whole journey from Greenland to Kjalarnes took only six half-days. This must, however, be dismissed, and it would have been pointless to try to spend such a short time on the journey. In that time it would not have been possible to travel much farther than the northern-most point of Labrador, and it is safe to say that Kjalarnes was not there. And even if the dubious interpretation is maintained that a *dægur* was 24 hours, not 12 hours or a half-day, so that 150 nautical miles or so might be sailed in a *dægur*, this leads to the conclusion that Kjalarnes could be no farther south than somewhere on the northeast coast of Labrador, such as Cape Porcupine, but this is, as stated before, quite unbelievable.

Furdustrandir

Once they had reached Kjalarnes in Nova Scotia, the travellers were growing close to their destination. By this time they were as far south as Leif when he stayed near Québec. So their anticipation must have been great. But Furdustrandir (Wonder Coast) is de-scribed in the saga as wild [*öræfi*] with a long shoreline and sand flats. I believe that the term *öræfi* is used here to mean wild land, unsuitable for settlement, in this case due to solid forests; Nova Scotia is almost entirely covered by dense forest, except where it has been cleared in recent centuries to use the land for other pur-poses. There is a strong similarity between this description and that of the land along which Thorfinn sailed westwards, probably the south coast of the Gulf of St. Lawrence, when he was searching for Thorhall the Huntsman. Chapter 11 of Eirik's Saga says:

They saw nothing but wild forest.

They may well have *wondered*, that along a long coast of this southerly land, the land should be so unpromising for settlement, but the saga attributes the name Wonder Coast to its being surprisingly long to sail along.

Some scholars who have considered the Furdustrandir have interpreted the saga's description to mean that the shore was a flat, more or less continuous sandy beach.[39] This is probably attributable to the word *strönd* sometimes being translated as "beach," hence "Wonder Beaches." This would severely limit the possible locations of Furdustrandir. But in Icelandic the word *strönd* does not apply only to sandy or shingle "beaches" but also to all kinds of shore and coastline: sand, stone, rock and steep cliffs. Since the "sand flats" are mentioned after the "beaches," it is reasonable to infer that the *strönd* ("shore") was long, while only some of it was sandy. Sandy beaches worth consideration are found, for instance, at Aspy Bay near the northern end of the east coast of Cape Breton Island. The last 30 miles of the coast of the island, before it grows deeply indented, have many sand and gravel reefs, and along the shore northeast of the saltwater Bras d'Or Lake there are also sandy stretches. Along the indented Atlantic coast of Nova Scotia there are extensive glacial moraines; sandy shores and saltmarshes have formed in the inlets, while headlands jut out between them: long shores and sand flats.[40]

There is nothing to contradict the hypothesis that Furdustrandir stretch along much of the eastern coast of Cape Breton Island and Nova Scotia, a distance of about 350 nautical miles. Since Thorfinn did not find it a promising land for settlement, it is not strange that he found it of "surprising length."

The exploratory foray of Haki and Hekja
On Furdustrandir, the shore becomes indented. This is a good description of the shore some distance from Kjalarnes, and now the

travellers begin to think of exploration. Chapter 8 of Eirik's Saga says:

> When Leif had served King Olaf Tryggvason and was told by him to convert Greenland to Christianity, the king had given him two Scots, a man named Haki and a woman called Hekja. The king told him to call upon them whenever he needed someone with speed, as they were fleeter of foot than any deer. Leif and Eirik had sent them to accompany Karlsefni.
>
> After sailing the length of the Furdustrandir, they put the two Scots ashore and told them to run southwards to explore the country and return before three days' [*dægur*] time had elapsed. They were dressed in a garment known as a *kjafal*, which had a hood at the top but no arms, and was open at the sides and fastened between the legs with a button and loop; they wore nothing else.
>
> The ships cast anchor and lay to during this time.
>
> After three days had passed the two returned to the shore, one of them with grapes in hand and the other with self-sown wheat. Karlsefni said that they had found good land.

Many people have regarded the story of Haki and Hekja as entirely apocryphal, and cast doubt upon this section of the saga: especially those, of course, who feel that it does not belong at this point in the story. The story of the runners' costumes is, however, remarkably detailed. Fridtjof Nansen, who otherwise gave no credence at all to the Wineland sagas (and died before the crucial L'Anse aux Meadows site was discovered), pointed out that *kjafal* might be the same as a garment called *cabhail* in Gaelic. A similar explanation for the etymology of the word is given in Asgeir Blöndal Magnusson's dictionary.[41] Or it could be derived from the Gaelic word *gjoball*, meaning a garment. It would make the best sense if the runners were Irish, but this need not necessarily be the case, especially since Gaelic dialect is spoken even today in some regions of Scotland. Matthias Thordarson found this story an ideal motif for the artist, while the same applies to many other aspects of the Wineland sagas.[42] Einar Haugen's book *Voyages to Wineland* includes a picture of the two Scots by F. T. Chapman, along with many other interesting pictures.[43]

Along most of the coast of the Gulf of St. Lawrence, woods grow close to the sea, as the Saga of the Greenlanders says. Photo Baldur Palsson.

"The country was wild with a long shoreline and sand flats." This description of Furdu-strandir applies well to the east and southeast coast of Nova Scotia. This photograph is from Ingonish on the way south from Cape North (Kjalarnes) on Cape Breton Island, where rocky shores alternate with sandy beaches. Photo Warren Gordon M.P.A.

In Bridgewater, Nova Scotia, about 80 km southwest of Halifax, the author found two species of wild grape: the riverbank grape (Vitis riparia) and the fox grape (Vitis labrusca). Photo Baldur Palsson.

At Malagash at the western end of the north coast of Nova Scotia are vineyards that bear the name of Hans Jost, who planted them in 1970. The vineyards produce award-winning wines which are served by Nova Scotians to foreign dignitaries. Photo Baldur Palsson.

The saltmarshes at Saint John would provide plenty of hay. The author believes this is the place Thorfinn Karlsefni called Straumsfjord. "The grass there grew tall," says Eirik the Red's Saga. Photo Baldur Palsson.

Reversing Falls. An obstacle in the Saint John River that flows through Saint John means that the river flows through rapids downstream at low tide, but reverses and flows upstream at high tide. The meander in the river (right) would have provided a convenient moorage, and an excellent farmstead site on the bank. Perhaps this is where Thorfinn Karlsefni stayed at Straumsfjord. Photo Baldur Palsson.

Eirík the Red's Saga says that one "could hardly walk without stepping on eggs." This grassland at the south of Grand Manan (Straumsey) was a breeding ground for thousands of seabirds until foxes that escaped from fur farms in the late 19th century reproduced and annihilated the bird colony. Photo Baldur Palsson.

Dulse on the beach at Dark Harbour on Grand Manan (Straumsey). When Thorfinn and his company fled from Straumsfjord to Straumsey due to the harsh winter, Eirik's Saga tells us that "their livestock improved there," perhaps due to good grazing on the shore. Photo Baldur Palsson.

Many kinds of flotsam and jetsam wash ashore at Whale Cove on Grand Manan: timber, even whales, as the name implies. Photo Baldur Palsson.

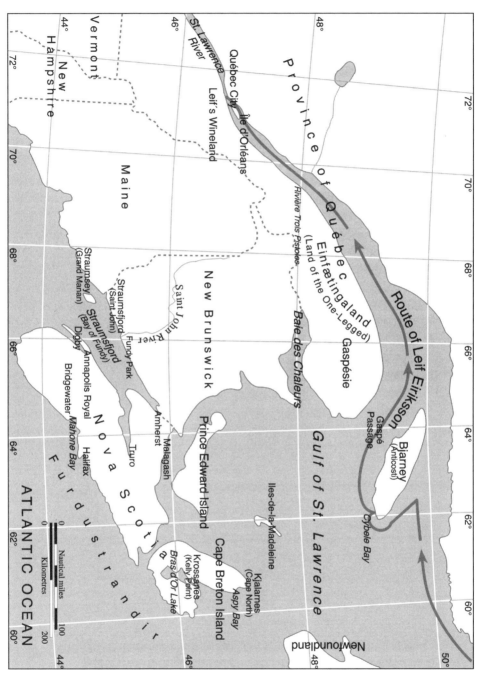

Gulf of St. Lawrence.

On a closer look, it is clear that this episode cannot be made to fit into the narrative better at any other point. While the manuscripts of Eirik's Saga are not entirely consistent, the clear implication is that they sailed into an inlet, and sent the runners off on their journey from there. They would undoubtedly try to find good moorage, and this could be found in many places along the southeast coast of Nova Scotia. The biggest and best of the harbours is at Halifax, which is said to be the second-largest natural harbour in the world, after New York. St. Margaret Bay and Mahone Bay, a little farther to the southwest, also provide good moorage according to sailing directions.

The statement that they entered the inlet when they had sailed along Furdustrandir may seem a little vague, as the runners then go on southwards. But perhaps this may be justified by the fact that it is never clearly stated where Furdustrandir ended.

But was there any chance that Haki and Hekja might find grapes and self-sown wheat at this point? They need not have existed in great abundance: the saga certainly never implies that they did. Each runner brought no more than a handful of each commodity. As stated above, wild rice, "self-sown wheat," is found in southern and western Nova Scotia: this is the species *Zizania palustris*, according to Fernald's manual of botany.[44] It is stated, however, that large expanses of wild rice are not found in Nova Scotia, except near Amherst in the northwest.[45] Wild vines, probably riverbank grapes, existed at three places in Nova Scotia in the 17th century, and at the same places in the 19th century. I shall return to this subject in the section on vines (see p. 211).[46] And in 1924 this species, riverbank grapes (*Vitis riparia*) with dark, sour, rather small grapes, was found at another location in Nova Scotia. This new area of vines, near Bridgewater on the La Have River, is about 80 km west-southwest of Halifax. The swift-footed runners could easily have reached this place on their journey.[47] If their point of departure was Mahone Bay, they would have been only 15 km from the place where the grapes grew. It is not unlikely that the runners had special instructions to search for these famous resources of Wineland, grapes and self-sown wheat, which had doubtless been discussed back at Brattahlid, and described as far as possible. The same species of vine is still found in the valley inland from Saint John at the Bay of Fundy, to which I shall return shortly. This is probably the same species as Cartier found along the St. Lawrence river, which still grows wild all over the St. Lawrence valley and north of Québec city.

Riverbank grapes ripen in August or September, which is precisely when Thorfinn may be estimated to have reached the area.[48] In addition, it is not unlikely that vines were more abundant in Nova Scotia a thousand years ago, and hence were easier to find than they are today, due to the white man's impact on the environment.

It is consistent with hardy grape vines growing in Nova Scotia, that modern viticulture is practised there in at least two places. In the small town of Malagash on the north coast, the Jost family grows prize-winning grape species on 35 acres (14 hectares).

The Halifax Natural History Museum had no information on riverbank grapes growing in Bridgewater, but we were advised to go there and ask around. We did so.

On Wednesday 21 August 1996 we woke up in Bridgewater in bright, fine weather. The river was smooth, and a scent in the air. There was some anticipation about what the day would bring.

We started by going to a travel agency, where we met friendly and helpful staff. They thought the best we could do would be to go to a museum run by the municipality, the Des Brisay Museum. A member of the museum staff said he did not remember hearing anything about wild rice being found nearby, but he recalled that some years before a man had come to the museum to ask about wild grapes. After some thought, he turned up a note, and referred us to the old Wile Carding Mill, which had been powered in the 19th century by water power from the Chases Brook. This is now a museum, where we met two cheerful ladies in the fine weather. They showed us two species of vines. They called one of them "Concord"; this grew on the front of the building, and reached a height of about two metres. This was the species Vitis labrusca, *the fox grape, which is hardly found farther north than southern*

*Maine. The grapes are tasty, and are used for winemaking, al-
though the taste of the wine is unusual. The plant had probably been transplanted to this location. But just across the
brook was a vine they called "Scuppernong," or* Vitis riparia,
*riverbank grapes. This vine was unusual in that it twisted
and turned its way right to the tops of the trees, although
nothing had been done to make the climbing easier. Hence it
was not unlikely that this was a wild plant. The ladies said
that the grapes were small and dark purple, and one grimaced
when we asked if they were sour. But they had considered using them for grape jelly.*

*We took a fine branch of each species. And Baldur took a pic-
ture of me in the role of Haki (or Hekja), holding my find. This
was precisely the area where we thought it most likely that the
Scottish pair had been sent out to explore. This was not proof,
of course, but it was a welcome clue that we might be on the
right track. That was all one could ask. We then set off straight
back to the museum in Halifax. We were cheered even more by
spotting a white-tailed deer hind on our way; the white-tailed
(Virginia) deer is said to have been introduced into Nova Scotia in the late 19th century. Marian Zinck at the museum promised to dry and press part of the vine branch, and send it to us
with a certificate identifying the species. The museum also received a sample of the species.*

*(And in due course, we received our dried samples of vines as
promised.)*

In view of this, the story of Haki and Hekja occurs at a natural
place in the account of Thorfinn Karlsefni's journey. Since wild
rice is found farther north than this, it would be unwise, to say the
least, to assume that it could not have existed here; and this may be
inferred from Fernald's manual of botany.[49] And although the two
Scots had found good things on the land, Thorfinn did not allow
this to tempt him. No doubt his mind was running on pasture land
for his domestic animals. Chapter 8 of Eirik's Saga continues:

After taking them on board once more, they sailed onwards,

until they reached a fjord cutting into the coast. They steered the ships into the fjord with an island near its mouth, where there were strong currents, and called the island Straumsey (Stream island). There were so many birds there that they could hardly walk without stepping on eggs. They sailed up into the fjord, which they called Straumsfjord, unloaded the cargo from the ships and began settling in.

They had brought all sorts of livestock with them and explored the land and its resources. There were mountains there, and a pleasant landscape.

They paid little attention to things other than exploring the land. The grass there grew tall.

"A fjord cutting into the coast" is a good description; after having sailed along the coast of Nova Scotia, which is indented with narrow inlets, they arrive at the wide Bay of Fundy between Nova Scotia and New Brunswick. William Babcock identified Grand Manan island in the mouth of the Bay of Fundy, which has an area of about 140 km², as Straumsey.[50] The existence of powerful streams or currents is supported by the fact that the Bay of Fundy has the greatest tidal range in the world; the difference between high and low tide is as much as 15 metres at the head of the bay, and eight metres at Passamaquoddy Bay, which lies to the west of the mouth of the bay.

An unusual kind of fishing has been practised at the Bay of Fundy, thanks to this huge tidal range. Nets were fixed along the shore, then visited between the tides with horse and cart, to reclaim the catch.[51] In the 1930s, the Americans had plans to build a huge tidal power station at Passamaquoddy Bay, west of Grand Manan. Similar plans have been suggested in Canada, especially regarding the Petitcodiac river at the head of the bay. But it was in Nova Scotia that such plans were first put into practice. This is the only tidal power station in North America, built as an experiment at the village of Annapolis Royal, the old provincial capital of Nova Scotia. It can generate up to 20 megawatts, but only when sea level is below average. Potential is however envisaged for a 1,400 megawatt power station, and another with 5,000 megawatt capacity farther up the bay. At the mouth of the Bay of Fundy, the

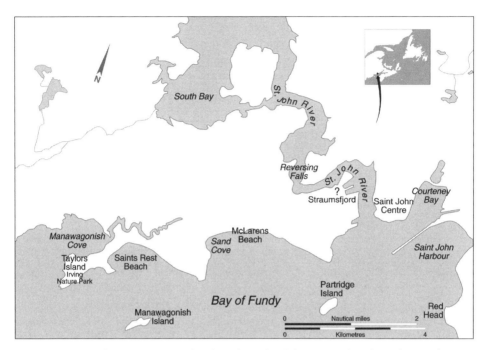

Saint John, New Brunswick, which the author believes may have been the site of Thorfinn Karlsefni's settlement in Straumsfjord.

tidal stream may reach a speed of 5–8 knots, especially on the west coast. And south of Grand Manan, sailing directions warn of strong currents. All this supports the theory that the Bay of Fundy could have been Straumsfjord, where there were "strong currents." [52]

At Straumsey, says the saga, one could "hardly walk without stepping on eggs." This description would, of course, apply to the breeding season in spring; 17th-century accounts confirm that the islands of the area teemed with birds. And as mentioned below, it is still possible to find islands densely populated by birds.

The saga says that they continued up into the fjord, where they unloaded their cargo and "began settling in." This phrase ("*bjuggust þar um*") suggests that they built houses here, as they would do subsequently at Hop. There is no indication that Leif's Wineland was at Straumsfjord, and the topographic description of the Saga of the Greenlanders lends no support to such a supposition. There are no shallows off shore, and grapes are not mentioned among the resources of the land: and one would have to travel a long way up the Saint John river from the town of Saint John to find them. This supports the hypothesis that Thorfinn had not reached the same area as Leif in Wineland, and that he had not accepted Leif's offer of loaning his houses in Newfoundland.

A promising place for a farm for Thorfinn would be by the Bay of Fundy, where the town of Saint John now stands, in New Brunswick. This has a harbour that remains completely ice-free all winter, one of only two in Canada: the other is Halifax.

On Friday 23 August we arrived at Saint John by the ferry Princess of Acadia *from Digby. There was a morning mist, confirming the fact that the bay is cold in summer due to the powerful currents from the ocean, that lead to cooling and condensation in the air. In the afternoon the mist lifted, and we could see down to the sea. Now we saw what I had hoped for: extensive saltmarshes. Saltmarshes are where the sea washes over low-lying shores at high tide, especially where clayey river sediments have accumulated at the heads of bays and in inlets. They are said to make for good hay-making, as they are often grassy, producing hearty hay that needs to be dried well. From the sea, a meandering channel led across the saltmarsh, which was dotted with small pools and puddles. The grass was knee-high in many places, fitting well with the description of Eirik's Saga that the grass "grew tall." The saltmarsh seemed to extend over an area of more than 200 hectares. Just a fraction of this would have been sufficient for Thorfinn, at least initially. But winter grazing would probably have been a problem, as when sea water flowed over the saltmarsh in winter, it probably froze solid. Then the only option would be to flee out to Straumsey island, if they had not gathered enough hay during the summer. We shall explore later what awaited them there.*

One evening we sat at a restaurant near the Reversing Falls; the name is derived from the fact that at low tide water flows down the river over a rocky obstacle, tumbling to form rapids or a waterfall; at high tide, on the contrary, the water pours back in the other direction, forming a waterfall on the upstream side. It was only possible to sail through at the brief period at the turn of the tide. It was an interesting sight. We also looked at the meandering river below the falls. This would have been an ideal moorage, where it would have been easy to beach a longship or knörr. At the top of the slope above, Thorfinn's and Gudrid's farmhouse might have stood. We were told that fresh water was plentiful.

Hay could have been gathered on and around the salt-marshes, while the riverbanks were grassy upstream. Good grassland was surely in short supply in this wooded country, and this must have made it difficult to find a suitable place for a farm. Although the hay would have to be transported some distance from the saltmarshes, it could easily have been carried by boat. One could imagine Thorfinn and his wife Gudrid, standing in front of their farmhouse with their first-born, looking out over the Reversing Falls in the glow of evening, while a zephyr of wind played across the water. It may have been so. We will never know for sure.

Most of the low-lying water-meadows along the Saint John River have been drained, making way for extensive potato farming. Herring, lobster, haddock and saithe are found in the bay in summer, the river abounds in salmon, there is trout in every brook, and game animals in the woods. "There were mountains there and a pleasant landscape," says the saga. Above the saltmarshes is a ridge, from whence distant mountains may be seen to the northwest; inland from Saint John is the most hilly land around the bay. This is now one of Canada's national parks, Fundy Park, which is about 12–14 km square, and thickly forested. This park is said to turn in the autumn to a sea of gold, ornamented in shades of red. "A pleasant landscape" indeed.[53] The most decorative of the forest trees is the sugar maple; and most forests in this region are equally colourful.

It is interesting to consider how well weather observations at Saint John fit in with the saga. The summers are warm, with similar temperatures to England or Denmark, though not mild enough

for viticulture, and the hardy wild riverbank grape grows only farther inland.

According to the saga, "they paid little attention to things other
than exploring the land" when they arrived at Straumsfjord.
Chapter 8 of Eirik's Saga says that in the first year

> They spent the winter there, and it was a harsh winter, for
> which they had made little preparation, and they grew short
> of food and caught nothing when hunting or fishing. They
> went out to the island, expecting to find some prey to hunt or
> food on the beaches. They found little food, but their livestock
> improved there. After this they entreated God to send them
> something to eat, but the response was not as quick in coming
> as their need was urgent.

Weather observations confirm that winters in Saint John are cold,
with heavy snows. Winter temperatures average between –5°C
and –8°C, with 17–26 cm of snow.[54]

On the island of Grand Manan, by contrast, the temperature is
two degrees higher on average in winter, so there is less snow. It
was an oversight on the settlers' part not to have made use of the
resources of Straumsfjord (abundant grass and game animals) in
order to lay in stores for the winter. They may perhaps have arrived too late in the year for haymaking, possibly due to high tides
on the saltmarshes. The following year they were better prepared.
They survived the winter, however. Spring comes relatively early
to this region, several weeks earlier than in Iceland or Greenland.

The statement that they "caught nothing when hunting or fishing" is interesting. This is consistent with the seasonal migration of
such fish species as cod, haddock and saithe in these parts. At the
beginning of winter, in late October, all handline and gill-net fishing on Grand Manan ceases, and does not begin again until the following May. During this dead period of midwinter, only shellfish
and some lobster are caught, but Thorfinn's men could hardly be
expected to have mastered these skills so quickly. The winter must
thus have been a hard one, lack of fish making things even more
difficult. But the fish returned in the spring, and, to judge by tem-

perature readings, seabirds had probably started breeding by April, providing plenty of eggs.

On Saturday 24 August we drove from Saint John to Blacks Harbour, where we took the car ferry to Grand Manan. Manan is a Native American word meaning "island place." The crossing took about one-and-a-half hours, and conditions were rather chilly at sea. The unusual shape of the bay means that some of the world's strongest currents flow there, with a constant influx of cold ocean water all summer. In winter the process is reversed, so that the cold waters of the bay are constantly mixed with warmer ocean water, and sea ice cannot form. What better name than Straumsey (Stream Island) and Straumsfjord (Stream Fjord)? Grand Manan is 25 km long from northeast to southwest, and widest at the middle, about 10km across. Hence it is big enough for the search for Thorhall the Huntsman, when he went missing, to have taken more than three half-days. The island is largely wooded, with many ponds and brooks, so Thorhall would have found plenty of water to fill his barrels when he sailed north and west in search of the land of wine.

We landed at North Head, quite a good harbour at the north end of the east coast. On our way south along the coast we were interested to see a saltmarsh, Castalia Marsh, approximately 50 hectares in area. This is where the islanders of Grand Manan spend leisure time and go birdwatching.

At the Grand Manan Museum in Grand Harbour, I found two issues of the Grand Manan Historian. *In the 1977 issue the editor, L.K. Ingersoll, says that in his childhood "sheep were kept the year round on Kent, Outer Wood and some smaller islands in the archipelago, requiring two roundups, one for shearing, and one later in the year for culling market lambs and mutton stock. Cattle, mostly younger steers to fatten for winter beef, were pastured in the same places for about six months of the year, requiring a roundup in the fall. Young boys were hired for a few pennies a day to help with the roundups, usually just a case of driving docile animals into a corral. Often, however, as happened when the writer was involved on two or three occasions as a young lad, a maverick would break away and elude its pursuers. Someone had liberated domestic rabbits on Outer Wood Island, and these had multiplied ten thousand fold in all colours of the rainbow. Chasing a half wild steer over the crags, and through the raspberry bushes, with herring gulls screaming overhead in the fog, rabbits flushed and running for cover, with the risk of tripping in the burrow of a rabbit warren, or that of Mother Carey's chicken (Leach's petrel), hooting and yelling to scare the steer in the right direction, was all heady stuff hardly matched by today's western classics on television.*

"More than that, it must not be forgotten that this whole process of natural husbandry of sheep and cattle added an additional dimension to the security and benefits of life in this part of the world, too often derided by well-meaning but grossly uninformed 'experts' on urban advantages."[55]

Among Thorfinn's company were men from the islands of Breidafjord in Iceland, where just such resources exist. Many of the islands are so small that the snow that fell on them was probably blown off by the wind. Kent Island, for instance, is only 200–300 metres across, and three kilometres long. Thanks to centuries of nesting seabirds, the islands were fertile, with abundant grass.

The Breidafjord men would have been quick to realise the value of the islands when they fled to Straumsey their first winter in Straumsfjord, and "their livestock improved." In addition, it may well have been possible to use the salt-water plants on the shores for grazing on the main island and the smaller islets. Tomorrow we will go looking for dulse, an edible seaweed, on the shore at Dark Harbour.

We went all the way south to the lighthouse at Southwest Head, where a considerable expanse of treeless grassland is found above a spectacular range of cliffs. Seagulls once nested here in their thousands: a report from 1806 says that there were no foxes, bears or other such predators on the island. Perhaps one "could hardly walk without stepping on eggs," as in Thorfinn's day? But Ingersoll says that foxes escaped from fur

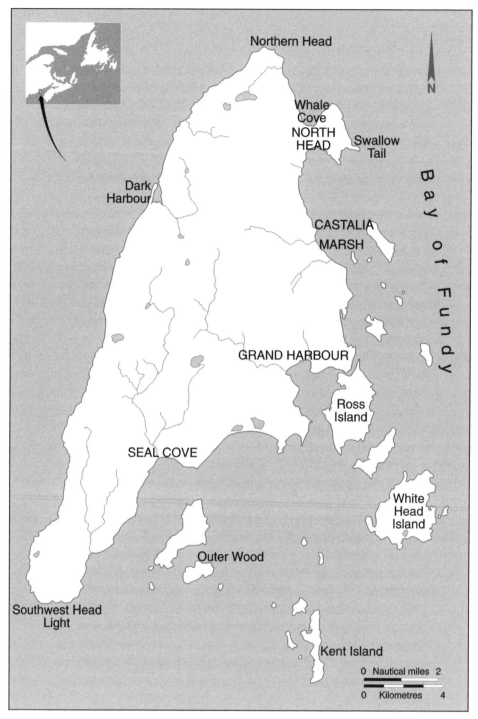

Grand Manan, which the author believes was the island of Straumsey in Straumsfjord.

farms in the late 19th century and reproduced fast. The bird colony disappeared. On Kent Island, however, where sheep were pastured, there were no foxes, and man has had less effect; the herring gull colony has been known to number 35,000 pairs.[56]

The following day we woke up in bright sunshine. About 2,000 people live on the island, and the population has declined somewhat in the past century. But the island boasts some 15 churches. At 11 am we peeked into a Baptist service. A welcoming worshipper took us in hand, and expected us to sing hymns straight from the page. When I asked him after the service whether he knew of dulse on nearby beaches, his interest flagged somewhat – not surprisingly. In the afternoon we went to Dark Harbour where dulse (Rhodymenia palmata), *a nourishing iodine-rich red alga, is harvested commercially. The tide was out, and we clambered down to the sea over slippery rocks, to take pictures of the dulse. This is not only excellent grazing for animals, but a tasty food for humans, that must have been welcomed by Thorfinn and his famished crew. We took a good handful with us.*

Then we went on to North Head. All around are cliffs, where Thorhall the Huntsman could have lain in hiding as he called upon the heathen god Thor, with the result that a whale was washed ashore. Just near North Head is a bay named Whale Cove, indicating that the stranded whale was not an isolated event; and no fewer than six companies on the island offer whale-watching cruises for tourists. Near Whale Cove, for instance at Swallow Tail lighthouse, the whale might have been thrown from the cliffs, after the whole company had eaten the whalemeat and fallen ill due to its "heathen" origins. But perhaps the version told in the Saga of the Greenlanders – that the whalemeat was plentiful and good – is correct. They may simply have thrown away the rotting remains when the spring brought fresh fish to eat.

We now leave the island of Grand Manan. Probably we will never prove that it is Straumsey. But nothing we saw indicates the contrary.

In the discussion above I have quoted the *Skálholtsbók* manuscript of Eirik's Saga. The corresponding part of the *Hauksbók* version is the one copied by Hauk himself; as stated above, he followed the original manuscript less scrupulously than the other two copyists. Thus the *Skálholtsbók* version should be regarded as a more reliable source for this part of the story. The difference is considerable.

According to the *Hauksbók* version, it appears that Thorfinn settled on Straumsey, and called his farmstead Straumsfjord. No mention is made of going out to the island to search for food, and grazing for the animals.[57] Hauk also omits the statement that there were mountains and "the grass grew tall." This is an excellent example of how a manuscript can become garbled in copying. I believe that Hauk's inaccuracies have misled those who have tried to guess where Straumsfjord was on the basis of his manuscript. The phrase "the grass grew tall" alone indicates that Straumsfjord could not have been up north in Labrador, or the north of Newfoundland. The account of sailing out to the island in midwinter also shows that there was no sea ice to hinder the travellers; this could not have been the case up north in the Gulf of St. Lawrence, let alone in Newfoundland or Labrador. But sea ice does not form in the Bay of Fundy, due to the powerful ocean currents.

The journey of Thorhall the Huntsman
After the first winter in Straumsfjord, a disagreement arises as to where exploration should continue:

> They then began to discuss and plan the continuation of their journey.
> Thorhall wanted to head north, past Furdustrandir and around Kjalarnes to seek Vinland. Karlsefni wished to sail south along the east shore, feeling the land would be more substantial the farther south it was, and he felt it was advisable to explore both.
> Thorhall then made his ship ready close to the island, with no more than nine men to accompany him. The rest of their company went with Karlsefni.

This journey planned by Thorhall in Eirik's Saga provides confirmation of the deductions made on the location of Wineland, on the basis of the Saga of the Greenlanders, i.e. that Wineland could be found by sailing into the Gulf of St. Lawrence. By the same token, the theory that Leif's Wineland and Thorfinn's Hop were one and the same is specifically excluded. But Thorhall must have been well aware that the grapes would not be ripe until the autumn, when it would be too late in the year to sail to Greenland. Hence he probably intended to return to Straumsfjord for the winter. This is why Thorfinn went searching for him the following spring, because he had not returned. The same route is described, from Straumsfjord, north of Kjalarnes and westward to Wineland. This demonstrates yet again that Hop was not the same as Leif's Wineland.

Before Thorhall sets off on his expedition, he declaims two verses, in which he complains that he has not had any wine at Straumsfjord as he had been promised, and mocks his companions for cooking whalemeat to eat. This would appear to indicate that he is heading for Wineland. However, in the second verse he says that he intends to go where their fellow-countrymen are, and this has been interpreted by some as indicating that he planned to go home to Greenland. But poetic language was often obscure, and he may simply have been referring to Wineland as "belonging" to Greenlanders.

Not only are the Saga of the Greenlanders and Eirik's Saga consistent regarding the location of Wineland. There is also evidence from Abbot Nikulas' writings, discussed further below, that Thorfinn went in search of Wineland the Good, and arrived at the place it was believed to be, but did not manage to explore or gather any resources. This is consistent with the account given in Eirik the Red's Saga of Thorfinn's search for Thorhall the Huntsman; he turned back before reaching Wineland, due to the threat of hostile *skrælings* or Native Americans. (The original meaning of the word *skræling*, used indiscriminately in the sagas to refer to both Native Americans and Inuit, is believed to be "man dressed in skins," derived from the word *skrá* = dried or withered skin.) In other words, Hop was not the same as Wineland. Hop was farther south than Straumsfjord, while Leif's Wineland was farther north.

The journey to Hop
This brings us to the journey southwards to Hop after the first winter. Chapter 10 of Eirik's Saga says:

> Karlsefni headed south around the coast, with Snorri and Bjarni and the rest of their company. They sailed a long time, until they came to a river which flowed into a lake and from there into the sea. There were wide sandbars beyond the mouth of the river, and they could only sail into the river at high tide.

The *Skálholtsbók* version of the saga says that there were islands (*eyjar*) outside the river estuary, while the *Hauksbók* version mentions sandbars (*eyrar*). If the original manuscript used a long-tailed *r*, it would have been easy for the young and inexperienced copyist Olaf Loftsson to confuse *r* and *j*. Most publishers have regarded the *Hauksbók* version as more reliable here, largely because a difficult sailing route into the river is more likely to go with sandbars than islands. This section was also written, not by Hauk himself, but by another copyist of the book, who appears to have kept more faithfully to the original. And if he was copying from the same original as that used by Olaf Loftsson, no doubt the lettering was clearer and more legible than when Olaf made his copy more than a century later.

Was Hop at New York?
Gathorne-Hardy maintained that Hop was at New York.[58] Let us consider whether this could be correct on the basis of Eirik's Saga.

The distance from the Bay of Fundy to New York is no problem. This is about 400 nautical miles, and they had the whole summer to make the journey – compared with perhaps 2,500 nautical miles they had sailed in the late summer of the previous year. In addition, this journey was all in coastal waters and mild conditions. Nonetheless, they might well be said to sail "a long time," as the distance was comparable to the "surprising" length of Furdustrandir. Also, Eirik's Saga subsequently recounts a tale of a long journey westwards from Kjalarnes to the Land of the One-Legged, which may have been from Cape North on Cape Breton Island, to the area west of the Gaspé peninsula.

It is interesting that at Hop they "built their settlement," and there is no mention of Leif's Camp at this location. From this one may infer that Leif's Camp was not at Hop. On a map, one can compare conditions at New York to the description above. The Hudson River flows from the far north to form a lagoon at the coast: *hóp* is the Icelandic word for a lagoon. The lagoon is what is now New York harbour, called Upper Bay – rather bigger than a lagoon named Hop in north Iceland, undoubtedly known to Thorfinn. This is where the Statue of Liberty now stands. The river then flows into the sea through the Narrows, which are justly named, one-and-a-half kilometres across. Beyond the river mouth is

New York.

Lower Bay, which has great sandbars on each side. Sandy Hook, on the southern side, is 20 kilometres long, while another sand bar projects from the north and east, ending in Rockaway Point. The distance between the two points is about 10 kilometres; this entrance to the lagoon has had to be deepened by canals. The largest is the Ambrose Channel, 600 metres across and 12 metres deep, leading all the way into the harbour. During this century, the land has subsided by the equivalent of 60cm in a hundred years, so it may have been even shallower in the past.[59]

The conditions at Hop and at New York thus appear to have much in common. No comparable location, with sandbars and a lagoon, has been suggested anywhere on the coast from New York north to the Bay of Fundy. Mount Hope Bay in Rhode Island has been a candidate, but there are islands, not sandbars, in the bay, and weather conditions are considerably cooler than they appear to have been at Hop. Babcock, who maintains that Hop was at Mount Hope Bay, admits that there is no lock-like bay, no sand-bars, and that ships can sail in without difficulty.[60] Chapter 10 continues:

> Karlsefni and his company sailed into the lagoon and called the land Hop (Tidal pool). There they found fields of self-sown wheat in the low-lying areas and vines growing on the hills. Every stream was teeming with fish. They dug trenches along the high-water mark and when the tide ebbed there were halibut [*helgir fiskar*] in them. There were a great number of deer of all kinds in the forest.
>
> They stayed there for a fortnight, enjoying themselves and finding nothing unusual. They had taken their livestock with them.

Then the Native Americans made a silent visit, after which the saga says:

> They remained there that winter. There was no snow at all, and all the livestock could fend for themselves out of doors.

Around New York, self-sown wheat and grapes would be in plentiful supply, and the description of the conditions in which these plants grow is convincing, as will be discussed later. The Icelandic term *helgir fiskar* (literally "holy fish") may mean some kind of flatfish; some flatfish species swim up large rivers, where they live in brackish water. One of these is the winter flounder (*Pseudopleuronectes americanus*), which is found between Georgia and Labrador, in water temperatures of 12–16°C. The winter flounder is 60 centimetres long in warm seas, and is excellent for eating. It is commonly found at depths between two and 37 metres,[61] but it can sometimes be caught at depths of as little as 15cm, when it burrows onto the sandy bottom, so only the eyes are visible.[62] But it is unlikely that the fish would feel at home there today, where a peaceful beach has been replaced by piers and quays, beneath skyscrapers and the Statue of Liberty, and all the brooks are covered by streets and buildings. Salmon is not mentioned at Hop, and salmon was probably never common in the Hudson River, although the river was once the most southerly habitat of the fish. Salmon is no longer seen there,[63] and is not found any farther south than the Connecticut River, as it does not thrive in warm seas. This is one of the factors indicating that Hop was a different place from Leif's Wineland, where salmon was plentiful.

The observation that no snow fell at Hop indicates that it cannot, at any rate, have been farther north than New York. Snow falls there most winters, admittedly, but there are occasional years, such as 1953, when average monthly temperatures did not drop below 3°C.[64] This is like the mildest of winters in southern Iceland, for instance the first months of 1964 in the Westman Islands, when hardly a flake of snow fell. To someone like Thorfinn, who came from northern Iceland where heavy snows are commonplace, this would be extremely mild. For comparison it is worth mentioning that at New Haven, Connecticut, a little north and east of New York, the temperature for the coldest month of the year, in the warm period from 1931 to 1960, averaged -1.3°C, similar to the temperature in Iceland's chilly Strandir area, while precipitation was much higher at New Haven. So a snowless winter could not be expected there, and hence Hop ought to be farther south. In view of this, together with the topographical description discussed above, the inference is that it is possible, indeed likely, that Hop was at New York. Later I shall argue that Hop could hardly be farther south, when we come to consider Thorfinn's expedition to search for Thorhall the Huntsman.

It was on 10 September 1998 that I arrived in New York with my grandson, Hjalti Baldursson. As mentioned above, the description in Eirik the Red's Saga of a river that flows off the land, through a lake and to the sea would indicate the Hudson River, and the sandbars and shoals at the entrance from the sea are also reminiscent of New York. But we were especially interested in exploring whether the specific conditions within the harbour might somewhere resemble those described in Eirik the Red's Saga, when Thorfinn settled at Hop.

The taxi driver who drove us from the airport told us that during the last winter there had only been one real snowfall. This is of course not much of a clue, but it would tend to support the idea that the statement in Eirik's Saga, that there was no snow during the winter Thorfinn spent at Hop, could apply to New York; at that time, the climate may be assumed to have been relatively warm.

The following day we went on a short cruise of New York harbour, between Manhattan and Staten Island; our guide was Clayton Tinsley who had, earlier that summer, been working on an archaeological dig in Iceland. There was a southerly breeze off the ocean, roughening the surface of the sea. It must sometimes have looked just like this in the days of Thorfinn Karlsefni, but there is not much else in this city that has changed so little. But to the south we saw the two headlands on either side of the Narrows, one projecting from the west, from Staten Island, the other from the east, from Brooklyn. Either one of them could have been the headland that features in Eirik the Red's Saga, when the natives came "from the south around the point" then went away south around the point. Thorfinn's homestead ought thus to have been a short distance north of one or other of the headlands, at a place with good moorage, also providing a quick, safe entrance from the sea to the lake, if other qualities of the land were acceptable.

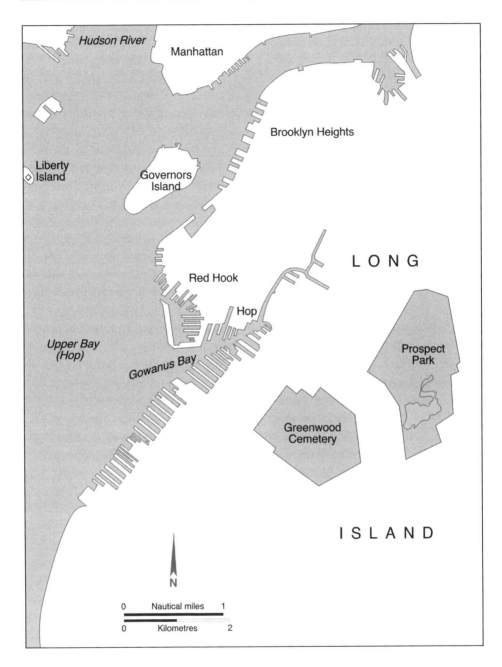

The author's idea of the location of Hop shown on a map of modern New York.

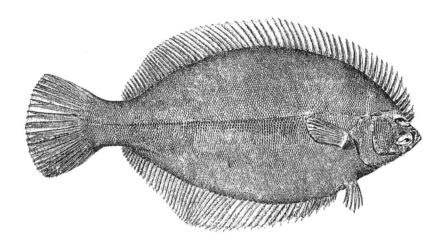

The winter flounder is a flatfish which is found on the coast of North America from Georgia to Labrador. It migrates into river estuaries when the temperature there is favourable. The winter flounder makes good eating, and this may be the "holy fish" caught by Thorfinn Karlsefni's company at Hop.

This is why my attention was caught by a small inlet on the east, which we found was called Gowanus Bay. This probably existed a thousand years ago, although the sea level has risen considerably since then. I was interested to find out whether various other topographic descriptions in Eirik the Red's Saga were consistent with this bay. This would not, of course, prove that Thorfinn had been here, but it would be interesting if the statements about Hop in the saga were consistent with one real place.

The following day we went to Gowanus Bay. We walked first along the west of the inlet, then to the east. The bay is about a kilometre in length; it lies southwest-northeast into Brooklyn, 200 to 500 metres across. Not only does it provide shelter from the ocean waves, but also from the turbulence that may form in the harbour itself in westerly storms. At the east of the bay are many large quays, from where ocean vessels sail. About 500 metres from the harbourside we saw that the land rose somewhat towards the east, in the direction of Greenwood Heights.

North of the heights is an area called Park Slopes, where the land slopes downwards to the lowland around the inlet. The words of the saga "vines growing on the hills" could apply here; the word "holt" which means hill in modern Icelandic, was probably used here in its ancient meaning of woods or woody hills. The ideal habitat of the fox grape (Vitis labrusca) *is at the edges of woods; New York is near the centre of its area of distribution on the east coast of the USA. If this was an area of deciduous trees, as indicated by the name Greenwood Heights, the saga's statement that there were "a great number of deer [animals] of all kinds in the forest" is believable.*

We discovered that from the head of the inlet, a strange canal or ditch stretched inland about one and a half kilometres, with four shorter canals branching off to the east, approximately 30–40 metres across. These were edged by stone walls, like the canals of Amsterdam. This was probably marshland that was drained and made more inhabitable by digging the canals, which must also have been convenient for boat transport. In the past, this wetland would have been ideal for wild rice (Zizania aquatica), *probably what Eirik's Saga calls "fields of self-sown wheat in the low-lying areas." New York is near the centre of the area in which this species is found; it grows in ponds of fresh or brackish water – as was probably the case here. When one looks at the canals inland of Gowanus Bay, there are indications that these were cut along the courses of brooks that flowed down the eastern slope, and into a small river that flowed at a slight angle into the bay. This makes the statement of Eirik's Saga "every stream was teeming with fish" more comprehensible. The account of the battle with the Native Americans also becomes clearer: Thorfinn's men are said to have fled upriver. There they found a cliff wall where they could put up a good fight. We could see no sign of such a cliff wall, but this was hardly to be expected, since the natural landscape has long since been obliterated by urban development.*

Conditions could well have existed by this bay for digging trenches along the high-water mark "and when the tide ebbed there were halibut [helgir fiskar] *in them." This is most likely* to have been *winter flounder* (Pseudopleuronectes american-us). *We met some people working at one of the businesses along the harbour, and showed them pictures of winter flounder, which they said was common along the coast. This was confirmed when we went to an exhibition of marine animals at Coney Island. At the harbour in Gowanus Bay, Hjalti saw a large number of fish fry in the water, but we could not identify the species. This shows, however, that conditions in the harbour are still tolerable for fish, in spite of modern pollution.*

It is not unlikely that the farmers who chose places to settle in the 17th century judged the land by similar standards to those of Thorfinn a thousand years ago. So it is an interesting clue that the first settlers in Brooklyn after the rediscovery of America settled precisely at Gowanus Bay, in 1636. These were Dutch farmers. Later they were followed by more Dutch settlers in Brooklyn, whose original name was Breukelen, which means marshland; this is the name of an area south of Amsterdam in Holland. It would be tempting to imagine that the canals inland of the bay were dug following Dutch examples; in the mid-seventeenth century, some of the canals for which Amsterdam is now famous were being dug.

From the fragments assembled here, we can now attempt to deduce with some accuracy where along the bay Thorfinn's men built their camp at the place they called Hop. It is difficult to place the location with accuracy, but on the western side of the bay, where Red Hook now stands, it would have been easier to prevent livestock wandering eastwards along Long Island. It must have been some distance along the inlet, since they had fled upriver from the Native Americans. Finally, the saga says that they built their booths up above the lake, with some of the huts farther inland, and others closer to the shore. It may be inferred that the ones close to the water were right on the shore, where the ships must have been moored or beached. This would make it easier to keep an eye on them.

Rather tired after our walk (especially the elder of us!), we took the subway back to our hotel in Manhattan.

On 13 September we went out to Coney Island south of

Brooklyn. From a tall viewing tower there are excellent views over the entrance to Lower Bay. A large freighter steamed through the Narrows under the Verrazano Bridge, a 1,300-metre suspension bridge, then eastward up the Ambrose Channel between the spits of Rockaway Point and Sandy Hook. On Coney Island is a broad, light sandy beach. Quite a number of people were enjoying the sun on the hot sand, and we followed their example – pale-skinned descendants of Thorfinn. Many took dips in the sea, although it was not very warm. There was a similar beach across the water at Rockaway Point, where there is quite a large community. To the south we could see the 20-kilometre-long sand reef of Sandy Hook in a haze; at the northern end is a US naval station. We could imagine Viking ships with their tall sails on this route between the spits described in the saga; their steersmen could have been proud indeed of their navigation across the broad Atlantic.

At the end of this trip to America, my attention was drawn to a book published in London in 1670, by a certain Daniel Denton, A Brief Description of New York.[65] *In his book, he urges English people to settle in the colony; the English had at this time recently captured the former New Netherlands from Dutch settlers. His account admittedly smacks of propaganda, but he claims to describe only what he has seen, and the value of his description is the greater because this was before any real urban development had begun. He extols the resources of Long Island, of which Brooklyn is the westernmost part. He mentions many kinds of fruit, including grapes, great and small, and an abundance of strawberries. He says that the island is thickly wooded, including such species as oaks, white and red, walnut, maple and birch, and that flowers are so plentiful that their scent carries out to sea. There are several rivers, some navigable, except along the south side of the island, where sand bars and shoals prevent sailing. There are, however, crystal streams, and one can hardly travel a mile without coming across a brook. The rivers he says are well furnished with fish, including trout, perch and eel, and he also mentions "Place," probably some kind of flounder or other flatfish, perhaps winter flounder. He makes no reference to salmon. Wild beasts mentioned by Denton include deer, bear, racoon, wolf and fox, as well as a multitude of wildfowl. There is no mention of "self-sown wheat," or wild rice, Zizania aquatica; the Native Americans of this region apparently made good use of the favourable conditions for growing maize, and for the English this unknown wild grain would hardly count as a major attraction. Otherwise, the description appears to be consistent with the details given in Eirik the Red's Saga. Denton says there are few Indians on Long Island, and that "it is to be admired how strangely they have decreased by the Hand of God" since the English settlement; he attributes this to combat among themselves, and to mortal diseases. A map in Colonial New York by Michael Kammen from 1975 shows various ancient Native American settlements and fortifications, including Coney Island, mentioned above, at the south of Long Island. From here the natives might have appeared from the south by the headland in the days of Thorfinn Karlsefni.*

On the basis of our slight research, it seems to me that a remarkable number of indications exist in New York that point to this being Thorfinn's Hop as described in Eirik the Red's Saga. It even appears that his homestead could have been at a specific place on Gowanus Bay, in the inner reaches on the west. Perhaps this may be accepted, at least as long as no better theory has been proposed?

Eirik's Saga says that Thorfinn and his company realised that, despite everything the land had to offer, they would be under constant threat of attack from its prior inhabitants. They then made ready to depart for their own country.

On the way from Hop to Straumsfjord, Thorfinn's men came across five skrælings in "skin sacks," whom they slew. This is an unexpected event, since Thorfinn is certainly not presented as a violent character. In the *Hauksbók* version of the saga, on which the translation of the sentence in this volume is based, the men are said to have been killed because Thorfinn's men believed they were outlaws. In my view, the version given in *Skálholtsbók* is more reasonable; this states that the skrælings were "sent from the land," which may be interpreted as indicating that they were spies. It remains, however, a rather inadequate explanation, unless the Wineland explorers knew of a skræling camp nearby.

In 1956–1978, Guy Mellgren and Ed Runge carried out archaeological excavations at Naskeag Point on Penobscot Bay in Maine, the easternmost of the United States. This is towards the north of the route from New York to the Bay of Fundy. The site is believed to have been the largest Native American community in Maine in the period 900–1500. Steven L. Cox at the Maine State Museum in Augusta, Maine, says that this place is one of the most beautiful on the Maine coast, and that from Naskeag Point one may observe practically all sea traffic along the coast.[66] Hence it is highly likely that Thorfinn and his men were aware of this Native American settlement. So when they came across the five skrælings nearby, by the sea according to *Hauksbók*, they may have feared that the Native American scouts were a threat to them, and hence felt that they must kill them.

On 18 August 1957 Mellgren found on this site a Norwegian silver coin, minted in the second half of the 11th century. Due to the dating of the coin, it can have nothing to do with Thorfinn's expedition. Another explanation, entirely possible, may be correct. This will be discussed in connection with the seventh Wineland expedition of 1121, made by Eirik Gnupsson, known by the nickname Upsi (saithe). He was the first bishop of Greenland.

On a headland Thorfinn's men spotted a large number of animals. The point looked like a huge dunghill, as the deer gathered there at night (in winter) to sleep. These were probably Virginia deer. The account does not contribute much to the narrative, but is primarily evidence that the story was told by an observant person with an interest in nature.

Thorfinn and his crew now returned to Straumsfjord. At this point, the writer of the saga expresses some doubt about the historical sources for chapter 11 of the saga, and mentions another version of the southward expedition. This authorial aside does him credit as an honest and conscientious historian:

Some people say that Bjarni and Gudrid had remained be-

hind there with a hundred [*tíu tugir*] others and gone no farther, and that it was Karlsefni and Snorri who went further
south with some forty men, stayed no more than two months
at Hop and returned the same summer.

The Icelandic term *tíu tugir* means literally "ten tens."

Heading for Leif's Wineland
When they arrived back at Straumsfjord in the spring, there was
no news of Thorhall the Huntsman. Chapter 11 of Eirik's Saga
says:

> The group stayed there while Karlsefni went on one ship to
> look for Thorhall. They sailed north around Kjalarnes Point
> and then westwards of it, keeping the land on their port side.
> They saw nothing but wild forest.
>   When they had sailed for a long time they reached a river
> flowing from east to west. They sailed into the mouth of the
> river and lay to near the south bank.

This is a clear topographical description, entirely consistent with
the account of the route described on the way from Greenland, and
also the account of Thorvald Eiriksson's journey. It is evident that
they sailed a long way along the south coast of the Gulf of St. Lawrence, either between Prince Edward Island and the mainland or,
more probably, north of the island and north of the Gaspé peninsula, after which they reached a river that flowed from the east;
most of the rivers in the region flow northward from the Notre
Dame mountains, while as one approaches Québec some flow
from the east towards the sea. An example is the Rivière Trois
Pistoles, which flows westwards to the sea two-and-a-half miles
west of the town of Trois Pistoles, at a latitude of 48.1°N.[67] At the
north of the river mouth the river is three metres deep along the
quay, more than deep enough for a *knörr*; to the west are mudflats,
from which rise large boulders. The journey here from Kjalarnes
might take six to seven half-days, and hence it is farther than the
route along the Furdustrandir or from Straumsfjord to Hop; all of
these routes are called "long" in Eirik's Saga. Thorfinn must have

believed that this was the route Thorhall would take in search of Wineland, which brings us back to the fact that Thorhall's quest for Wineland must have been based upon the knowledge or experience of earlier travellers to Wineland, which was easily available to him. He had also expressed in his verse a great interest in a better drink than spring water, and complained that no wine had passed his lips on the journey, when he set off on his journey north of Furdustrandir and Kjalarnes. As suggested above, it is probable that Thorhall intended to go to Leif's Wineland and return to Straumsfjord in the autumn.

Thorfinn must have thought so, at any rate, as otherwise there would be no reason to wonder what had happened to him and to send out a search party to the Gulf of St. Lawrence the following spring. But, since Thorhall travelled with a company of only nine, and mostly in the sheltered waters of the Gulf of St. Lawrence, he may have travelled in the ship's boat, as Thorvald Eiriksson's men did on their exploratory journey the summer after they arrived in Wineland.

As they lay to at the south bank of the river, they noticed a man who shot an arrow at Thorvald Eiriksson, which dealt him a fatal wound. They called the man one-legged. This episode is often dismissed as fantasy, but this is not necessarily so – or not entirely, at least. Native Americans apparently often wore fur cloaks in cold weather, and conditions may well have been cold when Thorfinn went on his search, probably as soon as the ice melted in the spring. The man may have appeared to them to be one-legged due to this garment, and this would suffice for them to call him one-legged. In addition, they do not appear to have seen the man at close quarters. There are many cases of superstition and fear leading to drastic illusions. The account may also be somewhat flippant, as the verse on the subject implies:

> True it was
> that our men tracked
> a one-legged creature
> down to the shore.
> The uncanny fellow
> fled in a flash,

> though rough was his way,
> hear us, Karlsefni!

The flippancy sits somewhat uneasily with the manner of Thorvald Eiriksson's death. It may perhaps be inferred from this that the account of the Saga of the Greenlanders is more accurate, i.e. that Thorvald was not on this expedition, but died at Krossanes on his own journey of exploration. But even if this was the case, the hostile "uncanny fellow" might be a sufficient indication of unfriendly inhabitants, giving Thorfinn reason not to go farther, after his unhappy experience with the Native Americans at Hop.

But the name Land of the One-Legged for the Gaspé peninsula is no more far-fetched than placenames such as Alfadalur (Elven Dale), Dverghamrar (Dwarves' Cliffs), Draugahlidar (Ghost Slopes) or Tröllakirkja (Trolls' Church) in Iceland. And in the region of Strandasysla is a farm named Einfætingsgil (Uniped Gully), after a one-legged trollwife who is supposed to have jumped over the gully, according to farmer Jon Sigmundsson.[68]

In this account, there is an apparent discrepancy in the fact that the one-legged man ran away northwards after his attack, although they lay at the south bank of the river, This may, however, be explained by the one-legged man having shot the arrow across the river. "South" could also have been miswritten for "north" in the original manuscripts from which *Skálholtsbók* and *Hauksbók* were copied.

In Land of the One-Legged, the travellers gain an interesting overview of the land they had explored in chapter 12 of the saga:

> They saw mountains which they felt to be the same as those near Hop, and both these places seemed to be equally far away from Straumsfjord.

This passage is largely missing from the *Skálholtsbók* version, but it is unlikely that Hauk's second copyist invented it, as he appears to have been a more conscientious copyist than Hauk himself. But it is true that the mountain range that runs along the Gaspé peninsula is the same as the one inland from New York, the Appalachians, although the northernmost part is called by a French name, Monts Notre Dame. This is undeniably a remarkably successful attempt at gaining an overall view of an area explored, without benefit of compass. The sea route from Straumsfjord to Land of the One-Legged is a circuitous one, first to the southeast, then to the northeast, then northwest, west and southwest. Thus, not surprisingly, the observation is not entirely accurate, but the distance as the crow flies between the mouth of the Bay of Fundy and the north coast of the Gaspé peninsula is about 250-300 nautical miles, while from the Bay of Fundy to New York is about 400 nautical miles. This is, however, no more inaccurate than estimates of the proportion of Iceland's length to its breadth in 16th-century maps, although far more experience had been gained by that time of navigation around Iceland, than of journeys around Wineland in the days of Thorfinn Karlsefni. This estimate of relative distance tends to support the theory that Hop was no farther south than New York. Climatic factors, however, indicate that it cannot have been much farther north than New York, as was explained above. In other words, Hop was probably no farther north, and no farther south, than New York, in addition to which the topography of the place supports the hypothesis; a river flowing from the north, a salt-water lagoon, the great sand-bars and shoals, the temperature, the marine life, the wild rice and the vines.

According to the above, Thorfinn did not travel quite far enough to reach the region which Thorhall the Huntsman believed was Wineland. This recalls a brief account in the manuscript AM 194 8vo, that Thorfinn went

> in search of Wineland the Good and arrived at the place where they believed it was and was not able to explore it or its resources.[69]

This assertion from the geographical treatise of Abbot Nikulas may refer to Wineland the Good only as the specific region where Leif built his (first) camp. This is consistent with the theory that Hop and Leif's Wineland were not the same place.

Land of White Men and Land of Skrælings

On the way home from Wineland, Chapter 12 of Eirik's Saga tells of Thorfinn's journey from Straumsfjord:

> They had southerly winds and reached Markland, where they met five natives. One was bearded, two were women and two of them children.
>
> Karlsefni and his men caught the boys but the others escaped and disappeared into the earth. They took the boys with them and taught them their language and had them baptized. They called their mother Vethild [Vætilld, Vethilld] and their father Ovaegi [Uvægi, Uvege]. They said that kings ruled the land of the natives [*Skrælingjaland*]; one of them was called Avaldamon and the other Valdidida [Avalldidida]. No houses were there, they said, but people slept in caves or holes. They spoke of another land, across from their own. There people dressed in white clothing, shouted loudly and bore poles and waved banners. This people assumed to be the land of the white men.

The description of the sailing route to Markland on a southerly breeze, probably from Kjalarnes, is consistent with conclusions already drawn about the relative positions of Kjalarnes and Markland. Although sailing conditions off the coast of Labrador are often hazardous, sailing directions indicate that there are also good moorages which are relatively easy of access from the sea, and presumably Thorfinn could have made use of these to go ashore. The account seems to indicate contact between Native Americans and Inuit, and that the boys seized were Inuit.

Archaeological research shows that these peoples both lived on the east coast of Labrador, Markland. Eirik's Saga states that the man was bearded. This indicates that he differed from the indigenous people they had come across hitherto, and Native Americans have neither beard nor body hair.[70] The region called *Skrælingjaland* (Land of Skrælings) could thus be the coastal region of Labrador. There have, however, been Native American communities farther inland, until the 20th century, in the woods and along the rivers. In the northeast of Labrador they were largely Naskapi,

Sculpture by Asmundur Sveinsson of Gudrid Thorbjarnardottir and her son Snorri Thorfinnsson (Karlsefnisson), the first European child born in America. According to Eirik the Red's saga, he was born at Straumsfjord. The author suggests the hypothesis that this may have been where the town of Saint John now stands, by the Bay of Fundy. (The First White Mother in America by Asmundur Sveinsson, © Heirs of the artist/MYNDSTEF 1997. Owner: Reykjavik Art Museum.)

Wavelets ripple the surface of New York harbour. The view is southward, showing the Verrazano bridge across the harbour mouth, the Narrows. The author believes that the Native Americans came around the point on Long Island (left) to Gowanus Bay, Thorfinn's camp at Hop. Photo Pall Bergthorsson.

Thorfinn Karlsefni *by sculptor Einar Jonsson. Two exemplars of the statue exist, one at Hrafnista in Reykjavik, the other in Philadelphia. Photo Pall Stefansson.*

Thorfinn Karlsefni grew up at Reynines, later known as Stadur at Reynines or Reynistadur. Relatives of Thorfinn lived there in later times. Watercolour showing the Stadara river flowing east, then north, forming the headland (= nes) where the farmstead stands. (Reynistadur 1930 by Magnus Jonsson, © Heirs of the artist/ MYNDSTEF 1997. The painting is the property of Sigurdur Jonsson at Reynistadur. Photograph courtesy of the Skagafjord Historical Society.)

x

while Montagnais were found farther south and west. Both of these tribes belong to the Algonquin language group.

The Native Americans customarily hunted reindeer in autumn and winter, moving out to the coast in spring, when the reindeer migrate there for the breeding season. For a long time bloody conflict was common between the Native Americans and Inuits, and accounts written by missionaries as recently as the early 20th century describe the terrified reaction of the Inuit if they suspected that Native Americans were nearby.[71] The boys' description of their neighbours might well apply to Native Americans, especially their well-known war-cries and the poles and banners or flags they waved. Gathorne-Hardy says that most books on Native Americans mention poles and flags, and that in Schoolcraft's book there is a picture of a Native American banner, admittedly made of feathers, not cloth.[72] Gathorne-Hardy also mentions elsewhere that Native American chiefs generally carried a banner of white buffalo skin, and another of reddish leather, to show whether they came in peace, or with more warlike intentions.

The Inuit wore clothes of animal skin with the fur on the outside, and thus appeared generally dark, often wearing sealskin. But it is not unlikely that the Native Americans wore lighter-coloured clothing, and this might explain the Inuit boys' reference to their wearing white. An old painting of an Algonquin family, for instance, shows them wearing white furs. If dark skins, such as reindeer skin, are worn leather-side out, they appear lighter, and this was common among the Native Americans.[73] Gathorne-Hardy says that deerskins which he had seen tanned by the Indians were as white as kid gloves, before they were smoked, and that it was not uncommon for these unsmoked skins to be used to make robes worn on ceremonial occasions. He says that he himself has seen Native Americans in Labrador wearing these robes, decorated with faint red lines and patterns, and that he would regard it as entirely natural to say that those who wore them were "dressed in white clothing." Such a robe may be seen in the Museum of Natural History in New York.

It is therefore possible that the Land of the White Men was the inland region of Labrador, and hence that the name was not pure invention, as has often been maintained. It is true that people might well imagine that the land was elsewhere than the boys believed, especially after the account became garbled and confused with legends of "Ireland the Great." On the long coast of Labrador, it is hardly possible to point out one place rather than another as the location where Thorfinn met the five natives. But it could well have been Hamilton Inlet, while the Land of the White Men may have been at the innermost end of Lake Melville, which is actually an enormously long inlet.

The Inuit are generally believed to be peaceable people, without warlords or captains. But the explorer Frobisher met up with bellicose Inuit on Baffin Island. Under these special circumstances, where the Inuit were at daggers drawn with the Native Americans, it is not unlikely that they would need some kind of kings or leaders such as Avaldamon and Valdidida to lead them in their confrontations with the Native Americans.

It is of course highly likely that the four names given by the Inuit boys have not been accurately preserved; they may well have been inaccurate from the start, and after the saga had been passed down many times the spelling might well be a mystery. An example of the difficulty of coping with exotic names is the spelling of the names of Norwegian Vikings in a peace settlement made with King Ethelred the Unready of England in AD991.[74] One of them was a ferocious young man aged about 20, destined for kingship, Olaf Tryggvason. The others are believed to have been a certain Jostein and Gudmund Stigandason, but the document bears the names *Anlaf*, *Justin* and *Gudmund Stegitan sunu*. The names mentioned by the Inuit boys would not have been written down at once, so there was far more risk of their becoming distorted than the names of the Vikings in England, not least because the names were so very foreign (Old English and Old Norse, on the other hand, were quite similar). A search has been made for such names in Native American languages, but without results; this is hardly surprising if the names were actually Inuit.

An attempt is made here to link two of the names with the Inuit language. But the proviso must be stated that it is impossible to tell how the original writer and subsequent copyists pronounced the words. *V* could have denoted either a *v* or *u* sound, and *g* could be hard or palatal.

In a 19th-century dictionary of the language of the Labrador Inuit I found the word *uik* which means *husband*. This bears some resemblance to Ovægir (Uvægi, Uvege), who was the boys' father, the husband of the family. But in 1866 Rink suggested that the father's name was *uvia*, which means *her husband*. Knut Bergsland[75] suggests, on the contrary, that the Labrador form was closer to *uinga*, perhaps written *Uiga* or *Viga*. The word *wife* in the Inuit language of Labrador is *uilik* (Greenland pronunciation *ooihleek*), plural *uillit* (Greenland pronunciation: *ooihleet*).[76] It is perhaps rather far-fetched to say that these words resemble *Vethild*, but there is some similarity, allowing for natural distortion.

But there is another reason for concluding that the boys were Inuit. This is the statement that the natives met by Thorfinn in Markland lay in caves or holes. This may well apply to Inuit. In addition to their familiar igloos, they lived in houses which were largely underground. From the middle of these dwellings lay tunnels, where dogs were sometimes kept. The missionaries apparently did not enjoy crawling down the long tunnels. They counted themselves lucky if they escaped being bitten by the dogs, and soiling their hands in the dogs' droppings. They were less worried about the dogs licking their faces. The roof of the dwelling was made of driftwood or whalebone, covered with turf, while seal guts were used to make a window. These homes might well be described as caves or holes. When the igloos or earth dwellings were uninhabitable due to wet conditions, for instance at the spring thaw, people lived in sealskin tents.[77] When the natives who escaped are said to have "disappeared into the earth" this could well apply to their entering one of the entrance tunnels; and it would be quite natural to abandon the pursuit rather than follow them.

In support of this description of the Inuit homes, it is interesting to read Frobisher's account written on his expedition at Frobisher Bay at the south of Baffin Island in about 1576:

In the large land opposite Warwick Island we saw the humble dwellings, or rather burrows, of the savages in this area, and it is true that we could not but be astonished by these poor and pathetic homes. It seemed that they sought shelter in these underground dwellings for protection against the harshness of the cold. They are two fathoms deep beneath the ground, and are circular like our furnaces. Also they are so close together that one might think they were the dens of foxes or rabbit warrens. In each dwelling is only one room, half of it a foot higher than the other, covered with large slabs of rock; the other is covered in moss, and doubtless performs the most undignified function of the home.[78]

This does not sound pleasant, but one should consider whether there was any better way of dealing with refuse and waste, rather than covering it with moss. Although Labrador is separated from Baffin Island by the Hudson Strait, Inuit homes in both places may be assumed to have been similar, and perhaps much the same as they were in Thorfinn's day, six hundred years before. It should be pointed out that "fathom" may not have had the same meaning as today. In the 15th century, for instance, a Genoa fathom was only 58 centimetres.[79] But to judge from comparable dwellings in Ammassalik in Greenland, the roof appears to have been at least high enough to permit walking upright.[80]

This account of natives in Markland, as far as it goes, must be acknowledged to be consistent with what is known of the ancient homes and ways of the Inuit on the Labrador coast. The land of the men who wore white, on the other hand, was probably in the forests of Labrador, and need not be pure invention. It is interesting that the name Land of the White Men (or Ireland the Great in the *Hauksbók* version) is not attributed to the explorers, but appears to be an addition or aside by the person writing the story down ("This people assumed to be the land of the white men."). From this it may be inferred that the narrator made no distinction between Native Americans and Inuits, calling them all "skrælings," although the captured boys clearly differentiated between their own people and Native Americans.

The proviso should be stated that the assumption is made here that Thorfinn's men met Thule folk or Inuit, and not their predecessors, the Dorset people. Little is known as yet of when this change took place. But what is known of the customs of the Dorset people does not exclude the possibility that these could have been the indigenous people Thorfinn and Gudrid encountered in Markland.

The worm-eaten ship

Eirik's Saga says that Bjarni Grimolfsson's ship entered a sea of worms and sank. The ship's boat, however, was coated in seal tar, which in the saga is assumed to provide protection against ship worms. Ludvik Kristjansson is of the opinion that the "tar" was seal fat, either alone, or mixed with tar.[81]

The ship worm is a species of bivalve (*Teredinidae*) that uses the shell on its end to drill into wood.[82] It causes most damage in warm oceans, where it can grow to a great thickness, and bore passages in the wood up to two metres long. In colder waters it is rarely more than a few inches long, and much thinner. Coal-tar creosote, a latter-day invention, has been regarded as the best form of defence against the ship worm. It sticks to the point of the worm's shell and blunts it. The "seal tar" probably had a similar effect. Damage to ships caused by the worms may go unnoticed for a long time, as this is generally invisible on the surface, although the timber may be crumbling from within. It is possible that Bjarni's ship had picked up ship worm in the warm seas, but that the damage was not revealed until they reached the Greenland Sea. This incident in Eirik's Saga may thus constitute proof that the ship had travelled much farther south than Newfoundland or the Gulf of St. Lawrence.

The journey of Freydis, Helgi and Finnbogi

After Thorfinn Karlsefni returned from his journey to Wineland, the Saga of the Greenlanders says that Freydis, daughter of Eirik the Red, set off on her ill-fated Wineland expedition, when she organised the massacre of the entire ship's crew of the brothers Helgi and Finnbogi, who had accompanied her. The saga tells that she would not allow the brothers and their followers to share the accommodation at Leif's Camp, so that they had to build their own house. If this was at L'Anse aux Meadows, this was probably when the third longhouse was added. From this it may be inferred that this was not where Thorfinn Karlsefni resided during his stay in Wineland, as his company, 140 to 160 people, was far too numerous for the existing two houses at L'Anse aux Meadows. Apart from this, Eirik the Red's Saga appears to be a more reliable (and especially more detailed) account of Thorfinn's expedition than the Saga of the Greenlanders. And no relics of domestic animals or buildings for them have been found at L'Anse aux Meadows.

There seems, however, to be nothing to contradict the supposition that Freydis spent the winter at L'Anse aux Meadows. The winter conditions are not described in the story of her stay in Wineland: the saga says that games and entertainment were held, until disagreements arose, and this continued for much of the winter. On the fateful day of the murders, the weather is described in detail; there is said to be a heavy dew, so that Freydis was damp and cold when she returned after her early-morning walk to Finnbogi's and Helgi's house. This gives little clue, however, as to where Freydis spent the winter. Admittedly such conditions would be highly unbelievable at L'Anse aux Meadows in the middle of winter. But there is nothing in the saga to contradict the supposition that the murders may have taken place in late spring. No human remains have been found at L'Anse aux Meadows, but Freydis would certainly have done her best to avoid leaving evidence of her wicked deeds.

The journey of Eirik Gnupsson

Although the journey of Eirik Gnupsson, first Bishop of Greenland, is not generally counted as one of the "Wineland journeys," there is every reason to do so here. According to the Book of Settlements, he was descended from Signy Valthjofsdottir, for whom the farm of Signyarstadir, W. Iceland, is named, and from Grimkel, the son of Bjarni Gullberi of Gullberastadir. Erik's great-great-uncle was Hördur Grimkelsson, founder of the Holmverjar clan, a vigorous but ill-fated man.[83] Icelandic annals record that Bishop Eirik went to search for Wineland in 1121.[84] The wording of the account implies that travel to Wineland had been in abeyance for a time.

Gustav Storm and others drew the conclusion that the bishop had intended to preach the Christian faith in Wineland. If so, it might indicate that people believed some Greenlanders or Ice-

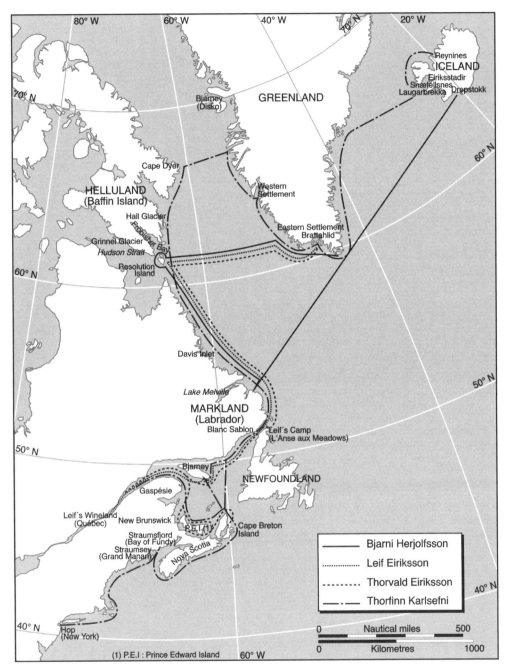

Routes of four explorers.

landers had settled permanently in Wineland. But if no such settlement was known to have existed, it must have been the Native Americans whom Bishop Eirik intended to convert to the true faith. At this time, stories of the Wineland expeditions, and descriptions of the route, must have been relatively well-known, and hence it is reasonable to suppose that the bishop found Wineland. But there is no mention of his return, and hence the inference is that his ship may have sunk, or that he may have fallen prey to other dangers, for instance in conflict with the Native Americans. Perhaps the memory of the five skrælings murdered a hundred years before by men from a Viking ship had been preserved among the Native Americans.

In the discussion of Thorfinn Karlsefni's journey to Wineland above, mention was made of archaeological research which revealed that a large Native American settlement was located on the coast of Maine in 900–1500. According to Steven L. Cox's description of the locale, it may be regarded as almost certain that Thorfinn would have been aware of the settlement. And this could support the account of the killing of five skrælings by the seashore, in Eirik's Saga.

Stefan Karlsson has pointed out to me that it is unlikely that Bishop Eirik's primary objective was to fetch valuable goods from Wineland, since in that case he could have sent other people rather than going there in person. But for purposes of a Christian mission, it would be natural for the bishop to go himself. He appears to have been consecrated by the archbishop in Norway, probably in 1112 or 1113, according to annals and to documents preserved in the Vatican.[85] The bishop's visit to Norway is crucial here, as will appear.

The bishop would naturally have gathered all available information on prior voyages to Wineland before setting off. Only a century had passed since the last Wineland expeditions, and so accounts of navigation and other sources were undoubtedly far more detailed than what has survived in the Wineland sagas. If Thorfinn had been aware of the large Native American community on the coast of Maine, it is probable that knowledge of it still existed in Greenland when Bishop Eirik was preparing for his journey. This major centre of Native American life would be an ideal place to preach the faith, and hence the bishop could have made his way there.

It is worth stating that the account of Bishop Eirik's search for Wineland is recorded in Icelandic annals which have proved to be highly reliable, for instance in their notes of when comets have been observed.

But there is no indication that Bishop Eirik ever returned from Wineland, and a few years later a new bishop, Bishop Arnold, had been consecrated.

This inevitably leads one to consider the Norwegian silver coin unearthed at Naskeag Point, or Goddard Site, as the place has been named after the man who first suggested a search for archaeological relics of Native Americans at this site. There is no doubt that the coin was struck during the reign of King Olaf the Quiet of Norway (1065–1080), a few decades before Bishop Eirik was in Norway.[86] A hole had been made in the coin, probably to hang it up as an ornament.

Most archaeologists who have discussed the coin have tended towards the view that it must have arrived in the New World via Labrador, probably from Greenland, and have been carried such a long way south via Native American trade routes. In support of this hypothesis, large quantities of quartz from Ramah, Labrador, have been found at Goddard Site: among other things, this was used for arrowheads. The hypothesis must, however, be regarded as far-fetched. Perhaps scholars invented this interpretation because the apparently reliable source on the journey of Bishop Eirik was not known to them.

And some scholars have been convinced that the Nordic mariners would not have sailed farther than the Gulf of St. Lawrence.

But my theory is that Bishop Eirik retraced the route of Thorfinn Karlsefni, which had been passed down to him, from the Western Settlement, across the Davis Strait, then south to Labrador, to the island of Anticosti, then across the St. Lawrence to Nova Scotia. From here the route was clear, around Kjalarnes (Keel Point) to the Bay of Fundy, and south to Penobscot Bay, where the large Native American community was known to be. After this, the silver coin is the only evidence, whether Eirik parted with it willingly or under duress.

All in all, I regard the silver coin as one of the most remarkable relics of Norse exploration in the New World nine or ten centuries ago. The find of the coin enlarges considerably the extent of the area which archaeological evidence otherwise indicates as likely to have been explored by the Norse travellers. The coin is even more precisely dated than other finds, and is entirely consistent with medieval Icelandic sources.

The historical framework of the Wineland journeys
It is interesting to look back over the first four journeys to Wineland, and their historical framework. Each journey of exploration progressed farther, in a logical manner.

Bjarni Herjolfsson, the pioneer, finds Labrador, on the mainland of North America. If the distances mentioned in the saga are reasonably accurate, Bjarni cannot have travelled as far as Newfoundland; he appears to have sailed north of Labrador, then eastward to Greenland.

Leif Eiriksson follows Bjarni's route in reverse, but travels farther and sails to Wineland, probably near Québec, where he builds a camp. He then builds large houses which are called Leif's Camp, probably not in Wineland itself, as stated in the saga, but at L'Anse aux Meadows. The following summer he returns to Greenland.

Thorvald Eiriksson follows Leif's route, to Leif's Camp, then explores the land south of the Gulf of St. Lawrence, first on the west, reaching Cape North (Kjalarnes), and then Big Bras d'Or on the east coast of Cape Breton Island, where New Campbellton now stands. There he is killed by a Native American arrow.

On these first three journeys, it appears that the travellers headed first for the south of Baffin Island from Greenland, presumably after having travelled some distance north of the Eastern Settlement. They probably returned by the same route, a journey of at least four half-days across the Labrador Sea. But it is not until Thorfinn's journey that a safer, coastal, route is chosen. Greenlanders who went north to hunt had an opportunity to gather information on this route once they knew there was land in the west. Thorfinn sailed much farther north up the coast of Greenland, to a point where a journey of two half-days would take him across to Baffin Island.

Thorfinn Karlsefni goes on past Leif's Camp. And instead of following the St. Lawrence inland to Wineland, he sails from Anticosti southwards across the Gulf, to Kjalarnes (Cape North), then goes on southwards, to the Bay of Fundy and then to New York.

This is a logical historical progression, which supports the theories put forward here regarding individual parts of the sailing routes. One leader after another makes use of the experience of those who went before, and adds to it in a logical manner.

When Freydis sets off for Wineland with the brothers Helgi and Finnbogi, further exploration appears not to be on the agenda; they headed for a known place, probably the same place as Leif found on the first Wineland journey.

Where was Wineland?

The hypothesis has been put forward here that Leif, and especially Thorvald, explored the south coast of the Gulf of St. Lawrence from Québec as far east as Cape Breton Island. In this context, it is interesting to observe how Finnur Jonsson (1858–1934) interpreted the exploratory journeys of the sons of Eirik from Brattahlid:

> The geography of Wineland in the Saga of the Greenlanders is also very unclear; one receives the impression of a coast that faces north, indented with several fjords lying towards the south.[87]

According to the theories explained here, this could be a correct interpretation of the geography of the Saga of the Greenlanders, if what is being described is a north-facing shore, i.e. the southern coast of the Gulf of St. Lawrence. But Finnur Jonsson appears not prepared to admit that the Gulf of St. Lawrence is being described; he is so bound by the preconception that the southeast coast of North America is being described, that he regards this as an example of the inconsistency of the Saga of the Greenlanders, and dismisses it with scorn.

When Leif is on the way to his first staging post, he travels westwards between the island and the headland that extends northwards from the mainland, but he does not discover wild vines until he has travelled farther. The headland is probably the Gaspé peninsula. Nor is there any mention of Thorvald, Leif's brother, finding vines when he travelled eastwards along the coast and east of Kjalarnes.

Sigurdur Stefansson may have had this headland in mind when he depicted the *Promontorium Winlandiæ* extending northwards from Wineland on his map of 1590, distinguishing it from Wineland proper.[88] Gustav Storm believes that there is no indication that Sigurdur Stefansson had access to any other sources than the sagas themselves, and that no more is to be gained from the map than modern readers themselves can read out of the sagas.[89] This may be true, but if so, this interesting inference by Sigurdur Stefansson is something that modern readers have failed to deduce from the sagas.

But the vines were found in other places on the mainland south of the St. Lawrence river, at Hop and also where Haki and Hekja made their exploratory journey, probably in Nova Scotia. The southern and western limits of the large land, Wineland, naturally remained unknown. In the 20th century, wild vines are still found in Nova Scotia, and also throughout the St. Lawrence valley south of Québec, as well as along the east coast of the USA. The name Wineland need not imply, of course, that vines grew throughout the country, any more than Markland (Forest Land) was all wooded, or Iceland always icebound, let alone that Greenland is green from shore to mountaintop. In all these cases, the name is derived from one attribute of the country.

Hence it is possible that Wineland, in the broadest sense, might be regarded as referring to the whole of the area of the eastern seaboard from the Hudson River, north and east to Nova Scotia and west to the St. Lawrence. It is also possible that the precise location was rather unclear; it might sometimes mean the region found first by Leif Eiriksson, at the head of the Gulf of St. Lawrence. This might explain the assertion in the geographic treatise of Abbot Nikulas that Thorfinn Karlsefni did not succeed in exploring Wineland the Good.[90] But it is also conceivable that the statement means merely that Thorfinn had to abandon his attempt at settlement, as recounted in both the Wineland sagas.

The chronology of the Wineland journeys

It was mentioned above that Bjarni Herjolfsson's journey to the

New World probably did not take place until shortly before 999 AD. According to Eirik the Red's Saga, Leif could have travelled to Norway that year, and back to Greenland in 1000, to undertake his Christian mission, whatever sceptics may think of this scenario. The story of Leif being carried off course and to America on that same journey is, however, less credible. In order to reach a region where grapes grow, he would have had to travel as far as the inner reaches of the Gulf of St. Lawrence. A provident and intelligent man like Leif would have been more likely to try to reach Greenland as soon as possible, rather than beginning exploration of an unknown land so late in the year, without knowing where he was or whether he would ever reach home. In this sense, the account of Bjarni Herjolfsson's adventures is far more believable. So it is probable that, with regard to Leif's journey, the far more detailed narrative of the Saga of the Greenlanders should be regarded as more reliable. The ruins at L'Anse aux Meadows, which are now generally believed to be Leif's Camp, are also a modern confirmation that Leif spent a winter there, contrary to what Eirik the Red's Saga states. It is probable that in the brief summary of Leif's travels given in Eirik's Saga, Bjarni's journey is partly transferred to Leif.

After this, the events and Wineland journeys can be traced more or less in accord with the Saga of the Greenlanders. This would indicate that the Wineland journeys were spread over a period of at least 16 years, from 998 or earlier, until 1013.

A possible chronology of the Wineland journeys might look something like this:

Bjarni Herjolfsson sights Labrador	*before 999*
Leif Eiriksson to Norway	*999*
Leif preaches Christianity in Greenland	*1000*
Leif sets foot in Wineland	*1001*
Leif returns from Wineland	*1002*
Thorvald to Wineland	*1002*
Thorvald's expedition returns from Wineland	*1005*
Thorstein Eiriksson carried off course	*1006*
Thorfinn Karlsefni to Greenland	*1007*
Thorfinn marries Gudrid	*1007–1008*

Thorfinn to Straumsfjord	*1008*
Thorfinn's son Snorri born in Straumsfjord	*1008*
Thorfinn at Hop	*1009*
Thorfinn searches for Thorhall the Huntsman	*1010*
Thorfinn returns to Greenland	*1011*
Freydis, Helgi and Finnbogi to Wineland	*1012*
Thorfinn to Norway	*1012*
Freydis returns from Wineland	*1013*
Thorfinn from Norway to Iceland	*1013*

If anything, the journeys may have been spread over more years than suggested here. Longer periods may have passed between expeditions, and there may also have been other expeditions which are not recorded in the sagas.

Gudrid's genealogy and the chronology

Although tradition and the sagas claim that Wineland was discovered in or around 1000 AD, problems arise with dating from other sources. Gudrid's genealogy is traced in the sagas, both back to the settlement of Iceland in the late 9th century, and down to historically-documented bishops around 1200.

It has been suggested that the age gap between Gudrid and her great-grandson Bishop Thorlak Runolfsson (b.1086) is unreasonably long, if Gudrid gave birth to her son Snorri in Wineland around 1008, as I have assumed here. From this point, some historians argue that the Wineland voyages must have taken place rather later than AD 1000, perhaps around 1020.[91] Hence it is worth considering the evidence of Gudrid's genealogy as a whole.

Some authors have felt it was unlikely that Vifil of Vifilsdal could have been Gudrid's grandfather. He first appears in Iceland as a serf in the service of Aud the Deep-Minded, who settled in Iceland around 890 AD. It is true that it is difficult to reconcile this with Gudrid, his granddaughter, being of marriageable age more than a century later, around 1000 AD, if the generations were normally spaced. But it is not impossible, as there may be considerable departures from the norm, although this is perhaps an extreme example.

It is interesting that Vifil, unlike Aud's other freed serfs, was not allocated a farm at once, although he asked for one. This could indicate that he was very young, though determined. He could perhaps have been born about 880, but not have been regarded as competent to run his own farm until about 900. It is not clearly stated when he had asked Aud for land of his own. Is it impossible that his granddaughter, Gudrid, could have been born 100 years after him? This is admittedly unlikely, but not unknown, in the case of a son's child.

If we look at the family tree of Snorri Björnsson of Husafell, we see that his son's son, Thorstein, was born 104 years after Snorri. Thorstein's son, Kristleifur, was in turn 105 years younger than his grandfather, and many similar cases may be found in the Borgarfjord area, the region best known to this writer.

Hence it is possible that Thorbjörn, son of Vifil, was born around 930, and his daughter Gudrid around 980. If they went to Greenland around 1005, as the above chronology suggests, Thorbjörn would have been over 70; he says in the saga that he has lived a long life at Laugarbrekka before leaving Iceland. But he could well have had the good health and courage to undertake the journey at this age, especially since he was motivated by pride.

It may also be regarded as unreasonable that the generations descended from Snorri, son of Gudrid and Thorfinn, were so widely spaced that his grandson, Thorlak Runolfsson, Bishop of Skalholt, was not born until 1086, if Snorri was born in 1008 as suggested here. The difference between their ages would be 78 years. But this is not unknown in the case of a daughter's child.

For instance, in 1933 a child was born who was the youngest of farmer Gudmundur Sigurdsson's daughters' children; born in 1847, he was 86 years older than his granddaughter. And Gudmundur's wife, the child's grandmother, was even older, born in 1843, and hence 90 years older than her granddaughter. In addition, my own grandmother was 81 years older than the youngest of her daughters' children.

To judge from such examples, it is impossible to say with certainty that the genealogy of Gudrid and her great-grandson Bishop Thorlak cannot be reconciled with the dating of the Wineland journeys, but some confusion may have arisen somewhere along the way, so this aspect of the dating remains something of a problem.

1   William Hovgaard 1914.
2   William Hovgaard 1914.
3   William O. Field 1975.
4   Olafur Halldorsson 1978.
5   Olafur Halldorsson 1978.
6   *St. Lawrence Pilot* 1969.
7   Kristleifur Thorsteinsson, personal communication.
8   Asgeir Svanbergsson, personal communication.
    Haraldur Agustsson, personal communication.
9   *St. Lawrence Pilot* 1969.
10 Hugh R. MacCrimmon and Barry L. Gots, 1979.
11 Gudni Gudbergsson, personal communication.
12 Thor Gudjonsson, personal communication.
13 *Canadian Climate Normals 1961–1990* 1993.
14 Helge Ingstad 1985.
15 William Hovgaard 1914.
16 Gunnar Marel Eggertsson, personal communication.
17 Gudmundur Olafsson, personal communication.
18 William Hovgaard 1914.
19 William H. Babcock 1913.
20 Gwyn Jones 1986.
21 G.M. Gathorne-Hardy 1921.
22 Camille Rousseau 1974.
23 Claude Roy, personal communication.
24 Birgitta Wallace 1991a.
25 *St. Lawrence Pilot* 1969.
26 C.C. Willoughby.
27 *St. Lawrence Pilot* 1969.
28 William Hovgaard 1914.
29 Kristjan Eldjarn 1968.

30   Olafur Halldorsson 1978.
31   Kristjan Eldjarn 1978.
32   Sven B.F. Jansson 1945.
33   Olafur Halldorsson 1982.
34   Roald Morcken 1977.
35   William Hovgaard 1914.
36   Gwyn Jones 1986.
37   *The King's Mirror* 1917.
38   D.D. Hogarth et. al. 1994.
39   William H. Babcock 1913. Mats G. Larsson 1992.
40   *Nova Scotia Nature Map* 1993.
41   Asgeir Blöndal Magnusson 1989. Fridtjof Nansen 1911.
42   Matthias Thordarson 1929.
43   Einar I. Haugen 1942.
44   M.L. Fernald et. al. 1950.
45   S.G. Aiken et. al. 1988.
46   Mats. G. Larsson 1992.
47   H.J. Scoggan 1978–79.
48   M.L. Fernald et. al. 1950.
49   M.L. Fernald et. al. 1950.
50   William H. Babcock 1913.
51   *Encyclopaedia Britannica.*
52   *Nova Scotia (South-east Coast) and Bay of Fundy Pilot* 1971.
53   *Encyclopaedia Britannica.*
54   *Canadian Climate Normals 1961–1990* 1993.
55   L.K. Ingersoll 1977.
56   L.K. Ingersoll 1977.
57   Sven B. F. Jansson 1945.
58   G.M. Gathorne-Hardy 1921.
59   *Encyclopaedia Britannica.*
60   William H. Babcock 1913.
61   Oskar Ingimarsson, personal communication.
62   G.M. Gathorne-Hardy 1921.
63   Oskar Ingimarsson, personal communication.
64   *World Weather Records.*
65   Daniel Denton 1670.
66   *Vikings. The North Atlantic Saga.* 2000.
67   *St. Lawrence Pilot* 1969.
68   Jon Sigmundsson, personal communication.
69   Olafur Halldorsson 1978.
70   Ian Wilson 1991.
71   Helge Kleivan 1966.

72   G.M. Gathorne-Hardy 1921.
73   Haraldur Olafsson, personal communication.
74   Snorri Sturluson 1991.
75   Helge Ingstad 1985.
76   Bolatta M. Vahl, personal communication.
77   Helge Kleivan 1966.
78   Louis Rey 1986.
79   Björn Thorsteinsson 1966.
80   Sigrun Stefansdottir, personal communication.
81   Ludvik Kristjansson 1982.
82   *Encyclopaedia Britannica.*
83   *Book of Settlements.* 1986.
84   Gustav Storm 1888.
85   Kolbjörn Skaare 1979.
86   Quoted by Thor Heyerdahl in his book *Ingen Grenser* (1999).
87   Finnur Jonsson 1915.
88   Helge Ingstad 1985.
89   Gustav Storm 1887.
90   Olafur Halldorsson 1978.
91   G. M. Gathorne-Hardy 1921. Olafur Halldorsson 1978.

HISTORICAL SOURCES

Sources other than the Wineland Sagas

Wineland is named in a number of sources other than the Wineland sagas, the oldest of which is Adam of Bremen's *History of the Archbishops of Hamburg-Bremen*. When Adam visited King Svein of Denmark shortly after 1065, he learned about Wineland. In his History, Adam emphasises the fact that his account is based on dependable sources. King Svein may perhaps have told the story after being visited by Audun of the West Fjords, who in the Tale of Audun is said to have brought him a polar bear from Greenland, and stayed "for a time" with the king.

It is worth quoting Adam's account of Wineland both in the original Latin and in English translation:

> Præterea unam adhuc insulam recitavit, a multis repertam in illo Oceano, quæ dicitur Vinland, eo quod ibi vites sponte nascantur, vinum optimum ferentes. Nam et fruges ibi, non seminatas, abundare, non fabulosa opinione, sed certa Danorum comperimus relatione (Gesta, IV, xxxix (38)).

> He [King Svein] told me too of yet another island, discovered by many in that ocean, which is called Wineland from the circumstance that vines grow there of their own accord, and produce the most excellent wine. While that there is abundance of unsown corn there we have learned not from fabulous conjecture but from trustworthy report of the Danes.[1]

There is scarcely room for doubt that the wine (*vinum*) is made from vines (*vites*), and not from any other berry, as has been suggested by some writers, in order to support the theory that the Wineland voyagers travelled no farther than to Newfoundland, where there were probably no vines. It would, admittedly, be an exaggeration to call the tart wine "excellent" which is made from the grape *Vitis riparia*; they may have found this along the St. Lawrence river, or elsewhere on the Gulf of St. Lawrence. On the other hand, the wines of the *Vitis labrusca* (fox grape), found in New England and farther south, have an unusual "foxy" flavour, but some Americans still prefer these wines to the more conventional wines of the world. The comments of Bishop Adam of Bremen could therefore be consistent with the theory that Thorfinn Karlsefni travelled as far south as New York, where fox grapes grew in abundance. This interpretation is more consistent with Eirik the Red's Saga than the Saga of the Greenlanders, which only mentions Thorfinn travelling as far as Leif's Camp. In this case, he could only have gathered the riverbank grapes of the St. Lawrence area.

The next-oldest source is in *Islendingabók* (the Book of Icelanders) by Ari Thorgilsson, known as the Wise, written in the early 12th century.[2] Ari the historian writes of Wineland as if it is well-known to all, but gives no account of how the country came to be discovered. Perhaps he did not think this was necessary, if he had already written an account of this elsewhere? Another interesting point is that he calls Eirik the Red "a Breidafjord man," indicating that Eirik was not born in Norway, as Eirik's Saga and some other sources say.

> The land which is called Greenland was discovered and settled from Iceland. Eirik the Red was the name of a Breidafjord man who went out there from here [Iceland] and took land in settlement at the place which has ever since been called Eiriksfjord. He gave the land a name, and called it Greenland, arguing that men would be drawn to go there if the land had a good name. Both east and west in the country [i.e. at both the Eastern and Western Settlements] they found the habitations of men, fragments of boats [of skin?] and stone artefacts, from which it may be seen that the same kind of people had passed that way as those that inhabited Wineland, whom the Greenlanders call Skrælings. When he began to settle the land, that was fourteen or fifteen years before Christianity came to Ice-

land [i.e. 985 or 986], according to what a man who had himself gone out with Eirik the Red told Thorkel Gellisson in Greenland.

Even if these passages by Adam of Bremen and Ari the Wise were the only sources on the discovery of Wineland, they would strongly support the idea of the Icelandic/Greenlandic discovery of America.

Wineland is also mentioned in the geographical treatise contained in manuscript AM 194 8vo in the Arni Magnusson Institute in Reykjavik. The information contained there is attributed to Abbot Nikulas "who was both wise and renowned, a good counsellor and articulate, with a good memory and well-informed." Abbot Nikulas, a contemporary of Ari the Wise, died in 1159. The manuscript states:

> [From] Bjarmaland extend uninhabited lands to the north, until one reaches Greenland. South of Greenland is Helluland, then Markland: then Wineland the Good is not far away, which some men believe is a part of Africa. It is said that Thorfinn Karlsefni cut wood for a *húsasnotra*, and then went in search of Wineland the Good, and reached where they believed it to be, but did not succeed in exploring or gathering any goods. Leif the Lucky was the first to find Wineland, and he found travellers at sea in peril and saved their lives by God's mercy. And he brought Christianity to Greenland, where it flourished so that a bishopric was established at the place named Gardar.[3]

Some of Nikulas' treatise has been treated with scepticism, and dismissed as later interpolation, such as the statement that Thorfinn Karlsefni did not succeed in exploring Wineland the Good, nor in gathering any goods there. Others have questioned the claim that Leif Eiriksson converted Greenland to Christianity. It is possible, however, that this scepticism is based upon far-fetched arguments, and even upon historical prejudices, rather than upon real proof. In fact there is nothing to show that both these statements, about Leif the Lucky and Thorfinn, could not be true.

Abbot Nikulas says that Leif the Lucky introduced Christianity in Greenland, without mentioning King Olaf Tryggvason in this connection. A book by an anonymous author, *Historia Norvegiæ*, tells that the Icelanders have "helped" Greenland by the Catholic faith.[4] Although worded rather obscurely, this could be a reference to Leif Eiriksson. Nor is Olaf Tryggvason's supposed role in this conversion or Christian practice mentioned here. It may thus have been a matter of opinion whether it was Leif or King Olaf who brought Christianity to Greenland, and it is not surprising that accounts are inconsistent. Views on this matter may have changed over time.

It should also be mentioned here that Icelandic annals tell of Bishop Eirik Gnupsson sailing to Wineland, as discussed on p. 102 above.[5]

The Wineland sagas as historical sources

The Wineland sagas, i.e. the Saga of the Greenlanders and Eirik the Red's Saga, provide an account of the discovery of the New World that is in many ways more detailed than those mentioned above. Translations of both sagas appear in full in this book (see pp. 235–276). With regard to some translation issues, see p. 11.

A letter-for-letter version of two manuscripts of Eirik the Red's Saga was published in 1945, edited by Sven B.F. Jansson.[6] In the following discussion, reference is made mainly to the *Skálholtsbók* manuscript. Stefan Karlsson, former director of the Arni Magnusson Manuscript Institute, believes that this manuscript was penned by Olaf Loftsson around 1420.[7] Arni Magnusson, the 18th-century collector of manuscripts and books who preserved many Icelandic sagas from being lost, acquired this manuscript from Bishop Jon Vidalin of Skalholt.[8] Another vellum manuscript of the saga is extant, in *Hauksbók*, a collection of sagas compiled by Hauk Erlendsson in the early 14th century. Both Olaf Loftsson and Hauk Erlendsson were descendants of Thorfinn Karlsefni. Jansson's studies indicate that the text has been revised in some places in *Hauksbók*, especially those written by Hauk himself. In some cases the text is so different that important aspects of the story are changed. This appears to be the origin of some dubious interpretations of the saga that have been put forward, by those who have placed too much confidence in *Hauksbók* rather than *Skálholtsbók*. This is especially noticeable in the account of Thorfinn Karlsefni's journey. In Olaf Loftsson's text, on the other hand, there are more instances of the original text being misread, or carelessly transcribed. But it is an indication of Olaf's conscientiousness that he did not attempt to "correct" the text if it did not make sense to him, but simply copied. Reference to *Hauksbók*, however, may help us to correct some of Olaf's slips of the pen, especially in the sections not written by Hauk himself, but by his copyists. Whether or not both are copied from a common original, the lettering was probably easier to decipher when *Hauksbók* was written, in 1420, than a hundred years later, when the *Skálholtsbók* copy was made.

Both manuscripts tell by implication, in the same words, that Brand Jonsson, a descendant of Thorfinn, was Bishop of Holar. He was bishop in 1263–64. This may be regarded as indicating that the original or originals of the saga were not written down until the time of Bishop Brand. Olafur Halldorsson, however, regards it as likely that the saga was originally put into writing in the early 13th century.[9] But in my view the original of Eirik's Saga may have been older still, perhaps dating from the time of Ari the Wise in the mid-12th century. This will be discussed below.

The Saga of the Greenlanders exists in one vellum manuscript, *Flateyjarbók* (the Flatey Book). This derives from an older manuscript version of the saga, generally believed to have been written around 1200, or earlier.

The relative reliability of the two sagas, the Saga of the Greenlanders and Eirik the Red's Saga, has been hotly debated. Eirik the Red's Saga attributes the discovery of Wineland to Leif the Lucky, while the Saga of the Greenlanders says Bjarni Herjolfsson happened across the new continent. Gustav Storm maintained that Eirik's Saga was a far better source, while the Saga of the Greenlanders gave a distorted view of the Wineland journeys.[10] Before Storm's day, however, there had been a general consensus that the Saga of the Greenlanders was more reliable. Finnur Jonsson agreed with Storm.[11]

The impression, still predominant today, that Leif the Lucky was the first European to discover America, may probably be at-

tributed to the ideas of the late 19th century, although no convincing arguments were put forward to discredit the account of Bjarni
Herjolfsson's journey in the Saga of the Greenlanders. Fridtjof
Nansen regarded both sagas as largely fiction, and made little distinction between them.[12] Sigurdur Nordal believed that the sagas
were

> so unrelated each to the other, that the most natural interpre-
> tation appears to be, that they are both written at around the
> same time, but in different regions of the country. Eirik the
> Red's Saga follows the interpretation that may be traced to
> Gunnlaug Leifsson, also upheld by Snorri Sturluson in
> *Heimskringla*, that it was Leif Eiriksson (the missionary!) to
> whom the honour of finding Wineland belonged; while the
> Saga of the Greenlanders mentions instead a man otherwise
> unknown, Bjarni Herjolfsson; in spite of specific unlikely as-
> pects, this could well be an older and more authentic tradi-
> tion. [13]

Jon Johannesson went much farther, believing that the Saga of the
Greenlanders was much older, and hence a more authentic and reliable source, and in recent decades most scholars have tended to
subscribe to this view.[14] But Olafur Halldorsson, who is one of the
leading researchers of these sagas, has reached the conclusion that
neither of the Wineland sagas is derived from the other. He believes that they are both of similar age, and are based upon stories
passed down orally, some aspects of which are common to both
sagas.[15]

Different objectives
In this book, neither the Saga of the Greenlanders nor Eirik the
Red's Saga is presumed in advance to be more authentic than the
other. Undeniably, however, Eirik's Saga appears to give a generally more detailed and accurate account of Gudrid Thorbjarnardottir and Thorfinn Karlsefni; they seem to be the focus of the
saga, while Eirik the Red's life in Iceland is also recounted in some
detail. The Saga of the Greenlanders, on the other hand, apparently gives a fuller account of the other travellers to Wineland:

Bjarni Herjolfsson, Leif, Thorvald and Freydis. This must be borne in mind when individual passages of the narrative are assessed.

How many journeys were made to Wineland? According to the Wineland sagas, they numbered only five, or six if Thorstein Eiriksson's failed attempt is counted. It is possible, however, that only the most interesting of the pioneering journeys were recounted in the sagas, and that more voyages were in fact made. And it is a matter of opinion whether the later journey of Bishop Eirik Gnupsson should be included.

As a matter of interest, let us compare the number of words used to recount each Wineland journey, in Eirik the Red's Saga and the Saga of the Greenlanders. Thorstein Eiriksson's unsuccessful journey is included here.

	Eirik the Red's Saga	Saga of the Greenlanders
Bjarni	0 words	585 words
Leif	104	383
Thorvald	0	753
Thorstein	331	121
Thorfinn	3295	1051
Freydis and Co.	0	1167

This table gives quite a clear impression of the contrasting emphasis of the sagas, and the authors' differing objectives. The Saga of the Greenlanders seems to be meant as a summary of the Wineland journeys in general, with relatively equal coverage of each journey. Eirik the Red's Saga, on the contrary, appears to be composed as a detailed account of Thorfinn Karlsefni's exploration. Other journeys to Wineland are scarcely mentioned, with the exception of a description of Leif's voyage, in 104 words. Some account of previous journeys was unavoidable in Eirik's Saga, in order to explain how Thorfinn came to know about Wineland before going there, and had such detailed information about the place that he set off with the intention of settling. Neither saga indicates that Leif made more than one journey to Wineland. But in view of the fact that the account of Leif in the Saga of the Greenlanders is far more detailed, it seems reasonable to regard this as the more reliable version. It is interesting that, although Eirik the Red's Saga all but ignores other journeys to Wineland, it gives a long account (longer than in the Saga of the Greenlanders) of Thorstein Eiriksson's failed expedition. The obvious explanation for this is that Thorstein was the husband of Gudrid Thorbjarnardottir, who plays a far more important role in Eirik's Saga than in the Saga of the Greenlanders.

Gudrid appears to be the focus of Eirik the Red's Saga, to the point that some readers have felt it was Gudrid's saga, rather than Eirik's or even Thorfinn's.[16] This would be consistent with my hypothesis that Eirik's Saga is originally based largely upon Gudrid's own accounts of her travels, although the saga must also have drawn on other sources. The passages dealing with Breidafjord, Gudrid's home territory, are detailed, and demonstrate familiarity with the region.

At the end of the Saga of the Greenlanders, the accounts on which the saga is based are attributed to Thorfinn Karlsefni. But this assertion need not necessarily be taken literally. The material on the background of Thorfinn's wife, Gudrid, is brief and unclear, for instance, in the Saga of the Greenlanders. This may perhaps be explained by the tale not being written down directly from Thorfinn's narrative; the story may have been passed down orally before being recorded in writing. But the overview of Wineland voyages presented in the Saga of the Greenlanders was certainly within Thorfinn's power to have passed on to his fellow-countrymen. Before setting off on his own adventures, it would have been in his interest to seek out all possible information on those who had already journeyed to Wineland. This does not mean, however, that the sagas could not have become somewhat distorted in the transmission, before being written down.

While the two sagas are to some degree complementary, the discrepancies between them are sufficiently important to cast some doubt upon both. But it is difficult to decide between them; both are to some extent credible, especially with regard to the convincing descriptions of topography and ethnic details, both in America and in Greenland. So the most reasonable course seems to be to accept both, without rejecting more of either saga than is strictly necessary.

In the discussion of the sagas in the previous chapter, short passages were quoted to illustrate various points. If only these chapters are included, the author may sometimes appear to be quoting selectively to support his/her own theories, and some writers have fallen into this trap. For this reason, the translated texts of both the Wineland sagas, the Saga of the Greenlanders and Eirik the Red's Saga, are appended in their entirety to this book, so that the reader can make up his/her own mind about the texts, and the conclusions drawn from them here.

The sagas are both well worth reading, both as history and as literature; some readers may prefer to read the sagas before reading the arguments of this book.

Origins of the Saga of the Greenlanders

Professor Jon Johannesson argued in *Nordæla*, a miscellany published in 1956 in honour of Professor Sigurdur Nordal, that the Saga of the Greenlanders was older than had been believed until that time.[17] His principal argument was that the saga does not mention Leif Eiriksson's alleged Christian mission to Greenland; he argued that this would surely have been mentioned if the saga had been written in the 13th century, when this story had become common belief. He conjectured that the tale of the missionary Leif might have originated with Gunnlaug Leifsson the Monk, author of a now-lost saga of King Olaf Tryggvason, believed to have been written around 1200.

This theory, based largely on negative rather than positive argument, cannot be regarded as convincing. There is no proof of what Gunnlaug the Monk wrote in his book, as it has not survived, and even if the writer of the Saga of the Greenlanders knew of this story of King Olaf, he might have deemed it irrelevant to the story he was telling. His primary purpose is clearly to tell of the Wineland voyages. He mentions the conversion of Greenland to Christianity, admittedly. But in his view journeys to and from the Nordic countries are not newsworthy, in comparison with the journeys to the New World. What the author of the Saga of the

Greenlanders did not write about the conversion cannot be re-garded as a crucial argument on the age of the saga, but only a "feeble handhold" as Olafur Halldorsson put it.[18] Essentially, the authenticity or otherwise of Leif Eiriksson's Christian mission to Greenland is not important here.

A stronger handhold seems to be provided by another argu-ment Olafur Halldorsson has used to ascertain the age of the Saga of the Greenlanders. He points out that, at the end of the saga, three bishops are listed who are descended from Thorfinn Karls-efni and Gudrid Thorbjarnardottir. These are the same bishops as are named at the end of Eirik the Red's Saga. But they are listed in a different order. Thorlak Runolfsson, the oldest of the bishops, is mentioned first in Eirik's Saga; as will be discussed below, it is pos-sible that this may be taken as an indication that the saga origi-nated partly with him. In the Saga of the Greenlanders, on the other hand, Brand Sæmundarson is the first named of Thorfinn Karlsefni's descendants, although he was the youngest of them. Olafur Halldorsson believes this may have been because the au-thor was personally connected in some way to Brand, who was bishop at Holar from 1163 until his death in 1201. Bishop Brand Sæmundarson is also mentioned in an interesting context in Sturl-unga saga:

> Almost all the sagas concerning events which took place here in Iceland were written before Bishop Brand Sæmundarson died; but those sagas which concern events which took place later were little written, before the *skáld* [poet] Sturla Thordar-son dictated the Sagas of the Icelanders. For this he drew on both the knowledge of wise men who lived during his early years and also on some materials written by those who lived at the same time as the sagas relate.[19]

While this does not directly state that the Sagas of Icelanders were written on the initiative of Bishop Brand, this could be the infer-ence. Which leads us to ask the question: could Bishop Brand Sæmundarson, who died in 1201, have had the Saga of the Green-landers recorded in writing? The bishop was in a good position to do so, surrounded by clerics at the bishopric of Holar, and with connections to monasteries at Thingeyrar and Munkathvera; the abbot at Munkathvera was Björn Gilsson, a kinsman of Brand and also a descendant of Thorfinn Karlsefni. This could support the hypothesis, put forward by such scholars as Sigurdur Nordal and Olafur Halldorsson, that the sagas were written independently of each other. It remains unclear, however, whether Bishop Brand was personally involved in the writing of the Saga of the Greenlanders. The background of his ancestress Gudrid, wife of Thorfinn Karlsefni, is described differently in the Saga of the Greenlanders and in Eirik's Saga. In the former she is said to have been married to Thorir the Norwegian when she arrived in Greenland, while the latter says she was unmarried. At any rate, there appears to be good reason to draw the conclusion that the Saga of the Greenlanders is considerably older than has generally been assumed, and that it was written no later than about 1200.

Origins of Eirik the Red's Saga

Professor Jon Johannesson was of the view that Eirik the Red's Saga was not written until after 1264, and hence was of considerably later date than the Saga of the Greenlanders.[20] This conclusion was based upon the genealogical table at the end of the book, where the names of the three bishops descended from Thorfinn Karlsefni and Gudrid are listed: Thorlak Runolfsson, Björn Gilsson and Brand Sæmundarson. Professor Johannesson points out that Brand is called "the first Bishop Brand," clearly to distinguish him from Brand Jonsson, also a descendant of Thorfinn and Gudrid, who was bishop at Holar from 1263. He concludes that the saga must have been written after 1264, and that this is consistent with the author of Eirik's Saga using *Landnámabok* (the Book of Settlements) in the *Sturlubók* version as a source. This has been the predominant view of scholars since Professor Johannesson's article was published in *Nordæla* in 1956.

Olafur Halldorsson has pointed out that both of Johannesson's arguments require a closer examination.[21] In the first place, Halldorsson states that the words "the first" may not have been in the original text. A copyist (not the author) may, at some time after 1264, have felt it necessary to add them in order to distinguish between the two bishops Brand, Jonsson and Sæmundarson.

In the second place Halldorsson points out that the writer of Eirik's Saga could have referred to an older version of the Book of Settlements than that found in *Sturlubók*. In support of this theory, the account of the pioneering settler Aud the Deep-minded in Eirik's Saga is not consistent with *Sturlubók*. It is clearly derived from the same source as was used for *Eyrbyggja saga*, which is certainly older than *Sturlubók*. Halldorsson also states that Eirik's Saga makes no mention of Leif having adopted the Christian faith from Olaf Tryggvason (as recounted in Snorri Sturluson's *Heimskringla*). Even Leif's baptism is not mentioned in Eirik's Saga. This discrepancy between the saga and *Heimskringla* could indicate that the saga is older than *Heimskringla*, although it does not constitute proof. Snorri Sturluson, author of *Heimskringla*, died in 1241. On the basis of this, there may be little difference in age between Eirik's Saga and the Saga of the Greenlanders.

In view of what has already been stated, especially with reference to the journeys of Thorfinn Karlsefni, it would be difficult to deny that Eirik's Saga is in many ways credible and consistent, often containing relatively accurate descriptions of nature and events. It is even reminiscent of travel books written in the 18th and 19th century, although the narrative is terse, and Eirik's Saga and the Saga of the Greenlanders are more consistent than has hitherto been believed. For this reason, among others, I think the possibility should be considered that Eirik the Red's Saga may be much older than Olafur Halldorsson's arguments indicate. One should also bear in mind the interesting reference in *Sturlunga saga* to Bishop Brand, although there has been no consensus on what to make of this.

Another factor here is that the Wineland voyages probably took place somewhat later than has generally been believed. The arrival of Thorfinn Karlsefni in Wineland, for instance, has generally been dated to about 1003. In the previous chapter, I suggested that a more likely date was 1008, and Olafur Halldorsson has even argued that the Wineland voyages may have taken place around 1020 or even later. This would mean that a shorter time had passed from the events until the writing of the saga, which may be a factor in the preservation of the story.

A patron of history at Skalholt

When Ari Thorgilsson the Wise wrote *Íslendingabók* (the Book of Icelanders), this was done on the initiative of Bishop Thorlak Runolfsson at Skalholt and Bishop Ketil Thorsteinsson at Holar, some time between 1122 and 1133. Ari is famed for his statement in the Book of Icelanders that one should "include that which is the more true," and no doubt the bishops aimed for the same standard of unbiased historical reporting. By taking the initiative in the writing of the Book of Icelanders, Bishop Thorlak may be regarded as pioneer and benefactor of Icelandic history writing.

In addition to this, he also ensured that the body of ecclesiastical law was enacted and recorded in writing. He and Bishop Ketil supervised the work, and these two "did and enacted much more in their time for the moral good of the people." Bishop Thorlak was a grandson of Snorri Thorfinnsson (and a great-grandson of Thorfinn and Gudrid), and it would be remarkable if he had not had relatively reliable stories to tell of his great-grandparents' adventures and attempt at settlement in the New World. One would also expect him to be interested in ensuring that an accurate account of these events was preserved for posterity. The recording of the Wineland story would be a project of similar nature to the writing of the Book of Icelanders or of the Book of Settlements, which was probably in preparation at the same period. Thorlak could have heard the stories from his mother, Hallfrid, daughter of Snorri Thorfinnsson.

A tale of Gudrid

It is easy to imagine Hallfrid at her grandmother's knee, hearing of Wineland directly from Gudrid Thorbjarnardottir, who is called "knowledgeable" in the saga; Eirik's Saga gives an interesting account of her ability to recite poetry. Gudrid is said to have chanted heathen *Varðlokur* (Ward Songs) at a feast at Herjolfsnes in Greenland, when Thorbjörg the "little prophetess" carried out her magic rites. The account of this event may have been passed down directly from Gudrid. This episode has been dismissed by some sceptics as invention; they point out that it is unlikely that the farmer at Herjolfsnes was a man named Thorkel. Many of the new settlements in Greenland appear to have been named for their founder; hence the master at Herjolfsnes must have been either Herjolf or his son Bjarni (who first saw the New World, according to the Saga of the Greenlanders).[22] This is quite true, of course, but the writer (or copyist) of the saga may have made a different mistake: probably regarding the name of the farm, rather than of the farmer.

The saga says that Gudrid and her father, Thorbjörn, had a difficult journey to Greenland, and did not arrive until the beginning of winter. Although dark nights and sea ice might prevent their reaching Eirik the Red's farm at Eiriksfjord, some distance up the west coast of Greenland, they could certainly have travelled farther than Herjolfsnes, at the southernmost point of the mainland. Hvalseyjarfjord, for instance, would probably have been free of ice. A friend and cousin of Eirik the Red, named Thorkel Farserk, lived at Hvalseyjarfjord; a strong and powerful man, he was master of most of the land between Eiriksfjord and Einarsfjord. Like Eirik, he appears to have been heathen, as he was buried on his own estate in a barrow by heathen rites, and, according to the Book of Settlements (*Sturlubók* version) haunted his old home ever after. As a friend of Eirik the Red, Thorbjörn would be more likely to seek shelter with Eirik's kinsman Thorkel, than with Bjarni and Herjolf at Herjolfsnes. The pagan feast of the saga could thus have taken place at Hvalseyjarfjord, and this would be consistent with the clearly pagan preferences of Thorkel, according to the saga.

By a strange chance, one of the few traces left at Hvalsey, a short distance from the farmhouse, is believed by some to be the remnants of a heathen barrow.[23] This reminds us of the tale of Thorkel; although no bones were found in the barrow, this need not disprove the connection, as in Greenland it became customary to collect the bodies of those who did not lie in consecrated earth, and rebury them in churchyards. Lika-Lodinn (Corpse Lodinn) made a living by this work later, and in Eirik's Saga the bodies of Thorstein Eiriksson and his men are transported back to Eiriksfjord from the Western Settlement for Christian burial.[24] The body of Thorkel may even have been transported to a Christian church-

Íslendingur ("Icelander"), a replica of the Gokstad longship, was built by Gunnar Marel Eggertsson and launched in March 1996. The ship is built of pine and oak, 23.5 metres long. Photo Gunnar Marel Eggertsson.

The gnomon or sólskuggafjöl is a navigational instrument described in early 19th-century Faroese sources. It resembles a barrel-base marked with concentric circles, with a central style or needle. By observing the length of the shadow cast by the style at midday, it was possible to deduce how far north or south the ship had travelled, while the length of the shadow at other times of day would give an indication of the direction of the sun. Gnomon made by Pall Jonsson. Photo Pall Bergthorsson.

Quadrant made by Indridi Einarsson of Hafnarfjord, based on a description in the 13th-century Rím II. *If a ray of sunlight shines through both slits, the weighted thread shows the solar elevation on a scale from 0 to 90°. If the sun is too bright to be viewed directly, the quadrant may be aligned so that the ray falls through the upper slit and onto the lower. Photo Larus Karl Ingason.*

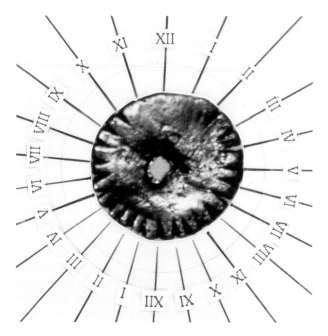

Sundial unearthed at Storaborg by Thordur Tomasson, probably from the 13th century. The grooves around the circumference may indicate the position of a shadow cast by a central style at each hour of the day at Summer solstice. The grooves are consistent with the correct calculated directions (shown by radiating lines). The largest interval between lines is at noon, 21°. The disc is 3.9-4.2 cm in diameter. Photo of sundial Björn G. Björnsson.

yard for burial in an effort to stop the restless wanderings of his spirit. Soil conditions at the Hvalsey churchyard are so unfavourable for preservation that only fragments of rotten bone and cloth have been found there. Widespread archaeological excavations in Greenland have not revealed any other sites which could be remnants of heathen burial sites. In the yearbook of the Icelandic Antiquarian Society of 1966, Thor Magnusson, former Keeper of National Antiquities, described a pagan burial barrow found in Patreksfjord in Iceland.[25] The grave had been disturbed somewhat, but stones appeared to have been arranged around it, as in the case of the barrow in Greenland. No well-preserved human bones were found in the grave, and they had probably been removed.

The account of the feast hosted by Thorkel indicates that the source of the story could be Gudrid herself; the description of the prophetess's clothing, and of Gudrid's own part in the proceedings, is so detailed. There would appear to be no reason to seek out more complex explanations.

The placename Reynines

It has often been maintained that Gudrid is the real "hero" of Eirik the Red's Saga, and this supports the hypothesis that Gudrid herself was the source of the story.[26]

The discussion of the name of Reynines in Skagafjord is interesting, as it could indicate an early date for the saga. When Reynines is first mentioned, as Thorfinn Karlsefni's old home, Reynistad is introduced as "… the place now named Reynines." Reynines is mentioned twice in Eirik's Saga, in the *Skálholtsbók* version. The *Saga of Grettir* also refers to "Reynines." This saga is based upon tales from Grettir's own time in the 10th and 11th century.[27] The estate was subsequently known as Stad, Stad at Reynines or Reynistad. It is not clear when the change of name took place. Magnus Stefansson of the University of Bergen believes that this was shortly after 1100, in the time of Bishop Gissur Isleifsson, who started to apply the word *staður (stad)* to estates with churches. The word *staður* is used of the episcopal seat at Skalholt in Ari the Wise's Book of the Icelanders.[28] No doubt it took some time, however, for such changes of name to be accepted.

Heiðarvíga saga (The Saga of the Killings on the Heath), which re-counts events that took place around 1000, mentions Thorfinn Karlsefni's father, Thord Horse-head, "who lived at the place now called Stad in Skagafjord."[29] This indicates that the change of name must have taken place such a long time before this saga was writ-ten that the writer is not at ease using the old name Reynines, al-though the sentence is supposed to be a direct quotation, spoken at the time of the saga. The sentence clearly indicates that the place formerly had another name. The Saga of the Killings on the Heath is sometimes counted among the oldest of the sagas of the Iceland-ers, from the end of the 12th century. Jonas Kristjansson maintains that it can hardly have been written later than the early 13th cen-tury. On this basis, Eirik's Saga would appear to be even older.[30] Bjarni Gudnason, however, believes that the Saga of the Killings on the Heath was written later than has hitherto been believed. Sturlunga saga first mentions the place in 1183, when it is called Stad without comment. At this time, the place belonged to Thor-geir Brandsson, a descendant of Thorfinn.

The phrase in Eirik's Saga about the place "now named" Reyni-nes indicates that a change of name was planned and imminent when the saga was written. It seems to me that this phrase points to an early date for the writing of the saga, perhaps even in the first half of the 12th century, and that it was written in south, rather than north, Iceland. Someone who was aware of the bishops' plans for changing placenames to *staður* would be a likely author of the saga.

Could Bishop Thorlak Runolfsson himself have written Eirik's Saga? He was fully competent and capable of writing the saga, or at least of editing. The saga is believed to have been written by a cleric – or at least some chapters of it. So there is nothing to contra-dict the hypothesis that Eirik the Red's Saga was one of the very first books written in the age of the written word, even though the saga has only been preserved in copies, perhaps with later addi-tions and changes.

The role of Ari the Wise

Ari the Wise confirmed, in his genealogical table at the end of the book, that he was the writer of *Íslendingabók* (the Book of Iceland-ers). Such genealogical identification by authors became something of a fashion in manuscripts, for instance in the case of Hauk the lawman and others who copied the Book of Settlements. There may therefore be a clue to the authorship of Eirik's Saga in the placing of the genealogical descent of Bishop Thorlak Runolfsson first at the end of the book. This is followed by the genealogies of other bishops, Björn Gilsson and Brand Sæmundarson, who were also descended from Thorfinn Karlsefni, and indirect reference is made to Abbot, later Bishop, Brand Jonsson. It is conceivable that in the original version of the saga, only Thorlak was mentioned, in acknowledgement of his part in the recording of the saga; in subsequent copies, including the manuscript from which *Hauksbók* and *Skálholtsbók* were copied, other, later bishops descended from Thorfinn may have been added. Such genealogical additions are known in copies, especially in the case of the Book of Settlements, as mentioned above.

Finnur Jonsson and others believed that Eirik's Saga was written on the Snæfellsnes peninsula in west Iceland; their conclusion was based on the author's accurate knowledge of topography and people in the region.[31] An indication that this may be so is the argument of Sven B.F. Jansson, regarding an unusual local locution: on the south of the peninsula, it is customary to speak of going "out" along the peninsula when one travels west, but "south" when one travels eastwards.[32] This usage also occurs in Eirik's Saga. But the greater confidence that may be placed in topographical descriptions of the New World, the less one need be surprised at accurate descriptions of Snæfellsnes. If the saga was written by, or at the behest of, Bishop Thorlak at Skalholt, he could have reinforced his knowledge every three years, when he made his regular visitations to the churches of Snæfellsnes, where the saga is partly set. In addition, he could consult his friend and retainer, Ari the Wise, regarding the accuracy of the descriptions of topography and human society, as Ari was likely to be well informed about Snæfellsnes, where he is believed to have served as a priest. And, not least, it is possible that the saga was written down by Ari the Wise himself, under Thorlak's supervision. It is probable that the section of the Book of Settlements which has been inserted into Eirik the Red's Saga was the work of Ari the Wise, so that the interpolation would have been an easy matter.

Was Eirik the Red not from Norway?

The section of the Book of Settlements in Eirik's Saga is somewhat inconsistent with the account of Eirik the Red's descent and origins in the Book of Icelanders; this states that Eirik was from Breidafjord. No reference is made to his having come to Iceland from Norway with Thorvald Asvaldsson, and settled at Drangar on Hornstrandir, as is asserted in the *Sturlubók* version of the Book of Settlements (chapter 89).[33] The account of Eirik's Norwegian origin has generally been accepted as the "correct" version. Chapter 158 of *Sturlubók*, however, tells of Thorvald Asvaldsson's settlement in Iceland without mentioning Eirik. *Sturlubók* also states that Thorkel Farserk, who settled at Hvalseyjarfjord in Greenland, was a cousin of Eirik the Red on his mother's side. But there is no indication that he travelled from Norway with Eirik and his father Thorvald, as one might expect. On this basis, Olafur Halldorsson proposes the theory that Eirik was indeed from Breidafjord, as Ari says. He may have been from Drangar: not the same Drangar as Thorvald Asvaldsson, but another place of the same name at Skogarströnd on the Snæfellsnes peninsula. In addition, *Flóamannasaga* (the Saga of the Floi People) states that Eirik the Red, a courteous young man, was at the court of Earl Hakon of Hladir shortly after Hakon came to power, probably soon after 970. This is consistent with Eirik's probable age. The saga calls him an "Icelander," and this is in agreement with Ari's description in the Book of Icelanders.[34] The Saga of the Floi People is, admittedly, regarded as one of the less reliable sagas, but is nonetheless based to some degree on recognised sources, including the Book of Settlements. The saga is also believed to contain some traditional tales. And this indicates that it may be one of the sagas retold on the basis of older stories.[35]

To judge from the above, Eirik sought fame and fortune in Norway, before returning to Iceland. This may perhaps have been the basis of the claim that he was Norwegian. The statement (error?) that he was the son of Thorvald Asvaldsson at Drangar on Hornstrandir may have been added to a manuscript of the Book of Settlements by mistake, and thence been adopted into copies of Eirik's Saga. The original writer of Eirik's Saga may have had nothing to do with it.

Better conditions could hardly have existed for recording the story of Eirik the Red than in the days of Thorlak Runolfsson and Ari the Wise. The contradictory evidence of the fact that the genealogies at the end of the saga are traced from Thorfinn and Gudrid, not only to Thorlak Runolfsson but also to later bishops of the line, need not be important. The additional genealogical material may well have been added at a later stage, as demonstrated in other instances.

The hypothesis put forward here, that Eirik the Red's Saga was written in the first half of the 12th century, cannot of course be proved. But I cannot see that it is any more far-fetched than other conjectures on the dating of this controversial saga.

And there is nothing new in the supposition that Eirik the Red's Saga and even the Saga of the Greenlanders may have been based to some extent on older written sources. Olafur Halldorsson has suggested that stories of Gudrid may have been written down in a work compiled to support the claims of Bishop Björn Gilsson of Holar, one of Gudrid's descendants, to be canonised. This idea appears to have arisen just before 1200, in the days of Bishop Brand Sæmundarson.[36]

Where did the original manuscripts used by Hauk and Olaf come from?
Mention was made above of the fact that the texts of Eirik the Red's Saga in *Skálholtsbók* and *Hauksbók* are believed to be derived from one or more manuscripts that cannot have been written earlier than 1263–1264, when Brand Jonsson was bishop of Holar, as both manuscripts make an indirect reference to him, in that Bishop Brand Sæmundarson is called "the first" Bishop Brand.

It is interesting to note how unassuming this reference to Bishop Brand is, since he was a descendant of Thorfinn and Gudrid, like the other bishops listed at the end of the saga. And it would thus have made sense to specify the connection. Is it possible that this copy was made by Brand Jonsson himself, who inserted this modest reference to himself? This would not be inconsistent with his character as depicted in *Sturlunga saga*, where he is generally mentioned in connection with peacemaking efforts in this era of strife and bloodshed. *Svínfellinga saga* (the Saga of the Svinafell Clan, part of the Sturlunga saga compilation) says:

The priest Brand Jonsson was consecrated abbot in the same year as Hakon's coronation. He governed Thykkvibær [monastery] in Ver, in the east; he was a splendid chieftain and a good clergyman, sensible and popular, powerful and benevolent. At that time he enjoyed the greatest good fortune of all men who then lived in Iceland. His mother was Halldora, daughter of Arnor, and Halldora's mother was Gudrun, the daughter of Bishop Brand Sæmundarson.[37]

When Brand's kinsman Thorgils Skardi made plans to travel north and seize power, Brand did all he could to discourage him, even though it could have meant Brand's vindication for murders of his kinsmen. He placed high ideals above pride, and human principles above ambition:

For harm will come to many innocent men on this expedition, and it will therefore not be fitting for me to give consent to it; furthermore, it may be that I will be so moved by indignation against some men that if I say much in this affair I will not be as careful of my words as I should be.[38]

Brand is believed to be the translator of *Alexander's Saga* from the Latin, for which he has been highly praised.[39] Although it cannot be regarded as a weighty argument, Eirik's Saga and Alexander's Saga share a stylistic peculiarity. Close to the end of *Alexander's Saga*, Galterus is quoted as saying, on the fall of King Cyrus:

Ho, ho, the joy of this world is ephemeral, and it is often seen how transitory it is.

And book three includes a section on the wise man Zoroas the Egyptian, who had foretold his own death from the stars; determined to fall to the royal sword of Alexander, he dares the great man to slay him. Alexander replies:

Ho, ho, what a wonder is here, he says. Whoever you are, I tell you to live, and not to degrade by your death a place of such great arts; neither my hand nor my sword shall ever be polluted by such a wise brain.

And the same exclamation is used twice in book six of *Alexander's Saga*.

In chapter five of Eirik the Red's Saga (*Skálholtsbók* version), when he falls from horseback, breaking his ribs and wrenching his shoulder, Eirik exclaims: *Ai, ai* (Ow, ow), however this was actually pronounced. In the following chapter, Sigrid, wife of farmer Thorstein in Lysufjord, exclaims *O* when she sees a gathering of ghosts, including herself. This use of exclamations is rather unusual in saga literature.

This argument for Bishop Brand Jonsson's role in the writing of Eirik's Saga is admittedly relatively weak, but, in view of his descent from the main characters of the saga, the idea is well worth considering. Halldor Hermannsson went so far as to suggest that Brand Jonsson could have been the author of Eirik the Red's saga.[40] But, as indicated by the arguments above, I think this is unlikely, and the saga is probably far older.

Consistency of the Wineland sagas

Hitherto, the focus of this book has been largely on the points of consistency between Eirik the Red's Saga and the Saga of the Greenlanders. Now let us consider some of the points which have been regarded as problematical.

It has often been seen as contradictory that Leif is supposed to have discovered Wineland, but only after Bjarni Herjolfsson's journey to the New World. As mentioned above, these accounts need not be contradictory; the Saga of the Greenlanders provides no basis for the inference that Bjarni travelled any farther than Labrador. There is nothing to contradict the assertion that Leif was not only the first European to step on Wineland's shore, but also the first to see it, even if Bjarni Herjolfsson was the first European to see Labrador, a part of the North American continent.

Both sagas recount that Thorvald, the son of Eirik the Red, died of an arrow wound sustained when on board ship. This consistency is important, but the details of the incident, and its timing, are far from consistent. In the Saga of the Greenlanders, Thorvald is said to have died on an expedition he led himself, while according to Eirik's Saga he travelled with Thorfinn Karlsefni's expedition to Wineland, and died there. As pointed out above, the account of Thorvald in the Saga of the Greenlanders is much more detailed and accurate, and thus more credible, and it also fits in well with the rest of the account of the expedition. The attack on the Greenlanders by the Native Americans, for instance, takes place as a logical consequence of their slaughtering the men Thorvald's company found sheltering under their leather boats on the shore. In Eirik's Saga, on the other hand, no reason is given for the one-legged man's attack on Thorvald. The flippancy of the verses on the one-legged man in Eirik's Saga hardly seems consistent with the tragic event. Hence the Saga of the Greenlanders appears to be a more reliable source than Eirik the Red's saga with regard to the death of Thorvald.

As discussed above, when the Saga of the Greenlanders states that Leif and his men spent the winter at the same place as they found the vines and other resources, this appears to be an error; they seem to have spent the winter at L'Anse aux Meadows. The saga's assertions regarding frostless winters would hence be based, not on experience, but on the travellers' assumption that the winters would be mild at Québec, since the summer was so warm and the land so productive. This is directly implied by the statement: "it *seemed to them* the land was so good that livestock would need no fodder during the winter." And this was not an unnatural assumption, since summer temperatures in Québec are similar to those in England, where the mildness of the climate means that domestic animals can stay out at pasture all year. In fact, winters in Québec are cold, with subzero temperatures and heavy snow, due to the continental climate.

The Saga of the Greenlanders recounts the death and Christian burial of Thorvald Eiriksson in Wineland as follows:

Greenland had been converted to Christianity by that time, although Eirik the Red had died before the conversion.

This has been interpreted to mean that Eirik was dead before the new faith was adopted, and hence that he could not have been opposed to it, as stated in Eirik's Saga. A possible, though rather far-fetched, interpretation of the sentence is that Eirik died before *himself* being converted, i.e. that he remained heathen until his death, although Greenland had largely adopted the Christian faith.

The Saga of the Greenlanders also states that Eirik the Red died the winter after Leif's return from Wineland. If Leif was spreading the Christian faith, as stated in Eirik the Red's Saga, this could have taken place during the summer and autumn, and hence before Eirik's death. It is, however, more likely that Leif had begun his mission of conversion before the expedition to Wineland, and hence that Eirik lived two years after the conversion to Christianity. This would be consistent with the statement of Eirik the Red's Saga that he was "reluctant to give up his faith." After this, the saga tells of Thjodhild (Eirik's wife, Leif's mother) having a church built, and then refusing to sleep with her husband because he was a heathen. Thus the two Wineland sagas are not as inconsistent as they may appear initially. But the discrepancy remains that Eirik's Saga says that Eirik was still alive when Thorfinn Karlsefni arrived in Greenland, while the Saga of the Greenlanders says he was already deceased. No conclusion will be drawn here on which is more likely to be correct.

Another stumbling block is the fact that the Saga of the Greenlanders makes no mention of Leif Eiriksson's journey to Norway, which is documented in various other writings. This is, however, not an important factor. The writer of the Saga of the Greenlanders may well have known of Leif's journey, but not have seen any necessity to include it in the saga. As mentioned above, the aim of the Saga of the Greenlanders appears to be to give an overview of the Wineland journeys, but not of voyages to other countries, such as Norway. Such journeys were relatively commonplace, and thus not much was said about them. The conversion to Christianity is, however, mentioned in both sagas, but this was of course a more important event than Leif's journey to Norway *per se*.

In contradiction to the claim that Leif the Lucky introduced

Christianity into Greenland on behalf of King Olaf Tryggvason, the point has been made that it is not until the 13th century that manuscripts begin to mention Greenland as one of the countries converted by Olaf. Defeated and killed in 1000, King Olaf was not an object of any great veneration immediately after his decease, as his memory would not have been honoured by the new rulers. Abbot Nikulas' geographical treatise does not mention Olaf in its account of Leif's mission. Nor is Olaf mentioned in the *Historia Norvegiæ*, when the Icelanders are said to have "helped" the Greenlanders with the Catholic faith.[41] This may well be a reference to Leif, who was probably born in Iceland. Later, when tales of the missionary activities of Olaf Tryggvason gained currency, it is quite probable that his name became associated with the conversion of Greenland. Eirik's Saga does not say that Leif was baptised at Olaf's court, although *Heimskringla*, Snorri Sturluson's history of the Norwegian kings, says so.

Eirik's Saga states that Thorfinn Karlsefni stayed at Straumsfjord, Straumsey and Hop. According to the Saga of the Greenlanders, on the contrary, he settled at Leif's Camp, which Birgitta Wallace believes was at L'Anse aux Meadows.[42] This is not credible, for various reasons. In the first place, no traces have been found there of domestic animals – no ruins of sheepsheds or cattlesheds, no pollen to indicate cultivation of grass. In the second place, Birgitta Wallace's research indicates that neither Inuits nor Native Americans were present at L'Anse aux Meadows at the time, so Thorfinn could not have found himself in conflict with the aboriginal population. In the third place, the cold climate of northern Newfoundland would not be a tempting prospect for Icelanders to set up a farm. The conditions are similar to those in the harshest regions of northern Iceland. In the fourth place, it is unlikely that Thorfinn would have gone to Leif's Camp intending to settle permanently, as there are various indications in the saga that Leif regarded himself as having first claim there. The account given in Eirik's Saga must be regarded as more credible, as it gives a far more detailed account of Thorfinn's journey. And if Thorfinn did not call at Leif's Camp, where there was accommodation for no more than 60–70 people until Helgi and Finnbogi built more houses, it is credible that his expedition consisted of 140–160 people – although the three vessels would have had to be fairly large. All these arguments tend to support the assertion that Eirik's Saga is a better source on Thorfinn's journey than the Saga of the Greenlanders. With regard to other Wineland voyages, however, the Saga of the Greenlanders appears to be a superior source in most instances.

1   Gwyn Jones 1986.
2   *Book of Icelanders* 1986.
3   Olafur Halldorsson 1978.
4   *Historia Norvegiæ* 1950.
5   Gustav Storm 1888.
6   Sven B. F. Jansson 1945.
7   Stefan Karlsson, personal communication.
8   Matthias Thordarson 1929.
9   Olafur Halldorsson 1978.
10 Gustav Storm 1887.
11 Finnur Jonsson 1915.
12 Fridtjof Nansen 1911.
13 Sigurdur Nordal 1968.
14 Jon Johannesson 1956.
15 Olafur Halldorsson 1978.
16 Olafur Halldorsson 1978.
17 Jon Johannesson 1956.
18 Olafur Halldorsson 1978.
19 *Sturlunga saga* 1970–74.
20 Jon Johannesson 1956.
21 Olafur Halldorsson 1978.
22 Olafur Halldorsson 1978.
23 Joel Berglund 1982.
24 Olafur Halldorsson 1978.
25 Thor Magnusson 1967.
26 Olafur Halldorsson 1978 and 1985.
27 *Saga of Grettir, Complete Sagas of Icelanders* 1997.
28 Magnus Stefansson, personal communication.
29 *Saga of the Killings on the Heath, Complete Sagas of Icelanders* 1997.
30 Jonas Kristjansson 1978.

31   Finnur Jonsson 1915.
32   Sven B. F. Jansson 1945.
33   Olafur Halldorsson 1978.
34   *Saga of the People of Floi, Complete Sagas of Icelanders* 1997.
35   Jonas Kristjansson 1978.
36   Olafur Halldorsson 1978.
37   *Sturlunga saga* 1970–74.
38   *Sturlunga saga* 1970–74.
39   *Alexanders saga mikla* 1945.
40   Halldor Hermannsson 1966.
41   Olafur Halldorsson 1978. *Historia Norvegiæ* 1950.
42   Birgitta Wallace 1991a.

HOW DID THEY REACH WINELAND?

Ships and sailing speeds

The Wineland journeys would have been inconceivable a thousand years ago, had the mariners not had at their disposal ships of sufficient size and seaworthiness – their longships and more especially the *knörr*, the Viking freighter, which Nordic shipbuilders had developed for long ocean journeys. The sagas contain considerable information on the structure of these ships and their qualities, but these sources were interpreted with indifferent success until relatively recently. It was not until the late 19th century, and also in recent years, that important archaeological finds made it possible to reconstruct these ships, and test their seaworthiness. In the late 19th century, two well-preserved Viking ships were excavated at Gokstad and Oseberg in Norway, and more vessels have been recovered since. This made it possible to carry out realistic tests on accurate replicas of real vessels.

One of the crucial qualities of the ships was their sailing speed. This is well described in *Vatnsdæla saga* (the Saga of the People of Vatnsdal), which gives an account of Ingimund of Hof in Vatnsdal being given a ship by King Harald Fairhair. Harald says:

> "Here is a ship called Stigandi [High Stepper] which we consider the best ship of all upwind under sail and a better voyaging ship than any of the others, and this is the one which I choose for you. It is a fine vessel, though not a large one."
>
> Ingimund thanked the king for the gift. He then took his leave with many tokens of friendship.
>
> He soon discovered how fast a ship Stigandi was.
>
> Then Ingimund said: "The king's choice of ship for me was a good one, and rightly it is called Stigandi, stepping through the waves as it does."

The Icelandic says that the ship "beats" well, referring to the vessel's efficiency at tacking into the wind, which was an important quality in unfavourable wind directions.[1]

Sailing speed is important in an evaluation of the credibility of the accounts of the Wineland sagas and other ancient writings. The speed was commonly expressed in terms of the number of *dægur* a certain journey took. Thus the concept of a *dægur* expresses distance, rather than time.

What's in a dægur?

To most Icelandic speakers today, the obvious answer to this question is that a *dægur* is 12 hours. This has, however, given rise to considerable debate, and most of the historians who have discussed Viking ships in recent times have asserted that a *dægur* was 24 hours. When the sagas state that the distance between Stad in Norway and the East Fjords of Iceland (about 545 nautical miles) is a seven-*dægur* journey, it is simple to calculate that the average speed was 6.5 knots, i.e. 6.5 nautical miles per hour. But some people have assumed that, although all the sources indicate that a *dægur* was 12 hours, this cannot be correct in this case. They infer from this that the speed must be divided by two in order to be credible.

This is difficult to accept. Definitions of the word *dægur* may be found in at least eleven places in old literature, rather more than those quoted in Fritzner's dictionary.[2] These are five examples from the Icelandic Encyclopaedia (*Alfræði íslensk*), three from the King's Mirror (*Konungsskuggsjá*), one from Snorri Sturluson's prose *Edda*, one from Snorri's *Heimskringla*, and one from *Heiðarvíga saga* (the Saga of the Killings on the Heath). In all cases, the clear meaning is 12 hours.[3] An attempt is made in Fritzner's dictionary to cite one of the examples from the Icelandic Encyclopaedia to support the theory that a *dægur* could be 24 hours. At the same time, it is acknowledged that the text is garbled. The same definition of a *dægur* appears in the Icelandic-English dictionary of Cleasby and Vigfusson, as well as the dictionaries of Sigfus Blöndal, Arni Bödvarsson and Asgeir Blöndal Magnusson: a *dægur* is 12 hours.[4] The Cleasby-Vigfusson dictionary, however, states the exception that in the Book of Settlements *dægur* "seems to be used of the astronomical day," i.e. 24 hours. But where does this assertion of Cleasby's come from? According to Gustav Storm, C.C. Rafn and others invented this interpretation of the word *dægur* in order to "rescue" the credibility of the sagas.[5] By this he means that Rafn could not believe that the Viking ships travelled as fast as they in fact did. Storm himself was in disagreement with Rafn's interpretation, and referred to ancient definitions of the word *dægur*. Storm's views on this are especially interesting in that he put them forward before any experiments had been made with the sailing speed of the first replica of the Gokstad ship, in 1893.[6]

The words *dagur* (day) and *dægur* can both mean "day" in the sense of the daylight hours, for instance when travelling overland, and resting overnight. This occurs in the account of Haki and Hekja in Eirik the Red's Saga, and also in the name of the heath Tvidægra (Two-*dægurs*), which is derived from the fact, recounted in the Saga of the Killings on the Heath, that Bardi Gudmundsson crossed the heath in two days, resting overnight in between.[7] Although a "day" may sometimes be the same as a *dægur*, it seems clear that *dægur* invariably means 12 hours in Old Icelandic.

Norwegian scholar Roald Morcken asserted that the word *dægur* meant 12 hours until the end of the 10th century, but that the meaning changed to 24 hours after that.[8] No doubt he is arguing here from Norwegian custom. But this is not consistent with the King's Mirror, written in Norway in the mid-13th century, which is in agreement with all the Old Icelandic sources.

The *knörr* was probably the vessel most used on the sailing routes between Norway, Iceland, Greenland and Wineland. Various information on their sailing speeds exists from the saga-writing age. It is natural to attribute particular importance to the sources on the ocean route which was undoubtedly most travelled at this time, the passage between Iceland and Norway. According to these sources, the journey between Stad in Norway and Horn in East Iceland (about 545 nautical miles) was a seven-*dægur* voyage. The Book of Settlements, Abbot Nikulas' geographical treatise and Ivar Bardarson's description of Greenland are all consistent on this point.[9] The Icelandic Encyclopaedia adds more detail, i.e. that the journey from Stad in Norway to the Faroe Islands took four *dægurs*, then another three *dægurs* to Horn on the East Fjords of Iceland; this proportion is remarkably accurate.[10] This is equivalent to 78 nautical miles per *dægur*, or a speed of 6.5 knots (nautical miles per hour). A nautical mile is 1,852 metres.

The *Sturlubók* version of the Book of Settlements says that from Langanes in northeast Iceland to Svalbardi is a four-*dægur* ocean journey. This is probably a reference to the "Svalbardi" discovered in 1194, now known as Jan Mayen. Again according to *Sturlubók*, the route across the strait from the Snæfellsnes peninsula, west Iceland, to Greenland is a four-*dægur* journey. On the basis of the speed calculated for the route from Stad to the East Fjords, Jan Mayen ought to be four *dægurs* from Iceland, as should Greenland from Snæfellsnes; the figures are entirely consistent.

The *Sturlubók* manuscript of the Book of Settlements states that from Reykjanes in south Iceland to Jölduhlaup in western Ireland is a five-*dægur* ocean journey. It would, however, be reckless in the extreme to attempt to sail to Ireland directly from Reykjanes. A more credible explanation is that a ship might, under unusual circumstances, cover the distance in the time in strong favourable winds, at a speed of 11 knots – and more probably a longship than the heavier *knörr*.

But it is more likely that the five-*dægur* ocean passage applied only to the sector of the journey across open sea, not counting the coastal part of the route. A parallel may be found in Thorfinn Karlsefni's journey to Wineland from Brattahlid in Greenland. This included three two-*dægur* passages sailing across open sea, but the saga gives no information on the duration of the long coastal journeys in between. The five-*dægur* ocean journey from Reykjanes to Jölduhlaup could thus indicate that ships first sailed eastwards along Iceland's south coast, and then across the ocean to the northernmost islands of Scotland, a distance of about 400 nautical miles. This would in fact be a five-*dægur* journey. From the north of Scotland, a coastal route would then be followed southwards to Jölduhlaup, on the west coast of Ireland. It would be odd if the shortest route to the British Isles were not included in the navigational information, as the Book of Settlements specifies the shortest sailing time from Iceland to all other nearby islands and countries: to Greenland, Jan Mayen, the Faroes and Norway.

The *Hauksbók* manuscript of the Book of Settlements contains a navigational detail, which may well appear questionable, that from Kolbeinsey island off Iceland's north coast, to the unpopulated area of Greenland, is a journey of one *dægur*. The correct distance would be something over two *dægur*. But it is worth bearing in mind that, even during warm periods, and in summers with little sea ice, such as during the years from 1919–43, a broad band of sea ice lies along Greenland's east coast. This means that it is not possible to sail more than one *dægur* in the direction of Greenland from Kolbeinsey. This may explain the reference in *Hauksbók*.

According to the geographical treatise of Abbot Nikulas (d.1159), it took seven *dægurs* to sail around Iceland "with a high wind, assuming the wind direction to be favourable all the time."[11] This is equivalent to a speed of nine knots, with high winds in favourable directions all the way, as the treatise states. Further details are given in the old Icelandic Encyclopaedia, i.e. that it takes one *dægur* to sail from Horn in the East Fjords to Hjörleifshöfdi, another to Reykjanes, a third to Bard, a fourth to Horn in the west, a fifth to Skagi, a sixth to Langanes, and a seventh back to Horn.[12] Thorarin Nefjolfsson travelled at a rather slower speed, averaging 7.5 knots, when he sailed from Møre in Norway to Eyrar, south Iceland, in eight *dægurs*. On this occasion he told the assembled representatives at the Althing (parliament) that he had left King Olaf Haraldsson four nights before – clearly indicating that a *dægur* was 12 hours.[13]

These sources on the sailing speed of Viking ships were put to the test when the replica *knörr*, *Saga Siglar*, set sail. A copy of a *knörr* that was excavated in Skulderlev, Denmark in 1962, the *Saga Siglar* was completed in 1983.[14] The *Saga Siglar* could sail at eight knots under a sail of 92 square metres, and achieved speeds of over 12 knots with favourable winds. The ship was sailed around the world by its owner, Ragnar Thorseth. In 1893 the longship *Viking*, the first replica of the Gokstad ship, sailed at speeds of up to 10 knots on the route from Norway to Newfoundland, and on one occasion it maintained an average speed of 11 knots for a 24-hour period.[15] The longship *Gaia*, another replica of the Gokstad ship, built in 1989–1990, reached speeds of 10 knots under a sail of 120 square metres; Gunnar Marel Eggertsson, who was helmsman on the ship, reports that the vessel sometimes reached speeds of 15 knots or more.[16] A replica of the Oseberg ship could sail at 10 knots with a sail of 100 square metres.

Another replica of the Gokstad ship, *Íslendingur*, the first vessel of the kind built in Iceland, was subsequently built by Gunnar Marel. It was launched in March 1996.

An expert at the Copenhagen Technical University, Wagner Smitt, has calculated that the Gokstad ship could sail at a speed of about six knots with a headwind at the prevailing force four to five (11–21 knots) travelling at an angle of 71° to the wind direction.[17] This means that the ship progresses at a speed of two knots, and must tack in order to maintain the right course overall. He also calculated that the Gokstad ship could have reached speeds of up to 14 knots. According to Gunnar Marel Eggertsson, both the *Gaia* and the *Saga Siglar* could be sailed closer to the wind than this indicates.

When a distance is given in terms of the number of *dægurs* it took to sail, there must be some assumption of standard conditions. If account were taken, for instance, of all the occasions when ships were carried off course, the result would be meaningless, and this would make it impossible to compare the distance of easy sailing routes, and ocean routes where the danger of getting lost is much greater. For instance, Jan Mayen is about as far from Iceland as Ammassalik, but it would normally take longer to find Jan Mayen, since it is a small island in a large ocean that tends to be foggy. On journeys back and forth on a certain route, favourable and unfavourable winds would tend to balance out in the long term, and the ship would drift equally far to port and to starboard. So it is reasonable to base calculations on typical weather conditions at the season, summer, when most travel took place. In the following table on the progress of a ship towards its destination, these conditions are assumed:

a) that the wind blows for an equal time from all directions.

b) that the wind is force 4–5 (average 16 knots), as is common in summer between Iceland and Norway.

c) that there are no delays due to being carried off course.

Wind directions	Ship's progress (knots)		Proportion of sailing time
	Longship	Knörr	
Headwind	2	1	$\frac{1}{8}$
45° headwind	6	5	$\frac{1}{4}$
Sidewind	9	8	$\frac{1}{4}$
45° tailwind	9	8	$\frac{1}{4}$
Tailwind	9	8	$\frac{1}{8}$
Weighted mean progress	7.4 knots	6.4 knots	
Distance sailed in 1 dægur	89 naut. miles	77 naut. miles	

Under these conditions, a longship will sail 89 nautical miles in a *dægur*, while the *knörr* will sail 77 nautical miles.

If we assume that most of the ships that sailed between Norway and Iceland were of the *knörr* type, these conclusions are consistent with the statement that the distance between Stad in Norway and Horn in the East Fjords could be sailed in seven *dægurs*, 78 nautical miles per *dægur* in average conditions in both directions. But this journey must naturally have taken longer on some occasions, and sometimes far longer, due to unfavourable winds and weather conditions. It is also probable that accounts of these difficult journeys are better preserved than those of uneventful passages.

English scholar W. Froude has put forward an empirical rule which indicates that sailing speed is more or less proportionate to the square root of the length of the vessel's waterline.[18] The length of the waterline of a *knörr* may be estimated at 16 metres, while that of a longship is about 22 metres. In addition to this, the wind speed is also important, of course. In keeping with the studies discussed here, I have made an estimate of the number by which the square-root of the length of the waterline must be multiplied, to indicate the speed under various conditions. I have made these calculations in collaboration with Gunnar Marel Eggertsson, who as stated above has built a replica of the Gokstad ship, *Íslendingur*, and has extensive experience of sailing both this vessel and the longship *Gaia*. In average wind conditions, with a wind speed of 16 knots, blowing equally frequently from each direction, I estimate this multiplication factor as 1.6, and 2 with a following wind all the way. With high winds throughout the journey, approximately 25 knots, the multiplication factor is 2.25, and 3 in optimum wind conditions, although these will hardly prevail for more than a few hours at a time. The results of these calculations may be seen in the following table:

Estimates of progress of ships and distance sailed in a *dægur*

	Knörr		Longship	
	Progress	*Distance in a dægur*	*Progress*	*Distance in a dægur*
Average wind from all directions	*6.4 knots*	*77 naut. m.*	*7.5 knots*	*90 naut. m.*
Average following wind	*8.0 "*	*96 "*	*9.5 "*	*114 "*
High following wind	*9.0 "*	*108 "*	*10.5 "*	*126 "*
Optimum wind	*12.0 "*	*144 "*	*14.0 "*	*168 "*

It is worth considering why people have been so reluctant to believe in the speeds attainable by these ancient Norwegian vessels. The elegant ships with their streamlined bow and side rudder had all but disappeared by the 14th century, to be replaced by the massive merchant vessels of the Hanseatic League and other traders. These had a deep draught and were relatively wide across the bow, and especially wide at the stern. Unlike the Viking ship, they were not streamlined and did not cut easily through the water, but they could carry a larger cargo, and hence they displaced the older vessels. When Icelanders who had travelled abroad, in the late middle ages and later, attempted to evaluate the descriptions of sailing speed in the Book of Settlements, they had no standard of comparison but these heavy, slow-moving ships. One can therefore sympathise with them in their inability to accept the information given. Unlike the modern reader, they did not have the advantage of learning from the remarkable experiments made over the past century with the sailing speeds and seaworthiness of Viking ships. It is also possible that the interpretation of the word *dægur* has been influenced by other Nordic languages, in which the cognate words *døgn* (Norwegian and Danish) and *dygn* (Swedish) have come to mean 24 hours in recent centuries.

The average distance covered in a *dægur* on the sailing route to

Wineland appears thus to have been about 75–80 nautical miles, the equivalent of a speed of 6.5 knots. In favourable winds, the speed may be assumed to have reached as much as 9 knots over 24 hours.

After many trials of replica Viking ships, it is now well-established that these vessels sailed fast, and were quite capable of covering an average of 150 nautical miles in 24 hours. The long-standing misinterpretation, that the word *dægur* in navigational descriptions in the Icelandic sagas must mean 24 hours and not 12, should thus have been thoroughly disproven by now. So it is disappointing to observe that in a new book from the Smithsonian Institution Press, excellent scholars are still maintaining this old theory. Thus they appear to believe that the distance called a two-*dægur* passage in the Wineland sagas, across Baffin Bay, the Labrador Sea and the Gulf of St. Lawrence, is about 280 nautical miles and not approximately 150.[19]

The matter of sailing speed and the significance of the word *dægur* has been discussed at such length because the interpretation of many aspects of the sagas is contingent upon the question of the speed attained, or attainable, by the ships. This justifies translating the word *dægur* as half-day.

Navigation in the Viking Age

Navigation in medieval times was of course made more difficult because the seafarer had no compass. The lodestone, which can be used to find the magnetic north, was not introduced until the 13th century. Thus it was vital to use other means of finding the right course, and deducing the location of the ship. An important skill here was knowledge of the changing position of the sun in the sky; in the light summer nights of the north, stars were of little use for navigation. The Pole Star, however, was generally visible on clear summer nights, south of the 58th parallel.

There is no doubt that helmsmen did their utmost to use the knowledge available to help their navigation, and it is probable that they observed the movements of heavenly bodies. In all likelihood, they could measure the elevation of the sun in some way. Some indications of this will be considered next.

Astronomy

It is clear that some astronomical knowledge existed in Iceland. Ari the Wise (1067–1148) recounts in *Íslendingabók* (the Book of Icelanders) that Thorstein the Black has made corrections to the Icelandic year of 364 days by the addition of a *sumarauki*, seven days added to the calendar in summer every five or six years, on the same principle as the modern leap-year day, February 29. The *sumarauki* was probably introduced in the mid-tenth century. In order to make this amendment, Thorstein would have required fairly accurate astronomical observations.[20]

In the first half of the 12th century, a century after the Wineland voyages, a man named Oddi Helgason, often called Star-Oddi, lived in the Thingeyjarsysla region of north Iceland.[21] He reported such precise observations of the changing elevation of the noon sun through the year that they must have been based upon instruments of considerable accuracy. The unit Oddi used for measurement is available to all: the diameter of the sun's disc, which is the equivalent of about 32 minutes of arc. He called this unit a *solarhvel* or sun-disc. Oddi observed that from the summer solstice the midday sun sank by half the solar diameter (about 16 minutes) in the first week, one diameter in the second week, one-and-a-half in the third, two in the fourth and so on, following this simple mathematical principle until the equinox. In the eighth week, therefore, the sun's elevation should drop by four solar diameters. By the same token, the solar elevation at noon was traced from winter solstice to equinox. Star-Oddi's calculations are normally within about 0.1 degrees in summer, but somewhat less accurate in winter, and especially around the equinoxes. This knowledge would have been highly useful to seafarers who intended to sail along a line of latitude, and had to bear in mind that the elevation of the sun rose or fell, even if they remained at the same latitude. This simple rule of thumb must have been of considerable help, provided that solar elevation could be measured. This is an excellent example of practical astronomy and mathematics at work in olden times. Such calculations are not, so far as I know, found in contemporary sources from other countries.

Oddi also determined bearings with great accuracy; his observations of the direction of the sun at dawn and dusk in his home region at different seasons of the year are precise to within one-third of a compass point. These observations of dawn and dusk were of great importance for time-keeping on land during the winter, but had less significance for navigators, at least in summer, when the sun hardly set. Eirikur Briem of the University of Iceland calculated that Oddi counted dawn or dusk when the centre of the sun's disc was 14° below the horizon.[22] Observations carried out by the present author in 1995–6 and 1996–7 show that at the point of dawn or dusk it is scarcely possible to distinguish the horizon or single clouds from the sky.

Solar elevation on Kroksfjardarheidi

A short section of the Greenland Annals, derived from the *Hauksbók* manuscript, was called *Prestaskipsreisa* (Pastors' sea voyage) by Jon Gudmundsson the Learned (1574–1658). This is an account of solar elevation on a heath known as Kroksfjardarheidi in West Greenland. It states, among other things, that the sun was as high at midnight as at home in the settlement when it was in the northwest.[23] This reference was probably to the settlement of Gardar, where the travellers subsequently went.

It is possible that this information may be used to deduce how far north Kroksfjardarheidi was. The observation was made on St. James' Day (25 July) after 1264, but before 1280. It may be assumed that the reference to Gardar applies to the same season of the year; otherwise the comparison would be meaningless. If the declination of the sun was between 20 and 23.5 degrees, i.e. in the brightest period of the summer, this would indicate that Kroksfjardarheidi was at a latitude of about 70°N. This ought thus to be located either on Disko Island or on the Nugssuaq peninsula directly east of it. This is a credible conclusion. It is not unlikely that Kroksfjardarheidi was the Nugssuaq peninsula. The rock, landscape and vegetation, especially on the east of the peninsula, are very similar to those found on Iceland's basalt heaths, known as *heiði*.[24] Heather and other heathland vegetation reaches up to an altitude of 6–700 metres. The name Kroksfjord (Hook Fjord) may well apply to the bay around the east of Disko Island; the name would be apt. This does not constitute proof of the location of Kroksfjardarheidi. But it does demonstrate that the solar elevation was measured in various directions, both in the south and north of Greenland's west coast, when people of Icelandic origin lived there. This form of comparison could hardly have been made without some form of instrument.

Shaft-high sun

The section on Christian law in the lawbook *Grágás* contains a detailed definition of when the sun was "shaft-high." *Kristinréttur* (Christian Law) was first recorded under the aegis of Bishops Thorlak Runolfsson of Skalholt and Ketil Thorsteinsson of Holar in the period 1122–1133:

> A chieftain is to come to a spring assembly in time to roof his booth on a Saturday before the sun is shaft-high and to be ready then to go to the formal inauguration of the assembly. If he works longer he is fined.
>
> The sun is shaft-high when a man standing on the shore where land and sea meet, with the tide half out, can look out to sea – assuming it is clear weather – as the sun is sinking and visualise a spear, of such a length that one could reach up to the socket, and viewed, as it were, at a distance of nine paces ["feet"], with its point touching the sun and the butt of the shaft touching the sea.[25]

When the chieftains assembled for their spring session, the assembly and its surroundings were consecrated on the first evening of the gathering. At this time of year, the sun is not "shaft-high" until evening, when it is much lower than at nones.

The spear head above the socket was probably about 30 centimetres long, while the average man was about 1.72 metres tall.[26] A man can reach a good 40cm farther than his height, however, so the spear ought to be about 2.40m long. The expression "nine feet" must here mean nine paces, which is the main meaning given in the Sigfus Blöndal and Asgeir Blöndal Magnusson dictionaries.[27] The later meaning of the word "foot" in the modern sense does not fit here, as if the sun were this high in the sky it would not be evening. The length of pace of a man of average height, walking at moderate speed, is estimated at 75cm; this is an ancient unit of measurement, the *passus* used by the Romans.[28] The distance from the spear is thus 6.75 metres. Hence the proportion of the height of the spear to the distance is about 0.36, and the elevation of the sun 20°. The socket of the spear shaft must have been aligned with the horizon; otherwise the words "assuming it is clear weather" would be meaningless. The spear may have been placed in such a way that the observer's eyes were level with the spearhead socket; an observation was then made of when the point touched the sun. An easier method would be to note when the shadow of the spear was nine paces. The result would be similar whether the man was tall or short, as the length of pace would normally be in proportion to the man's height.

Spring assemblies were held over four to seven days in the fifth to sixth week of summer, i.e. between 7 and 27 May by the Julian calendar. By the modern (Gregorian) calendar, this would be between 17 May and 6 June. At this time of year in Iceland, the sun is at an angle of 20° at about the time it is in the west, or a little later. This is consistent with the assembly being consecrated in the evening. But whether this conclusion is correctly calculated or not, the description in *Grágás* demonstrates that people at that time understood the connection between the elevation of the sun and the time of day, and strove to find simple methods of measuring solar elevation on land, even when they had no instruments but the human body itself. For seafarers it was of course more important to be able to measure the elevation of the sun, and preferably by more accurate means.

How Abbot Nikulas measured the elevation of the Pole Star
Abbot Nikulas' geographical treatise, dating from the 12th century, gives a delightful description of how to measure the elevation of the Pole Star by adopting imaginative physical positions, when one had travelled as far south as the river Jordan:

> Out by the Jordan, if one lies down on a flat surface and raises one's knee and one's fist atop it, and raises the thumb of the fist, the Pole Star will be seen at the same height, and no higher.[29]

Experiments show that Nikulas' method produces an accurate

Measuring the elevation of the Pole Star by the Jordan in the 12th century. Abbot Nikulas of Munkathvera describes this method of measuring the elevation of the Pole Star, and hence the latitude. Drawing by Bjarni Jonsson.

reading, of about 33°. But it should be borne in mind that a thousand years ago the Pole Star was 6° from the Pole, so that two observations would have been necessary, one in the night and one in the morning. This is yet another example of inventive ways of measuring the elevation of heavenly bodies, not least in view of the fact that this measurement was made by night.

Similarly, I have heard from Hjalmar Finnsson that during his boyhood in the West Fjords of Iceland he learned the method of measuring the elevation of the sun or a star by extending a clenched fist at arm's length. When he sailed from Iceland to New York during World War II, he observed the elevation of the Pole Star by this method. According to my own observations, a clenched fist with raised thumb is equivalent to about 15° of elevation. The thumb thus represents 7°, and each of the other fingers 2°. This will, of course, vary somewhat according to the size and build of the observer. It cannot be stated with any certainty that this method was practised continuously in Iceland from the days of Abbot Nikulas, or even longer, but it is quite possible. Although the method is not precise, the elevation of the sun relative to its elevation at noon gives a fair indication of the direction of the sun, if the measurement is always carried out in the same way. I shall return to this subject below.

The Faroese gnomon (sólskuggafjöl)

The ancient Greek Anaximander is believed to have used a vertical pointer (*gnomon*) on a horizontal plane to measure the elevation of the sun as early as 575 BC.[30] This was possible on dry land, but such an instrument would be of little use at sea, due to the rolling of the vessel. In the Faroe Islands in the 19th century, a description was written of an instrument to measure the elevation of the sun, the *sólskuggafjöl* (sun-shadow dial), which appears to solve this problem to a considerable degree.[31] (See picture on p. xi). The circular dial was kept horizontal by floating it on water in a container held steady by a standing man. It was marked with concentric rings. From the centre of the dial, a needle or style projected, casting a shadow when the sun shone. The height of the style was said to be adjustable to allow for the variable elevation and declination of the sun by season. The length of the shadow at midday could be measured by the rings, so that changes in solar elevation from day to day could be estimated. If this instrument was accurately made, and of sufficient size, it could have been as precise in some ways as the quadrant, discussed below. It seems that a container of water was used in the same way when the magnetic needle was first used; the magnetic needle or lodestone was fixed to a small piece of wood which floated on water. It is possible that this method was adopted because of previous experience of the sun dial, which may have been older than the compass, and could have been used by Viking navigators. But it is difficult to say whether such an instrument existed at the time of the sagas.

As will be discussed below, various items that have been attributed to the Nordic Greenlanders have been discovered in the Buchanan Bay area of Ellesmere Island, off the west coast of northwest Greenland, at a latitude of about 79°N.[32] Among them is part of a small barrel-base, with three concentric circles marked around the centre. The disc, originally about 19cm across, is well preserved, except that the centre is missing, so it is not possible to tell whether there was a hole for a style. Another, less regularly-shaped, piece of wood was found nearby; this is also part of a barrel base with three concentric rings, with a clear hole at the centre. The third piece of wood, of oak, with two or more probably three concentric circles near the edge, and another circle closer to the centre, was found in Marshall Bay in Greenland, a short distance north of Thule. The concentric circles appear to be placed at an average of 6.0, 7.3 and 8.6 centimetres from the centre, or at least at these proportional distances. My hypothesis here is that these Greenlandic items are gnomons. Obviously, when sailing north into the uninhabited reaches of west Greenland, it would have been helpful to observe the solar elevation, and hence the distance travelled from the home region in southern Greenland. Hence it is no coincidence that precisely on these sailing routes so many relics have been found that are reminiscent of the gnomon, although it is not impossible that the rings were merely decorative. If the central style was of a size to cast a shadow to the innermost ring at noon at the southernmost point of Greenland, the shadow would have reached about to the second-outermost ring in the Western Settlement, and close to the outermost ring north at Bear Island (Disko).

During archaeological excavations at Storaborg in south Iceland in 1981, Mjöll Snæsdottir found two pieces of wood which could be part of a gnomon.[33] One is marked with two concentric circles, with diameters of about 16.5cm and 19.2cm. On the other there is one circle, 27.2cm in diameter. This is, however, not conclusive.

The deck of the Gokstad ship, unearthed in Norway, is covered with circular markings that have been cut into the wood. Each consists of two to four concentric circles. Some stand alone, while others overlap. On the replica of the Gokstad ship in the National Museum of Iceland, I estimate that the diameter of the circles is on average 19, 31, 50 and 72 cm in the case of four circles, 23, 47 and 73 cm in the case of three, and 24 and 48 centimetres in the case of two.

So far as I know no explanation has been suggested for these circular markings on the Gokstad vessel, other than that they were purely decorative. But they are indisputably reminiscent of the

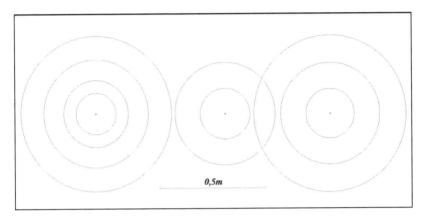

The deck of the Gokstad ship is covered with three forms of circular patterns. When the sun is in east or west, the shadow of a needle in the centre of the circle would be slightly more than twice as long as at noon. From this, the wind direction may be deduced, making it possible to steer a relatively accurate course.

Faroese gnomon, although there was no need for so many rings in order to observe the solar elevation. But because the limited space aboard the ship was used for so many tasks and purposes, even in battle, it is possible that it was regarded as helpful to be able to use any circular marking on the deck. Instead of a fixed style, a detachable pin or cone could have been used, attached by a small point into the centre of the circle. The rolling of the vessel means that the deck does not remain as level as would be desirable, but if the wind was not too high it would be possible to keep the ship fairly steady for taking a reading, by turning it into the wind, or downwind, while the observation was made.

These circles could have been used for two purposes; both to keep to a course along a line of latitude, and also to ascertain the wind direction three times a day, when the sun was in the east, south or west, as explained below.

By daily observations it was possible to sail in such a way that the shadow of the noon sun remained more or less the same day after day, i.e. the ship remained at the same latitude, sailing directly east or directly west. On longer journeys account had to be taken of seasonal variations in the elevation of the sun – except at the height of summer. Such adjustments could have been made by seafarers, if they were familiar with variations in solar elevation, as Star-Oddi was in the 12th century.

I believe that it would also be possible to use these circles on the Gokstad vessel in order to ascertain when the sun was in a certain direction, and hence to deduce the wind direction. Let us first consider the circles which are 24 and 48cm in diameter. If the shadow of a style in the centre reaches the innermost circle at noon, the shadow will reach the outer circle when the sun is in the east or west; in the summer, this produces an observation within one compass point of the true bearing, or 1/32 of the horizon. The pairs of circles with diameters 19 and 50 cm, 31 and 72, or 23 and 47, can be used in the same way. In these cases the deviation is less, and, interestingly, the deviations morning and evening cancel each other out. By these means, therefore, it would be possible to make an observation of when the sun is in the west or east, with considerable accuracy. The sun was, of course, in the south at its highest point. These observations could be used to indicate the wind direction. The vessel could then be steered according to this reading, until the next reading was taken. And these observations, unlike magnetic readings, needed no correction .

If the sky was reasonably clear, this instrument could thus facilitate navigation on various sailing routes, e.g. between Norway, Iceland and Greenland. It would be of no use, of course, if the sun was entirely hidden; I shall return to this problem below.

It should be clearly stated that there is nothing to prove that the seafarers of a thousand years ago exploited the potential of these circular patterns for navigational purposes. However, the information from the Faroes and Greenland, together with Norwegian and Icelandic relics, combine to provide an indication that some kind of gnomon was used for navigation. This was essentially the same as the ancient Greek *gnomon*, but adapted for use on board ship.

Quadrant

The Icelandic Encyclopaedia, *Rím II*, which is believed to have been written late in the 13th century, contains a fairly detailed description of a quadrant, an instrument for measuring the elevation of the sun or stars.[34] The instrument was in the shape of one quarter of a disc (see picture on p. xii). From the "sun corner" at the corner of the quadrant a lead weight hung from a thread, which passed over a scale marked on a 90° arc of the curved side. The description continues:

> The slits placed equally at the corners of the right-hand side of the quadrant bring the correct beam to the man's eye from the sun-corner, while the lead weight that hangs on its thread from the sun-corner shows variations in degrees as the sun rises and declines. The latitude of each place is seen by where the thread touches the degree of the quadrant at the autumn and spring equinox at midday.

This appears to mean that along the edge of the quadrant at both corners were slits or holes. In weak sunlight, the holes on the instrument could be aimed at the sun, but in bright sunlight this is difficult. In this case it is better to view the quadrant from the side, aligning it so that the ray of sun that shines through the slit closer to the sun falls directly on the other slit.

In this way the quadrant was more useful than the gnomon. The elevation of the Pole Star, which is equivalent to the latitude of the location where the reading is taken, could probably also be measured in this way, although only if there was enough light by night to allow for reading off the quadrant.

If a sun reading was taken at noon at the equinox, the latitude of the place could be deduced. If the declination of the sun was known, as it was to Star-Oddi, it would have been possible to pinpoint latitude by the solar elevation at all times of year. Morcken has estimated that by use of this instrument, readings could be taken within a deviation of half a degree on land, and one to two degrees at sea.[35] This is equivalent to half the width of Iceland from south to north, so such a degree of accuracy would be adequate to find Iceland when sailing along a line of latitude from Norway. It is my experience, however, that on land the deviation is 0.2 or 0.3 degrees.

This does not prove, of course, that the quadrant was in use around 1000 AD in the Nordic world, but it may well have been used long before it was recorded in writing. Star-Oddi, for instance, must have had some such instrument in order to make his remarkably accurate observations of solar elevation; he lived more than a century before *Rím II* was written.

It is probable that there was little difference in terms of accuracy between the gnomon and the quadrant. But the quadrant had the advantage that it would often be possible to measure the elevation of the stars, and also solar elevation when sunlight was not bright enough to cast a shadow, perhaps for days at a time. The quadrant was also useful for measuring the elevation of the sun when the sun was very low in the sky, whereas the bearing dial was less suitable for this. The position of the sun can sometimes be deduced from sunrays shining through cloud, even if the sun itself is invisible. This phenomenon is called crepuscular rays or "sun drawing water."

During summer, between the spring and autumn equinoxes, the direction of the sun can be deduced quite accurately from how much lower the sun is in the sky than at noon. According to the Icelandic almanac, the following table may be drawn up of the direction of the sun and solar elevation at 65°N in summer. The deviation is no more than one degree:[36]

Direction of the sun	*Solar elevation compared with elevation at noon*
Northeast	*42° lower*
East	*23° lower*
Southeast	*6° lower*
South	*0° lower*
Southwest	*6° lower*
West	*23° lower*
Northwest	*42° lower*

From the middle of Iceland (65°N), these figures drop some 4% for each degree of latitude to the north, and rise about 4% for each degree to the south.

Using the quadrant, it would thus have been possible to ascertain

This weather map shows conditions similar to those described in the King's Mirror (p. 182). First is an easterly wind, then southeasterly, southerly with foggy drizzle, then showers and perhaps thunderstorms in westerly winds, followed by cooler northerly or northeasterly winds. This knowledge of weather conditions would be helpful to navigators when the sun or stars were not visible.

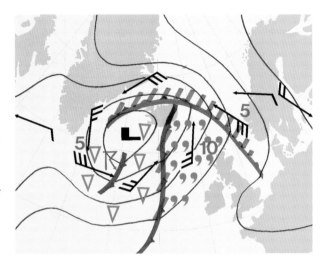

Lenticular clouds often form over mountains, and are visible from far out at sea, from a much greater distance than the actual mountains. West coast of Disko Island (Bjarney), W. Greenland. Photo P. Stahl.

Burls, a kind of tree tumour, form on the trunks of such tree species as birch, walnut and maple. The wood is dense and does not split easily, and hence it is ideal for making cups, bowls, etc. At L'Anse aux Meadows a small burl was unearthed, no doubt brought there from warmer climes. Thorfinn Karlsefni's húsasnotra (astrolabe?), made of mösur wood from Wineland according to the saga, may have been made from such a burl. Burl on a birch tree at the forest of Hallormsstadur, E. Iceland. Dimensions: 0.46 m high, 0.33 m across, and 0.21 m thick from centre of trunk. Photo Sigurdur Blöndal.

Icelandic construction methods in the turf walls of Leif's camp. The walls were built of turf cut into strips, wedges and blocks. The cavity of the double walls was filled with sand and gravel, and the walls were reinforced with crosswise strips of turf, as in Iceland and Greenland. Photo Gisli Gestsson. National Museum slide collection 727.

Kristjan Eldjarn (later president of Iceland, left) and Helge Ingstad at the excavations at L'Anse aux Meadows in 1961. Photo Gisli Gestsson. National Museum slide collection 692.

Bog iron in the Ellidaar river, Reykjavik. The Vikings used bog iron to make utensils, and there are clear traces of iron-working at L'Anse aux Meadows, probably to make rivets for ship repairs. Photo Pall Bergthorsson.

one's bearings throughout the day if the sun was shining, even if it could only be glimpsed through clouds. Once the direction of the sun had been ascertained, it would be possible to deduce the wind direction with fair accuracy, and steer a course on this basis. It appears unlikely that expert seafarers would not have learned to exploit this useful quality of the quadrant and other instruments for measuring the elevation of the sun.

Clues to the location of Wineland
Many attempts have been made to deduce the latitude of Leif's Camp from the Saga of the Greenlanders, which provides the following information about the duration of daylight at the winter solstice, in a famous passage:

> *Meira var þar jafndægri en á Grænlandi eða Íslandi. Sól hafði þar eyktarstað og dagmálastað um skammdegi.*

This sentence appears to be best understood as meaning that the duration of day and night was more equal than in Greenland or Iceland, and that at the darkest part of winter [*skammdegi*], the sun reached from *dagmálastaður* to *eyktarstaður*.

The word *reached* is here used to translate the Icelandic word *hafði* (literally "had").

Thus the sun was aloft from *eyktarstaður* to *dagmálastaður*. A less likely, and highly indefinite, meaning would be that the sun was aloft from *eyktarstaður* to *dagmálastaður* or longer.

But what is *eyktarstaður*? In the Christian Law section of the lawbook *Grágás*, *eykt* is defined in the following article:

> *Eykt* is the time when, if the southwest eighth of the sky is divided into three, the sun has passed through two parts and has one part still to pass.

The northern eighth is defined in *Grágás* as follows:

> The northern eighth extends from the sun's arrival midway between northwest and north to its arrival midway between north and northeast.

From this it is clear that north is between northnorthwest and northnortheast. The definition of *útsuður* (southwest) must thus be similar, i.e. between southsouthwest and westsouthwest.[37] Southwest would thus be the sector from 22.5 degrees west of south to 67.5 degrees west of south.

So when the sun is at *eyktarstaður* it should be 22.5 + 30 = 52.5 degrees west of south. The sun would thus have passed through two-thirds of the southwest sector. This is the place (*eyktarstaður*) where the sun was visible at midwinter during Leif the Lucky's stay in America. The term thus represents, not time, as many have maintained, but a direction. There is no simple correlation between place and time in this example.

But why should *eyktarstaður* have been defined in this unusual way? It is probable that an attempt was being made to work out when three hours had passed from noon during the busiest time of the year; after this time it was forbidden, on pain of punishment, to work on Saturdays, with the exception of routine everyday tasks. This was of course most important in summer, when the burden of outdoor work was greatest, except for daily care of animals. It was not only by Icelandic law that the holy day began at nones on Saturday. In various Norwegian laws, such as the Christian law of Frostathing, Borgarthing and Gulathing, the Sabbath is said to begin at nones on Saturday.[38] The word nones (Icelandic *nón*), from the Latin *nona hora*, means the ninth hour, counting from 6 in the morning, i.e. 3 p.m. Accurate calculations for the latitude of 65°N show that for the 185 days of the Icelandic summer by the old almanac, averaging 22 April to 23 October, the sun is normally close to *eyktarstaður*, 52.8° west of south, at 3 p.m. By defining *eyktarstaður* at 52.5° west of south, two objects were achieved; that the legal provisions on the Sabbath were observed with fair accuracy, and that legally permissible working hours would be utilised to the utmost.

In order to reach this remarkable conclusion about *eyktarstaður*, an effective means of measuring time had to be available. I shall argue below for the likelihood that water-clocks may have existed in early times in Iceland, and that sloping sundials, that show the correct time in relation to the changing position of the sun, may have been available.[39] It would also have been possible to use a sundial similar to the one found by Thordur Tomasson at Storaborg, south Iceland, which will be mentioned below (see p. 165).[40] If some such instruments did exist, experts would no doubt have been appointed to pinpoint *eyktarstaður* when the laws were passed. Before clocks arrived in Iceland, and until the 19th century, the passage of time was often measured by how long a given quantity of lamp oil (fish-liver oil) lasted.[41] In this way, the most learned of men could work out the direction of the sun when three hours (one-eighth of the day) had passed from noon – or, of course, six or nine hours. On the same principle as the position of *eyktarstaður*, one may deduce that *dagmálastaður* was 52.5° east of south.

But the achievement of finding *eyktarstaður* is nonetheless remarkable, given only such simple instruments and man's own inventiveness.

But where is the place where the observation in the Saga of the Greenlanders of the duration of daylight was made? In brief, in spite of centuries of speculation, no-one has been able to answer this conundrum.

The first attempt was made by Arngrimur Jonsson the Learned (1568–1648).[42] Next was Thormodur Torfason (1636–1719),[43] then Pall Vidalin (1667–1727) and Bishop Finnur Jonsson (1704–1789).[44] It was not until the late 19th century that Gustav Storm made a correct analysis of what *dagmálastaður* and *eyktarstaður* meant.[45] With the assistance of astronomer Hans Geelmuyden, he concluded that the observations of the duration of daylight applied to a latitude of 50°N, which is equivalent to northern Newfoundland. They saw no reason to calculate the latitude with great precision, and in any case Storm did not believe the result was of much use. He felt that this northerly country could not have been the land of vines and self-sown wheat.

Storm tried to salvage the calculation by concluding that the duration of daylight at Leif's Camp was from *dagmálastaður* to *eyktarstaður* or longer, i.e. that the location could be anywhere south of 50°N. This left the field wide open. Most subsequent scholars have followed his example.

But I am certain that the brilliant Storm would soon reach a solution if he could come back to life in the present day. He would realise that the ruins found at L'Anse aux Meadows by Helge Ingstad must be Leif's Camp, because this was the gateway to Wineland, although this is not literally stated in the Saga of the Greenlanders. He would probably agree with my conclusion above that the duration of daylight there was neither more nor less than from *dagmálastaður* to *eyktarstaður*. One would observe that the estimated latitude of Leif's Camp as calculated by Storm and Geelmuyden is only one-and-a-half degrees south of L'Anse aux Meadows. This is a small deviation. And further calculations, following the more precise methods used in almanacs, reveal an even smaller deviation. They count sunrise and sunset at the point when the upper edge of the sun, not the centre, touches the horizon. It transpires that at L'Anse aux Meadows, the sun sets at 51.5° west of south on the shortest day of the year. This deviates by only 1° from the *eyktarstaður*, 52.5° west of south. And there would be no deviation at all if one defined *skammdegi* (the darkest part of the winter) as the six weeks of midwinter rather than the single day of the winter solstice. But even without further calculations, the solution to the puzzle may be regarded as found: the famous statement on the times of sunrise and sunset in Wineland applies to Leif's Camp, at what is now L'Anse aux Meadows.

But is it reasonable to presume that Leif's company could have made such accurate observation of the direction of sunrise and sunset, or is this pure coincidence? Bearing in mind that they were seamen, who had to make precise observations of the position of the sun in their work, one may safely assume that their readings were not far off. In this context, one may recall the remarkable precision of Star-Oddi's observation of the direction of dawn and dusk, when the sun was about 14° below the horizon. In his observation, the deviation averaged not more than two-and-a-half degrees, and never exceeded 3.7 ° according to the calculations of Eirikur Briem.[46] It is considerably more difficult to ascertain the direction of the sun at dawn and dusk than at sunrise and sunset; hence one may assume that the deviation would be no more than one or two degrees if readings were taken as accurately as by Star-Oddi. He lived, admittedly, about a century later, and thus may have had better instruments at his disposal.

The conclusion of all this, with all the provisos mentioned above, is that the observation made by Leif's men on the duration of daylight supports other evidence that they spent the winter in the "large houses" at L'Anse aux Meadows in Newfoundland, following their expedition up the St. Lawrence valley. This can also be seen as an indication that the changing position of the sun and other navigational skills were well known to the Vikings.

A sundial from Storaborg

In the Skogar Folk Museum in south Iceland is a small but interesting copper disc, unearthed by Thordur Tomasson, curator of the museum.[47] It was found at Storaborg, south Iceland, at a point where the sea is eroding the soil. It was found at a depth that indicates it may date from 1200–1300. The disc has an almost square hole in the centre, probably for some kind of style that would cast a shadow in sunlight, and 24 grooves marked around the circumference. But it would appear that three of the grooves have been marked so slightly as to be scarcely visible. If the dial is placed in a horizontal position, the direction of the sun can be read from the shadow cast by the needle. The most probable application of the dial was to show solar time at the summer solstice. The grooves are most consistent with this time of the year, and this is the season when the sun is most likely to be visible around midnight. In order to read the correct solar time, the grooves have to be unevenly spaced. Between 11 am and 1 pm, for instance, the sun progresses 21° along the horizon per hour, but the progress is only 13° between 8 and 9 pm at the summer solstice, at the latitude of 63.5°N, as at Storaborg in south Iceland. I have calculated these different timings, and shown them on a diagram upon which the dial has been superimposed. They are so consistent with the grooves on the sundial that the deviation is never more than one-and-a-half millimetres (4–5 degrees) from the correct point. (See picture on page xii). This sundial would not be useful at any point much farther north or south. It is interesting that the shadows of 6 am and 6 pm are not opposite each other on the dial, nor should they be at the time of the summer solstice.

It is worth mentioning that the sundial would also be useful in midwinter, but it would have to be turned the other way, so that the longest gap between hours was at midnight and not midday. At the darkest time of the year, the hours of daylight are so few, that the dial could only be used for about three hours in the middle of the day.

The craftsman who made the sundial would appear to have been an expert upon the movements of the sun. The instrument was probably made by trial and error, marking the point of the shadow from the central needle each hour. In this case the craftsman would have required a relatively accurate clock. Chronometers and clocks in the modern sense did not exist at this time. But various methods could be used, nonetheless.

It is possible to discern the correct solar time by means of a sundial. This differed from the horizontal dial in that the disc sloped in accord with the sun's course. A needle placed at right angles in the middle of the dial was aligned with the Pole Star, which enabled the circle to be divided into exactly 24 hours. It is probable that the ancient Greek scientist Ptolemy, who lived in the second century AD, used such a sundial in Alexandria, as he used an instrument that cast a shadow on surfaces that sloped at different angles.[48] The other method of measuring the passage of time was the water-clock (which will be discussed below), or burning fish-liver oil, as mentioned above. But whatever the method used by the instrument-maker at Storaborg, this modest little dial appears to be an important find, indicating skill and inventiveness. It should be reiterated that the unclarity of the grooves for 11 am, midday and 1 pm is still a problem with regard to the hypothesis proposed here. But the grooves corresponding to the eight *eyktamörk*, discussed below, were clear enough. With all provisos, the disc may be taken as an indication that people were well aware at this time that equal periods of three hours cannot be indicated by equal intervals of solar directions. This implies familiarity with the changing position of the sun. The same knowledge is probably the basis of the definition of *eyktarstaður* found in *Grágás*, although this makes reference to general summer conditions, rather than to the position of the sun around the summer solstice.

When such a sundial had been made, it could be taken around to different farms, in order to fix suitable *eyktamörk* – these were certain mountains or other landmarks which could be used as indications of the time, in conjunction with the position of the sun.

Eyktamörk in Iceland

As mentioned above, before the days of clocks and watches, ordinary Icelanders kept track of the time of day by observing when the sun was over a certain mountain, hill or other landmark. These time-landmarks were called *eyktamörk* (*eykt* = a period of three hours, *mörk* = signs. Singular form: *eyktamark*). In the mid-eighteenth century, *eyktamörk* all over Iceland were studied by two scholars, Eggert Olafsson and Bjarni Palsson. They had no chronometer, but estimated the time (incorrectly) by assuming that 3, 6 and 9 am and noon should be when the sun was in the northeast, east, southeast and south respectively, and in corresponding directions in the afternoon. But to their surprise the actual *eyktamörk* were not consistent with this theory; when the sun was over the *eyktamörk*, their estimated time was as shown in column 2. It is possible to deduce from this what the correct solar time was, on average, at the summer solstice. This is shown in column 3.

"Folk-time"	*Estimates by EO and BP*	*Correct solar time*
6 am	*4:30–5 am*	*5:22 am*
9 am	*7:30 am*	*8:20 am*
12 noon	*10:30–11 am*	*11:05 am*
3 pm	*3 pm*	*2:17 pm*
6 pm	*6 pm*	*5:13 pm*
9 pm	*8 pm*	*7:31 pm*

This demonstrates that, contrary to what Eggert Olafsson and Bjarni Palsson concluded, the period between the *eyktamörk* was almost exactly three hours, with one exception, between 5:13 pm and 7:31 pm. They noticed the phenomenon that the last *eyktamark* of the day was relatively early in the evening, but assumed that this was for practical reasons. Their theory was that this reflected a feeling that the working day should be no longer than this; in addition, by this time, in many areas of the country the sun would soon be setting behind the mountains to the northwest. "Folk time" was an average of 40 minutes ahead of the true solar time; this would be practical for domestic tasks. But in order to achieve such good results, it was necessary to choose landmarks that were unevenly spaced around the horizon, at intervals varying from 40° to 50–60°. This may be deduced from the time calculations made by Eggert Olafsson and Bjarni Palsson; it demonstrates that the connection between the movements of the sun and time was familiar long before chronometers were known in Iceland.

A German scholar, Konrad Maurer, quotes a clergyman in Eyjafjord, north Iceland, around 1850, as saying that *eyktamörk* are fixed by observing the path of the sun at the summer solstice. This is consistent with the conclusions of Eggert Olafsson and Bjarni Palsson, and also with the sundial found at Storaborg, and it supports the hypothesis that such a sundial was used to fix *eyktamörk* at individual farms.

Water-clock

The ancient Egyptians used primitive water-clocks as long ago as 1400 BC, and this means of measuring time was later improved by the Greeks and Romans, who called it a *clepsydra* (water-thief). In one form of these, flowing water was maintained at a steady level in a vessel, so that the water pressure at the bottom remained constant. The water then flowed slowly through a hole in the bottom of the vessel into a vertical cylindrical container, in which was a float that showed the rising water level. By experiment it was possible to find the total rise in water level during a whole day, which could be divided by 24 to show hours, or other units of time. Vitruvius describes a water clock in which the float moved a sprocket wheel that turned a hand, as on a modern clock face.[49]

The accuracy of such clocks was limited, of course; one of the variables is that water flows faster in hot weather than cold. The deviation caused by this would, however, be minimal at sea, where temperatures fluctuate less than on land.

What is the chance that the water-clock was brought from southern to northern Europe? It must be counted as possible. The Vikings travelled as far south as Africa and Constantinople, and there is no doubt that they would have been interested in this technology if they came into contact with it. In later times, water-clocks were known in the Faroes and in northern Norway, and I have noted a sixteenth-century reference to a water clock in Iceland. The instrument had been known from ancient times, and this makes it more likely that it was used in the Viking Age of navigation, when the need for a chronometer was especially great.

In the Faroes, an account of a Faroese water-clock, known as *Ketil undir og ketil á* (Pot under, pot on top), was written down in the early 19th century.[50] This is described as a round copper "engine," hollow inside. In the centre, a hollow bowl or sphere was fixed, according to the account. The sphere was filled with water which flowed down into the "engine" for 3, 12 or 24 hours, after which it is said to have been turned over. On the sailing route from Norway to the Faroes, the day is said to have "followed" (*fylgt með*) by a third of an *eykt*. This meant that the clock appeared to "gain" an hour, on the basis of such observations as sunrise and sunset. A gain of about 50 minutes would be more accurate than 60. This phenomenon is familiar from modern air travel, as the sun rises and sets an hour later for each 15 degrees of longitude travelled westwards. By trial and error, the water-clock could be used to discern how far the ship had travelled west or east, just as the sundial could show whether the ship had drifted northward or southwards. Longitude could thus have been deduced from this, but hardly with any great accuracy.

Uwe Schnall believes that the Faroese account of the water-clock does not justify the inference that water-clocks were used in the Viking Age.[51] But Olaf Helseth makes a passing reference in his writings (1938) on yachts in Salten, Norway after 1814, to water-clocks being used on these vessels until the nineteenth century.[52] When accurate ships' chronometers and pocket watches became available, however, water-clocks were gradually displaced.

When the present author learned of the sundial from Storaborg, mentioned above, he went in search of sources on Icelandic water-clocks. At the University of Iceland Institute of Lexicography, the word was recorded, with a reference to a historical document.[53] This showed, among the possessions of the church of Krysuvik in 1570, a *vatzklucka* or water-clock. No comment is made on this item in the inventory, and hence it does not appear to have been an unfamiliar instrument. Another water-clock was in the possession of the church of Hvamm in Kjos. These sources may cast a new light on Icelandic chronological measurements in the middle ages; it is unlikely that the most prosperous landowners would not have acquired such an instrument, since it existed in isolated Krysuvik. And the seafarers of the Viking Age would have had yet more cause to acquire a water-clock. It is not impossible, however, that the term "water-clock" may have been used of some other item, such as a water vessel.

Sun stone
Old writings sometimes mention a "sun stone" which appears to have shown the direction of the sun in overcast conditions.[54] This could be based upon the fact that the molecules of the air polarise sunlight to some extent, especially 90° from the sun, e.g. in the sky overhead when the sun is low in the sky. Some minerals can be used to discern this polarised light in the atmosphere. The sky must be clear directly overhead, although the sky around may be cloudy. The sun should preferably be low in the sky, at an elevation from 30° above the horizon to 7° below. At sea conditions sometimes arise when fog obscures the sun, but the sky can be seen at the zenith. This instrument could be useful under these circumstances. One of the minerals that can be used is Iceland spar (a form of calcite) which still exists in some quantity in Reydarfjord, east Iceland, and also cordierite, a transparent blue crystal found in Kragerøy in Oslo Fjord. Cordierite must be held up and turned in a vertical plane; the methods vary according to the crystal used. But finding the sun is not sufficient for orientation, whether the sun is viewed through a sun stone or is directly visible. One must also know the time of day. This is easy on dry land, where landmarks are familiar, but is far more difficult at sea. However, even at sea the direction of the sun at sunrise and sunset is fairly well-known, according to the time of year. Between these times, the time elapsed must be estimated. Fortunately this kind of estimate is not difficult if careful observations are made. The deviation of the estimated wind direction would then only be 15° per hour of deviation. If a water-clock was available, even more accuracy could be achieved. Should such estimates of the direction of the sun and time of day continue for a number of days, one would expect the deviations to cancel each other out, and hence that the ship would keep more or less to its intended course. The guidance

Polarised sky light compass. In the 1950s, navigational aids of this kind were used in polar flights over Canada, in order to discern the direction of polarised rays of sunlight when the sun was invisible, or was below the horizon but not so low that the stars had become visible. Dane Thorkild Ramskou believed that the sun stone mentioned in the sagas could have fulfilled the same function, but there is no evidence that the sun stone was used at sea.

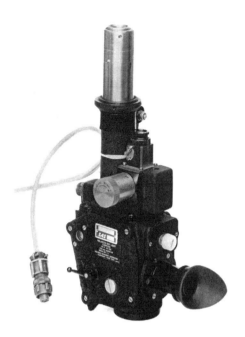

provided by the sun stone could be helpful in finding one's bearings when lost at sea, if the sky overhead cleared from time to time. But the usefulness of the sun stone should not be overestimated, because in this case the sun would normally be visible from time to time, and this would of course provide better guidance.

An indication of the usefulness of the sun stone is a modern invention, the polarisation or sky compass, based upon the same principle of polarisation of light in the upper atmosphere. This is used for aerial navigation close to the magnetic poles, where conventional compasses are unreliable.[55] The polarisation compass can be extremely useful when flying above clouds, in conjunction with an accurate chronometer.

Although it is arguable that the sun stone can be used to pinpoint the position of the sun, the old sources never directly state that this was done except on dry land. An account of this appears in the Tale of the Sons of Raudulf in the Greater Saga of King Olaf.[56] These events took place shortly after the time of the Wineland voyages. Sigurd Raudulfsson had told King Olaf that he could always tell the time, day or night, even if he could not see any heavenly bodies. The king had Sigurd tell him where the sun was, and tested him by having the sun stone picked up, and held up, "and he saw how the rays shone from the stone, in the direction that Sigurd had said." The narrative says, however, that the entire sky was overcast, and this is not consistent with the required conditions mentioned above. It is not unreasonable to conclude that the storyteller may have used a little poetic licence in his account, ignoring some clear patch among the clouds. But it is interesting to note that the sun stone is discussed as a familiar instrument for this purpose.

The Saga of Bishop Gudmund Arason states that the bishop gave a sun stone to Hrafn Sveinbjarnarson, and in the saga of Hrafn himself this is also stated, though without specifying the use of the stone.[57] But there could be a clue in the fact that when Hrafn and Bishop Gudmund sailed to Norway, Hrafn was the pilot, and guided the ship with "wisdom and good luck." A sun stone would have been an ideal gift to such a benefactor, even if its usefulness was limited.

Whatever the truth of the matter, it would appear unlikely that the sun stone was an important navigational aid, although it may have been of some use in exceptional circumstances.

A sundial or astrolabe from Greenland
In order to achieve greater accuracy in pinpointing the wind direction using the sundial, it has been suggested that an instrument found at Uunartoq (known to the Nordic Greenlanders as Siglufjord) in the Eastern Settlement of Greenland in 1948 could have been of use. This is a disc of oak, about 7cm across. Half the disc is missing. In the centre was a circular opening, 2cm in diameter.[58] Around the edge of the disc, teeth or leaves are marked. These number 16 per 158°, close to 36 around the entire circumference, spaced at variable intervals of 8 to 12 degrees. It has generally been maintained that there were 32 teeth around the circle, but this appears to have been based on inaccurate measurements. In order to make use of this instrument at sea, one would have to see the sun, and know the time. Its usefulness would therefore be limited. But on dry land it could be mounted based on accurate bearings. Star-Oddi may have used an instrument of this kind in order to

On the left is a fragment of an oak disc discovered by Christian Vebæk at Uunartoq (Siglufjord) in Greenland in 1948. The diameter is 7cm, and in the centre is a 2-cm hole. The instrument is not accurately made: the points around the circumference are 8–12° apart, averaging 10°. On the right, Gunnar Bjarnason has made a replica of the disc as a simple astrolabe (húsasnotra), *hung up by one side. The alidade or style is turned to the back, and pointed towards the sun, and for this purpose there is a sight on the alidade, as on a quadrant. Thus changing latitude can be observed from day to day according to the noon elevation of the sun, and the direction of the sun may be observed from the difference of elevation from the noon reading. This instrument was used on the Viking ship* Íslendingur *sailing from Iceland to New York in summer 2000.*

make his accurate observations of the direction of the sun at dawn and dusk at his home in northern Iceland.

This instrument has sometimes been termed the "Viking compass." It is maintained that on the disc are scratches which were used to find out the direction of the sun, according to the changing length of the shadow of the central needle. This must, however, be counted as dubious; the arcs in question disappear where the central hole is. Therefore they could not be used for observation around midday. Some people have even doubted whether the instrument was used for observing the direction of the sun at all.[59] If this were so, it would be more likely that the circle would be divided into 32 sectors, as on a compass, and not 36. It is more likely that it was used for measuring solar elevation, hung up by a hook on the side. Hanging it up would serve a similar purpose to the astrolabe discussed below. A hand or alidade which rotated on a central axis could have been used to point out the solar elevation, and observe its alteration during the day (see fig. p. 173). From this the direction of the sun at different times could be deduced, as with the quadrant, and this would also have made it possible to maintain the same solar elevation at noon, day after day, when sailing at constant latitude.

Dragon's tail or Scandinavian astrolabe?

On the Île de Groix south of Brittany in France, an ancient mound was excavated in 1906 by du Chatellier; it was the funeral pyre of a Norse chieftain in his ship, probably from the 10th century. An object found on the site was described as follows by Swedish archaeologist Arbman:

> … a circular band 2 feet in diameter with movable leaflike ornaments round the outside and three rings inside. It can have had no practical purpose and was evidently meant to be seen from both sides; it was not nailed onto anything else, for there are no holes. It seems most likely that this was the "dragon's tail," mentioned in the sagas, which balanced the figurehead at the bow.[60]

As the Norwegian scholar Morcken has pointed out, considerable imaginative effort is required to maintain that this was a dragon-tail affixed to the stern as shown in Arbman's book, in contradiction of what has just been said, that it was not nailed to anything. Morcken was of the view that it might even be some kind of navigational instrument, but said that further study was required to confirm it. This hypothesis will now be examined.

The objects from the Île de Groix are preserved in the Musée des Antiquités Nationales at Saint-Germain-en-Laye in France, whose director, M. Patrick Périn, has kindly sent me information about them.

A detailed drawing has been made by Müller-Wille of the object, which is made of iron.[61] Although considerably distorted by the ef-

The Groix artifact (Müller-Ville). To the right is a reconstruction, showing the shadow of a central needle.

fects of fire and the ravages of time, the lower half is quite well pre-served, and it is edged with "leaves" of some kind. Only two of the leaves clearly have holes in them, and a line between them appears to divide the circle into two equal parts, so that the centre of the object is halfway along the line. The leaves on this lower half appear to be placed at intervals of 11.25°, which would mean that they numbered 32 around the circumference of the object. Three arms, or more probably four, extend from the rim towards the centre; on each were three concentric iron rings, of which traces remain. It is improbable that these flimsy wire rings dangled unsupported. Perhaps there was a wooden disc or shield inside the ring, on which the whole object was fastened, which was destroyed in the fire.

Let us suppose that the object was suspended by its upper half, which is incomplete, so that the central line mentioned above was horizontal. If a needle or style projected from the centre of the wooden disc, it would cast a shadow out to the rim in sunny conditions, thus indicating the elevation of the sun, when turned so that the sun's rays fell on the edge of the instrument.

It is interesting that whenever the shadow falls on the centre of either of the upper wire rings, the solar elevation is similar to that at the Île de Groix at midday at the winter solstice (19° or 1.7 leaves of the circumference). But if the shadow falls on the centre of either of the lower rings, the solar elevation is similar to that at midday at the summer solstice at the Île de Groix (66° or 5.9 leaves of the circumference). It would have been convenient if these wire rings had identified that part of the ring where one might expect the shadow of the style to fall at midday on the French island, the home of a Norse chieftain. This could thus be a navigational instrument tailor-made for use at the same latitude as the Île de Groix.

This argument is based upon the assumption that most or all components served the purpose of measuring solar elevation. The loose piece at top left could be a continuation of the iron ring, although it lacks leaves, which would strictly speaking be unnecessary on this upper section. The fragmented piece at the top may have served to suspend the instrument. The only piece lacking is the style or pin in the centre, which could well have been made of a material that did not survive the funeral pyre. The size of the object is suitable for holding it in front of the legs, by extending the arms downward.

From solar elevation observed at noon, it is possible to deduce how far north or south the ship has progressed over each period of 24 hours, according to whether the noon elevation is higher or lower. One could sail along a line of latitude, to east or west, by maintaining the same solar elevation at noon day after day. The difference in solar elevation at midday and other times of day could also be used to deduce the direction of the sun, and hence which direction to steer the ship, as has been discussed above. This would be of great help once the ship was out of sight of land.

This is of course not an indisputable conclusion, but all in all it is possible that this object is a thousand-year-old navigational instrument from a Nordic sailing vessel, inventively conceived and useful, adapted to the local conditions. And there is nothing to show that such instruments may not have existed on other Nordic ships, as implied by various references in Old Icelandic literature. These are our next subject.

Húsasnotra – astrolabe
At the end of the Saga of the Greenlanders, a southerner from Brem-

en in Saxony is said to have asked Thorfinn Karlsefni to sell him his *húsasnotra*, when his ship lay at anchor in Norway waiting for a favourable breeze. The account seems to indicate that the *húsasnotra* was something one would expect Thorfinn to have aboard his ship. The southerner paid half a mark (about 250 grammes) of gold for the *húsasnotra*, which the saga says was made of *mösur* wood from Wineland; *mösur* wood will be discussed below

In the days of King Magnus the Law-Reformer (13th century), a ship's captain was paid half a mark of silver a month, the equivalent of one-sixteenth of a mark of gold. The *húsasnotra* was thus an object of great value, the equivalent of a captain's pay for eight months.[62]

Another interesting example from Fritzner's dictionary is from the Saga of Arrow-Odd. The saga tells that the *húsasnotra* of Odd's ship had "fallen apart," so that he went ashore with another man to cut wood for a new one. This demonstrates the importance attached by seafarers to renewing this item, and that good wood had to be chosen for it. Arrow-Odd's Saga is, admittedly, regarded as mythical, but such sagas often seek to portray daily life in a realistic manner.

The third example of the word occurs in manuscript AM 194 at the Arni Magnusson Manuscript Institute, in the geographical treatise. It states:

It says there that Thorfinn Karlsefni cut wood for a *húsasnotra* and then went in search of Wineland the Good, and arrived at the place where they believed it was, but did not succeed in exploring or gathering any goods.[63]

It would appear from this that cutting wood for a *húsasnotra* was an important part of the preparation for a sea voyage, and this could indicate that the *húsasnotra* had a practical application for sea journeys. It is interesting that this statement that Thorfinn had a *húsasnotra* is independent of the account in the Saga of the Greenlanders of Thorfinn's sale of the *húsasnotra*.

Fritzner's dictionary of Old Icelandic states that the *húsasnotra* was some kind of household ornament (*hús* = house, *snotra* = something pretty), but the examples quoted in the dictionary, and

A húsasnotra? The hypothesis is proposed here that the húsasnotra sold by Thorfinn Karlsefni for a high price was a form of astrolabe, an instrument that originated in Ancient Greece. Astrolabes, made of wood or metal, were used to measure the elevation of the sun and other heavenly bodies. The more complex instruments showed the twelve "houses" of the heavens, and could be used to determine the time, and latitude. The astrolabe (front and back) in the picture is Arabian, and dates from 984 AD, when Eirik the Red was settling in Greenland. From Astrolabes of the World by Robert Gunther.

here, do not support this conclusion, since all indicate the use of the *húsasnotra* aboard ship. So some alternative meaning should be sought.

Gustav Storm believed that the *húsasnotra* was an instrument for use aboard ship.[64] Morcken was of the same opinion.[65] He believed that *húsa* was a verb meaning to house or keep, while *snotra* was a reference to knowledge or wisdom, which is *per se* a reasonable suggestion. But this construction is not logical in Icelandic. A more natural form would be *snotruhús* or *snotruhýsi*, neither of which refers specifically to navigation.

But the word *hús* can have other meanings than a house or building. In the middle ages the word house (Latin *domus planetarum* = home of the planets) was used of the 12 "houses" of the astrological heavens. The oldest Icelandic example in the records of the University of Iceland Lexicographical Institute of the use of the word *hús* in this sense is in *Persíusrimur* (Ballad of Perseus) by Gudmund Andrésson, who died in 1654:[66]

> *Reikna ég annað regiment*
> *ræður lika stórum:*
> *himintungla hlaupið vent*
> *í húsum átta og fjórum.*

> (I reckon there's another power
> that has a lot to say:
> the movement of the heavenly bodies
> in their houses, eight plus four.)

In Danish and English examples of the word house used in the same sense are known from the 14th century onward. *Snotur*, used in modern Icelandic to mean "pretty," meant "wise, clever" at the time of the saga writers. On this basis, the word *húsasnotra* could mean "house lore" or "astronomical knowledge."

This brings us to the ancient instrument the astrolabe, which is believed to have been invented by the Greek Hipparchus (150 BC) or even Apollonius of Perga (c. 240 BC).[67] The word astrolabe means literally "a tool to take the stars," or "star instrument." Astrolabes were made of wood, and later metal. One of the known instruments of this kind was made by German astronomer Johann Müller, in 1462. This is a complex work of craftsmanship, suspended from a small ring; it is a kind of slide-rule. It includes discs with an alidade (a revolving hand) and viewer for measuring the elevation of the sun or stars, and it is also marked with the twelve star signs or houses. The elevation of the sun was measured first. Measuring the elevation of the sun at noon on a certain day pinpointed the latitude, while solar elevation at other times of day would give the time. This is of course useful at sea, if the sun is visible, as the wind direction can then be deduced. Professor Charles Jenkin resurrected this forgotten instrument, and introduced it as a teaching aid. It may thus, with some justification, be called the oldest scientific instrument still in use, and its place in cultural history is an important one.[68] This was undoubtedly a valuable and prized instrument, like the *húsasnotra* sold by Thorfinn Karlsefni for the equivalent of eight months' wages of a sea captain.

The Saga of the Greenlanders says that Thorfinn's *húsasnotra* was made of *mösur* wood from Wineland. Although the word *mösur* may have been used for a specific species of tree, its ancient meaning was also a burl growing as a tumour on a tree.[69] In Old High German, the word *Masar* means knotty wood or a lump or burl on a tree, and in modern German *Maserwuchst* also means such a burl. In Swedish, *masurbjörk* is a species of birch on which burls abound. These burls (see picture on page xiii) can be quite large, 30–60 cm across. The wood in them is ideal for making various items, such as cups and bowls, as the fibres are densely meshed together, and the wood is thus unlikely to crack. The German word *Maserholtz* refers specifically to this quality of the wood.[70] If the *húsasnotra* was something similar to the astrolabe described above, such wood would have been ideal for making this circular instrument. But the burls were rare, and this is consistent with the statement in Arrow-Odd's Saga that he went with a companion to search for material for making a new *húsasnotra*.[71]

Burls are found on birch, maple and walnut trees, among others. At the ruins of the Viking settlement at L'Anse aux Meadows in Newfoundland, a small burl from a butternut tree was found; this species is closely related to the walnut. It had been cut with metal tools.[72] In order to find this tree species, the Wineland travellers would have had to travel as far as Québec, or some distance inland in New Brunswick, to the upper reaches of the Miramichi or the St. John River. Québec is by far the more likely location for the find, since the sailing route there was direct, and vines also grew there. In fact there are many indications, as recounted above, that this is where Leif Eiriksson went on his Wineland journey.

If the *húsasnotra* was an astrolabe, the question is, how did it reach Scandinavia and Iceland from the Greeks or Arabs? There appear, however, to be some possible routes.

Arab sources on the astrolabe exist from the seventh century, indicating that the instrument had long been known; the oldest extant astrolabe is Arabian, from the year 984 AD, when Eirik the Red was exploring Greenland. Sources tell that Vikings from the

Nordic countries travelled south to the Mediterranean and harried this region. The instrument found at the Île de Groix, mentioned above, may be evidence of this.

In the early centuries of Iceland's history, Nordic warriors and merchants served in the Byzantine Empire; these were mainly Swedes, who sailed southwards via the rivers Dnieper, Danube and Volga. Known as *Varangians* or *Rus*, some of these men came from Iceland. Arab writers Ibn Fadlan and Ibn Rustah reported meeting Varangians around 920 and 940. Hence one may conjecture that Icelanders and other Nordic seafarers could have learned of these useful instruments from the Arabs, and acquired them, either by raid or trade.

From the ninth to the thirteenth century, considerable numbers of Varangians, including Icelanders, were in the service of the Byzantine Emperor in Constantinople. According to Sigfus Blöndal in his *Væringja saga* (History of the Varangians), this led to some cultural influence in the Nordic world; not much in literature, but more in terms of arts and crafts, ecclesiastical and worldly goods. Such goods could well have included the astrolabe.[73]

One of the Icelanders who served in the Varangian Guard was Gris Sæmingsson of Geitaskard; he is believed to have been in Constantinople around 970–980, and to have been awarded a sword and a gold-ornamented spear. Gris lived quite near to Thorfinn Karlsefni's home at Reynines. The main path across the mountains passed both estates. This demonstrates that there was ample opportunity for Thorfinn, the provident seafarer, a near-contemporary of Gris, to have gained access to an astrolabe or information about it, and even to have had one made from *mösur* wood brought from Wineland, as the saga says.

This is of course only a conjecture on the meaning and function of the *húsasnotra*, and perhaps the hypothesis may seem far-fetched. But one should not underestimate the results that could be achieved, even a thousand years ago, in utilisation of the knowledge and skills of scholars and craftsmen, in the interest of successful navigation at sea.

Midnight sun and dark nights
Undeniably, instruments and expertise were required for measur-

ing and utilising solar elevation. And it should be stated that direct references to such observations at sea are sparse. But in order to ascertain more or less how far north a vessel was, a method existed, and still does, that would undoubtedly have been useful to observant seafarers. When one travels southwards from Iceland in the summer months, one cannot help noticing that the nights grow much darker. Even within Iceland, a difference may be discerned; in Akureyri, north Iceland, nights are lighter in early August than in Reykjavik, in the south, although the difference in latitude is only one-and-a-half degrees. At the summer solstice, the sun is above the horizon at the Arctic Circle in the northernmost parts of Iceland and in Holsteinsborg in Western Greenland, while in northern Ireland and at Hamilton Inlet, Labrador, the sun is 12 degrees below the horizon, so that the light conditions would be only so-called "navigation twilight." There is still enough light to discern bearings, as the horizon can be seen in the north around midnight in clear conditions; the Pole Star is also clearly visible by night. The brightness or darkness of the night can hence be used to estimate how far north the vessel is located, and to steer a course accordingly. Even in poor visibility, the darkness of the night is an obvious clue. Bjarni Herjolfsson could have used this method to estimate his position when he had been carried off course, as stated in the Saga of the Greenlanders, even without benefit of any navigational instruments.

Altogether, there is much to indicate that the people of the Viking Age had access to extensive knowledge of the changing position of the sun, and all good seafarers must undoubtedly have tried to acquire such knowledge.

Characteristics of wind directions

But the real problem arose when the sun was not visible and the sky overcast for days at a time. Under these circumstances, familiarity with the kind of weather conditions normally experienced in certain wind directions could be useful. The King's Mirror tells of this in a poetic, though fairly realistic, way.[74] (See map on p. xiii). This appears to give quite an accurate description of the changes in the weather experienced when a deep depression passes over during the winter. The description is more applicable to western Norway than to Iceland. The conditions also apply to some degree to summer depressions, although the weather is usually milder and wind speeds lower. No doubt Icelanders gathered comparable information on the characteristics of various wind directions in Iceland, and it would be highly useful for seafarers to be familiar with the winds, and use this knowledge to steer a correct course.

The King's Mirror tells first of the east wind, describing the building of rain clouds, the first harbinger of the coming depression:

> He puts a cloud-covered hat on his head and breathes heavily and violently, as if mourning a recent loss.

Then the southeasterly blows with high winds and rain, which are known today as its usual accompaniment:

> Stirred by the distress of a resentful mind, he knits his brows under the hiding clouds and blows the froth violently about him.

The description of the south wind could be a reference to the foggy conditions that often occur in the warm sector between a warm and a cold front, often accompanied by drizzle:

> … wraps himself in a cloud-lined mantle in which he conceals his treasures and his wealth of warm rays and blows vigorously as if in frightened defence.

Then the southwesterly wind following a cold front brings the familiar showery weather:

> … sobs forth his soul's grief in heavy showers, … puffs his cheeks under the cloudy helmet, blows the chilling scud violently forward.

The westerly wind is often gusty, like the southwesterly:

> … puts on a black robe of mourning over which he pulls a cloud-grey cloak and, sitting with wrinkled nose and pouting lips, he breathes heavily with regretful care.

In the northwest wind we know that air masses that reach western Norway from Canada, via a route south of southern Greenland, are often accompanied by thunder in winter:

> … throws rattling hail violently about, and sends forth the rolling thunder with terrifying gleams of lightning.

The description of the north wind is probably primarily a reference to the falling temperature:

> … brings out a dim sheen which glitters with frost, places an ice-cold helmet on his head above his frozen beard, and blows hard against the hail-bearing cloud-heaps.

After this the northeast wind usually brings cold conditions without precipitation:

> … sits wrathful with snowy beard and breathes coldly through his wind-swollen nostrils.[75]

This means that seafarers could estimate the wind direction with some accuracy although the sun was not visible, even for days at a time. This table shows the correlation between wind direction and weather conditions a short distance off the coast of Norway:

Weather	Probable wind direction
High, whitish veil	easterly (later southeasterly)
Windy, rainy, not cold	southeasterly
Fog, drizzle, mild	southerly
Gusty winds, showers, cooler	southwesterly (or westerly)
Showers (and thunder), rather cold	westerly or northwesterly
Little precipitation, cold	northerly, northeasterly

The correlation between weather conditions and wind direction is, of course, not always this simple, and it was important to be familiar with all the possible variations of weather, in order to predict

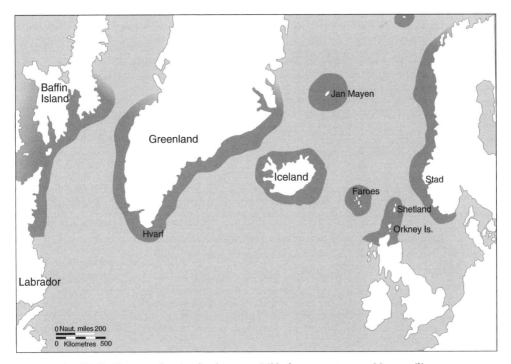

Map by Sibylla Haasum showing landmasses visible from out at sea on Norse sailing routes.

developments over the next day or two. This was useful when setting sail on short ocean routes.

Other navigational aids
But seafarers made use of various other phenomena to provide clues to their position, some of which will be mentioned below.

Seabirds, especially auk species and gannets, often fly out to sea in the morning, a distance of as much as 50–100 nautical miles, returning to shore at night. If they are carrying food, it may be regarded as certain that they are returning to their nests.[76] Seabirds can thus indicate the direction of the nearest land.

Floki's ravens. According to the Book of Settlements, Floki Vilgerdarson, one of the first people to attempt to settle in Iceland, carried ravens on his ship to guide him to the next land. When aloft, the birds can see much farther than the men aboard ship.

Whales. Some species of whale tend to keep to the continental shelf, while others are found in deeper waters. Birds and whales are mentioned in old navigational information as clues to the proximity of land.

Changing colour and temperature of the sea. At a point where warm and cool ocean currents meet, there is often a change of colour in the sea; the temperature may also change noticeably, e.g. off the East Fjords of Iceland or near the edge of the sea ice on the sailing route between Iceland and Greenland.

Sounds. The sound of crashing surf and even the chattering calls from birdcliffs may be heard far out at sea. Sound carries better downwind than upwind. Sounds carry particularly well downwind if the winds are stronger at higher altitude, and conditions close to the surface are relatively cold. On land, for instance, one may detect the wind direction by ascertaining from which direction the sound of a waterfall or surf is heard.

Odours may be carried long distances. The scent of new-mown hay has been known to be discernible 130 kilometres off the coast of New Zealand.[77] And when Tim Severin sailed his leather curragh *Brendan* to America in 1977, he could smell the scent of the pine forests of Newfoundland far out at sea.[78]

Mountains and mirages. Mountains of unusual shape, and especially high mountains, may provide landmarks. The accompanying map has been drawn up by Sibylla Haasum, showing the distance out at sea from which land may be sighted, on various Nordic sea routes.[79] The map clearly shows how a route may be charted in order to keep land in sight for the maximum amount of the journey. This is based upon excellent conditions of visibility. Mountains are visible, however, from much greater distances when mirages occur. Such conditions arise especially in summer, when the air near the surface of the sea is relatively cold, and warmer at higher altitude. Old sources tell that from the middle of the Denmark Strait both Greenland and Iceland were sometimes visible, and the ice cap of Snæfellsjökull, west Iceland, has been known to be visible from the sea, 500 km away to the southwest.[80] Mirage conditions are especially common in the northerly regions off West Greenland. At the narrowest point of the Davis Strait, no doubt both Greenland and Baffin Island are visible in such conditions from the middle of the Strait. This is precisely the route chosen by cautious navigators to Wineland from Greenland.

Cumulus and lenticular clouds. Certain cloud formations are typically found over land rather than sea, such as high banks of cumulus on bright summer days. Lenticular clouds, often in several layers one above the other, are frequently seen over mountains at all seasons, and can point to the way to land, which is itself invisible. See fig. p. xiii.

Iceblink. The glow reflected from expanses of ice at sea, or on a snow-covered land, can be reflected off clouds. In the summer of 1866, Arni Thorlacius saw such an iceblink over the Hunafloi bay in north Iceland from Stykkisholmur, over 100 kilometres away, both day and night.[81]

Wind waves at sea adapt quickly to changing wind conditions, but the underlying swell keeps to its course for much longer. A comparison between the two can often reveal whether the wind direction has changed. If land is nearby, one may often find the right course by following the swell, which flows towards land.

Sounding line. A sounding line could be used for measuring the depth of the sea. This would be vital inshore, especially when sailing in unfamiliar waters, for instance in exploration.

Island-hopping. It made sense to sail so as to keep within sight of islands and other landmarks as far as possible along the way, even if it meant sailing a longer distance. The most provident of seafarers appear to have chosen this approach. An example of this cautious method is Thorfinn Karlsefni's route from south Greenland to America, first sailing more than 1000 kilometres north up the west coast of Greenland, so that the crossing to Baffin Island would only take about 24 hours, before turning southwards along the North American coast. Such island-hopping is described in the instructions given in the *Hauksbók* version of the Book of Settlements for sailing from Hernar in Norway (an island northwest of Bergen, whose modern name is Hennøya) to Hvarf (Cape Farewell) in Greenland:

> From Hernar in Norway one must sail a direct course west to Hvarf in Greenland, in which case one sails north of Shetland so that one sights land in clear weather only, then south of the Faroes so that the sea looks halfway up the mountainsides, then south of Iceland so that one gets sight of birds and whales from there.

It would have been less risky to sail up to the Snæfellsnes peninsula in west Iceland, then west to Greenland, and turning south along the coast to sail around Cape Farewell. But it is also true to say that by choosing this more southerly route, the mariners would have had the advantage of being able to see the Pole Star in the later part of summer on clear nights. This was more difficult close to Iceland, due to the light summer nights.[82]

Most indications go to show that helmsmen employed many different ways of travelling safely across the ocean between Norway, the Faroes, Iceland, Greenland and Wineland.

1   *Saga of the People of Vatnsdal, Complete Sagas of Icelanders* 1997.
2   Fritzner 1883–1896.
3   *Alfræði íslensk 1–3* 1908–1918. *King's Mirror* 1917. Snorri Sturluson 1995. Snorri Sturluson 1991. *Saga of the Killings on the Heath, Complete Sagas of Icelanders* 1997.
4   Richard Cleasby and Gudbrandur Vigfusson 1975. Sigfus Blöndal 1920–1924. Arni Bödvarsson 1963. Asgeir Blöndal Magnusson 1989.

5   Gustav Storm 1887. C.C. Rafn 1837.
6   A.W. Brøgger and Haakon Shetelig 1971.
7   *Saga of the Killings on the Heath, Complete Sagas of Icelanders* 1997.
8   Roald Morcken 1977.
9   *Books of Settlements* 1964. *Sturlunga saga* 1970–74.
    Olafur Halldorsson 1978.
10 *Alfræði íslensk 1–3* 1908–1918.
11 *Sturlunga saga* 1970–74.
12 *Alfræði íslensk 1–3* 1908–1918.
13 Snorri Sturluson 1991.
14 Ole Crumlin-Pedersen and Olaf Olsen 1967.
15 Some of this information is derived from a press pack
    distributed to journalists in 1991, when three replica Viking
    ships were sailed down the east coast of North America, to
    Washington D.C.
16 Gunnar Marel Eggertsson, personal communication.
17 Sibylla Haasum 1974.
18 Sibylla Haasum 1974.
19 *Vikings. The North Atlantic Saga.* 2000.
20 *Book of Icelanders* 1986.
21 Björn M. Olsen 1914.
22 Björn M. Olsen 1914.
23 Olafur Halldorsson 1978.
24 Jon Vidar Sigurdsson, personal communication.
25 *Law of Early Iceand, Grágás* 1980.
26 Arni Björnsson 1990.
27 Sigfus Blöndal 1920–1924. Asgeir Blöndal Magnusson 1989.
28 Roald Morcken 1977.
29 *Alfræði íslensk* 1908–18.
30 *Encyclopaedia Britannica.*
31 Niels Winther 1875.
32 Helge Ingstad 1985.
33 Mjöll Snæsdottir, personal communication.
34 *Alfræði íslensk 1–3* 1908–1918.
35 Roald Morcken 1977.
36 *Almanak fyrir Ísland* 1996.
37 *Law of Early Iceland, Grágás* 1980.
38 Almar Næss 1954.
39 *Diplomatarium Islandicum* 1857 onward. *Encyclopaedia Britannica.*
40 Thordur Tomasson, personal communication.
41 Jonas Jonasson 1961.
42 Almar Næss 1954.

43   Thormodur Torfason 1715.
44   Almar Næss 1954.
45   Gustav Storm 1886.
46   Björn M. Olsen 1914.
47   Thordur Tomasson, personal communication.
48   *Encyclopaedia Britannica.*
49   *Encyclopaedia Britannica.*
50   Niels Winther 1875.
51   Uwe Schnall 1975.
52   Roald Morcken 1977.
53   *Diplomatarium Islandicum* 1857 onward.
54   Thorsteinn Vilhjalmsson 1990.
55   Torkild Ramskou 1969.
56   Thorsteinn Vilhjalmsson 1990.
57   *Sturlunga saga* 1970–74.
58   Thorsteinn Vilhjalmsson 1990.
59   Uwe Schnall 1975.
60   Arbman 1961.
61   Müller-Wille 1978.
62   Roald Morcken 1977.
63   Olafur Halldorsson 1978.
64   Gustav Storm 1887.
65   Roald Morcken 1977.
66   Gudmund Andresson 1949.
67   *Encyclopaedia Britannica.*
68   *Encyclopaedia Britannica.*
69   Asgeir Blöndal Magnusson 1989.
70   Haraldur Agustsson, personal communication.
71   *Arrow-Odd* 1970.
72   Birgitta Wallace 1991a.
73   Sigfus Blöndal 1954.
74   *King's Mirror* 1917.
75   *King's Mirror* 1917.
76   Arnthor Gardarsson, personal communication.
77   Sibylla Haasum 1974.
78   Tim Severin 1978.
79   Sibylla Haasum 1974.
80   Gwyn Jones 1986.
81   Arni O. Thorlacius 1867.
82   *Book of Settlements* 1986.

ARCHAEOLOGICAL EVIDENCE

Evidence from Greenland

The many archaeological sites in Greenland, most of them ruins of farms, serve *per se* to confirm much of what the Wineland sagas say about Greenland. These finds thus go to support the argument that the Wineland chapters of the sagas are also, broadly speaking, credible.

When Eirik the Red's farmstead at Brattahlid was excavated in 1932, there was some disappointment that no sign was uncovered of the church, mentioned in Eirik the Red's Saga, reputed to have been built for Thjodhild, Eirik's wife, "a fair distance from the house," after she was converted to Christianity by her son, Leif. This probably undermined belief in the credibility of the saga a little. But thirty years later the remains of a small church were found about 200 metres from the main farmstead, beyond a hillock. This undoubtedly served to restore confidence in the writer of Eirik the Red's Saga. At the south wall of the church, a grave was excavated, containing a jumble of bones. It transpired that the bones had belonged to twelve men, and a child aged 12–14. The men appear to have been taller than the other occupants of the graveyard. Olafur Halldorsson has, as mentioned on p. 50, proposed the theory that these could be the earthly remains of Thorstein Eiriksson and his crew, whom he had chosen "for their strength and size" to join his expedition, and who travelled to Lysufjord where some died of a fever. The bodies were transported back to Brattahlid for burial.[1] This is recounted in the Saga of the Greenlanders.

Eirik the Red's Saga tells us that Thorfinn Karlsefni landed goods from his ship at Brattahlid, where "there was no lack of good and ample outbuildings to store them." This is consistent with the excavation in 1932 of four large outbuildings.

In 1930 Danish archaeologists excavated the ruins of an old

farmstead at Ameralik in the Western Settlement, which may have been the property of Gudrid Thorbjarnardottir and of Thorfinn Karlsefni, after the decease of her first husband, Thorstein Eiriksson. At some depth in the main farm building, a lump of anthracite was found. This hard, shiny form of coal has not otherwise been found in Greenland. In Iceland there is no anthracite, only small deposits of lignite (brown coal), while coal is found in the far north of Norway, but not anthracite. Anthracite occurs, however, in two places on the east coast of the USA, in Rhode Island. Both these locations are on the route that has been suggested here as being travelled by Thorfinn Karlsefni from Straumsfjord to Hop. Although it does not constitute proof, the find of a lump of anthracite in Greenland can hardly be explained in a more probable manner than that it was brought back to Greenland by someone who had been in Wineland, perhaps one who had been in Thorfinn's company.[2]

A more decisive indication of links with America was found in an old churchyard near the farmstead mentioned above in Ameralik. This is an arrowhead of quartzite, which according to Danish archaeologist Jørgen Meldgård is clearly a typical Native American arrowhead.[3] A possible explanation would be that the arrowhead had been brought back to Greenland with the body of one of those who fell in battle with the Native Americans in the New World. According to the sagas, the Greenlanders of that time felt strongly about returning their dead for burial in hallowed ground, even over long distances. This could explain the fact that no heathen barrows have been found in Greenland, with the possible exception of one find in Hvalseyjarfjord.[4]

At Herjolfsnes (Ikagait), coffins have been unearthed made of larch, which grows in Labrador and Newfoundland, but was unknown in Scandinavia at this time. There is much to indicate that the Greenlanders sailed to Markland to fetch timber, as it was closer than Norway. In 1347, a Greenlandic ship arrived in Iceland; it had sailed to Markland, possibly to gather timber, and then been carried off course to Iceland.[5]

These archaeological finds add up to a strong indication of the credibility of the Wineland sagas.

Riverbank grapes (Vitis riparia) *are hardier, and grow farther north, than other species of wild grape in America, but they tend to be sour, and not suitable for making wine. But probably Leif had no better grapes to choose from. The riverbank grape vine climbs up tall trees, and may be seen near Québec and in various places in the St. Lawrence valley, and also in parts of Nova Scotia and New Brunswick. These grapes were found at Bridgewater, Nova Scotia, near where the author believes Haki and Hekja made their exploratory foray. Photo Larus Karl Ingason.*

Fox grapes (Vitis labrusca) *are wild grapes which still grow in the vicinity of New York, and north into southern Maine. Thorfinn Karlsefni and his company probably found such grapes. Wines have been made of fox grapes, but the "foxy" flavour is an acquired taste. Grapes found at Bridgewater, Nova Scotia, probably introduced by man. Photo Larus Karl Ingason.*

Wild rice (Zizania aquatica brevis) *found growing in shallow water close to the bank of the St. Lawrence river in Québec. Native Americans have eaten wild rice for thousands of years, and it is now a gourmet foodstuff on the international market. The "self-sown wheat" of Eirik the Red's Saga was probably wild rice, and the "grain cover" described in the Saga of the Greenlanders was probably for storing such grain. Photo Larus Karl Ingason.*

*The butternut (*Juglans cinerea*) is a species of walnut that grows as far north as wild grapes in Canada. Three butternuts were unearthed at the excavations at L'Anse aux Meadows, in addition to a small butternut burl. The nuts and burl must have been brought to L'Anse aux Meadows from some warmer place, e.g. from Québec, where these butternuts were gathered in the autumn of 1996. Photo Larus Karl Ingason.*

The sugar maple is a species of hardwood tree, which may be regarded as one of Wineland's most valuable resources. It is ideal for making musical instruments and for flooring. The tree also yields maple syrup. Photo Larus Karl Ingason.

The Native American Widow, *a statuette from a Micmac store in Nova Scotia. The skrælings slain by Thorvald Eiriksson's men were probably of the Micmac tribe. Photo Larus Karl Ingason.*

Archaeological finds in Arctic Canada

Although it is not directly relevant to Wineland, there are certain indications that Norsemen visited Arctic Canada at the time of Nordic Greenland.

Near Thule in northern Greenland, Nordic items have been found, including the barrel-base mentioned on p. 155, which may have been a navigational aid.[6] On Ellesmere Island opposite North Greenland, another two sites are known, both at 79°N. In 1977 on Skraeling Island off the Bache peninsula on the east coast of Canada, Danish-Canadian archaeologist Peter Schledermann found part of a breastplate, woollen cloth, ship's nails, part of a chessman and fragments of a barrel-bottom, which may have been used for navigational purposes. Radiocarbon analysis indicated that they dated from the 13th century. The idea has been suggested that this may be the remains of a shipwreck, or that the objects may have been brought to the place by Inuits, which seems less likely.[7]

About 200 kilometres farther west, both on the west coast of Ellesmere Island and in the south of Baffin Island, articles believed to be of Nordic origin have also been found.

This may indicate that there was more communication than has hitherto been believed between Greenland and the Arctic lands to the west during the time of the Nordic settlement in Greenland. It is not unlikely that these contacts continued for far longer than the actual Wineland voyages.

Archaeological finds in Newfoundland and Maine

The most tangible evidence of Nordic journeys to the New World is the remarkable discovery of a Viking-Age site, made by Helge Ingstad and his wife Anne-Stine at L'Anse aux Meadows, at the northernmost point of Newfoundland. Birgitta Wallace has written about these findings.[8] There are many indications that her conclusion is correct, that this was a gateway and place of ship repairs on Nordic journeys to Wineland about a thousand years ago. The archaeological finds themselves indicate this time-scale; among them is a ring-headed pin of a high-lead tin bronze, of a distinctly

West Norse type, common in the 10th century. Radiocarbon analysis is also consistent with this dating.

The buildings were of the Icelandic type: a timber framework supported walls and roof of turf. Most of the walls were of double thickness, with sand and gravel filling the cavity between the walls, and individual crosswise turves binding the two walls together. This was the same kind of turf construction as was used in Iceland and Greenland. The filling material between the walls was intended to drain away the water that flowed off the roof. The roof did not meet the wall at its outer edge, in the normal way, but at the middle of the wall. The long walls of the houses curve outwards, while the end walls are straight. In the residential buildings, there was a long hearth in the middle of the building, and benches along the walls, also used as beds.

A furnace hut has been found on the site, and signs of charcoal-burning pits nearby, similar to those found in Norway, and the same as have been used in Iceland until recent decades. There were many traces of iron-working, remnants of ships' nails that had been sliced through, chips of wood, and broken wooden objects. Items that seem to indicate fishing include containers of birch bark, often used to cover net weights, and nearby a pile of stones the size of an egg or fist. The *King's Mirror* advises that aboard ship one should "keep on board two or three hundred ells of wadmal [woollen cloth] of a sort suitable for mending sails, if that should be necessary, a large number of needles, and a supply of thread and cord."[9] This may explain why the finds at L'Anse aux Meadows included a fragment of a needle, a quartz needle-hone and a spindle-whorl of soapstone. It is difficult to tell what would have been spun using the spindle-whorl, because there is no sign of sheep or horses (hence sheep's wool or horsehair), but the voyagers may have taken wool or horsehair, or even flax, with them from Greenland or Iceland. Yarn made of three threads of horsehair was used in olden times in Norway for sewing sails. This was plaited, and hence stronger than twined yarns.[10] In Iceland, spinning horsehair was traditionally a man's task. The spindle-whorl found at L'Anse aux Meadows is admittedly rather smaller than those normally used in Iceland for spinning horsehair, but horsehair yarn was made in various thicknesses depending on its purpose. So it is quite possible that the needle, quartz needle-hone and spindle-whorl were all used by men, although some of the Wineland expeditions certainly included women – the group led by Freydis, Helgi and Finnbogi, for instance.

In the Gokstad ship, unearthed in Norway, the planking of the hull is tied to the ribs using spruce roots; these were also used for various other purposes on the ship, e.g. for strong fixtures on the sail, etc. At L'Anse aux Meadows, long spruce roots were found, wound in a bundle, for later use, and remarkably well preserved. Scraps of entwined roots were also found, which may have been intended for use on ships.[11] One of the reasons for this choice of location was probably the presence of bog iron, which was found by Icelandic archaeologist Dr. Kristjan Eldjarn at Black Duck Brook.[12]

It is entirely consistent with other evidence from L'Anse aux Meadows that Kevin P. Smith has found pieces of jasper there, used for lighting fires, which he believes were brought from Iceland or Greenland.

The settlement was clearly short-lived, since there is little sign of middens, and no trace of a graveyard. It was probably only inhabited for a few years. Nor are there any signs of byres for livestock; on this rugged peninsula the sea is blocked by drift ice until summer. Summer temperatures on Belle Isle are only a little higher than on the chilly north coast of Iceland, while in winter snows are heavy. The land is close to being barren, according to Helge Ingstad's description:

> ... small hills, bogs and a number of lakes. There is abundance of moss, lichens and willows, in some places a heavy growth of small wind-blown spruce trees, and grass in the sheltered areas.[13]

In addition to this, pollen analysis by Kari E. Henningsmoen at L'Anse aux Meadows does not indicate any major change in the climate over the past thousand years.[14] At the time of the Wineland voyages, the climate was probably similar to that of the warmer period of the 20th century (see below for discussion of climatic factors).

The Ingstads' archaeological work has won them a place in history. But Helge Ingstad has perhaps tended to be carried away by his enthusiasm for connecting the events and locations of the Wineland sagas to L'Anse aux Meadows and interpreting them to conform with the chilly climate of the place. This leads him to reject some of the essential features of the story; the name of *Vín*land (Wineland) is changed to *Vin*land (Pastureland), and the vines and self-sown wheat of the sagas are dismissed. But the Ingstads' remarkable discovery need not conflict in any way with the accounts of the resources of Wineland. Three butternuts from more southerly climes, together with a burl from a butternut tree, found at L'Anse aux Meadows, actually constitute a tangible clue that the Wineland voyagers travelled on to warmer lands, as Birgitta Wallace has pointed out.[15]

These relics of a Nordic (or, more specifically, Icelandic) settlement at L'Anse aux Meadows are a fact. Hence one would wish to be able to answer the question of why the houses were built. Birgitta Wallace believes that the settlement at L'Anse aux Meadows was a gateway to Wineland, a staging-post where goods were gathered together in summer and autumn, and where the seafarers could spend the winter, waiting for suitable conditions to sail home to Greenland in the spring, when the sea ice off Labrador thawed. This is good enough reason in itself. Wallace also points out that archaeological research shows that no Native Americans lived in the area at the time. It would have been difficult to find such a safe place on the Gulf of St. Lawrence or farther south in Wineland. Wood debris found at L'Anse aux Meadows, which had been cut with stone tools, appears either to pre-date or post-date the Norse settlement.

Birgitta Wallace has reasoned from the signs of settlement at L'Anse aux Meadows that the place was only inhabited for a few years. If we consult the Wineland sagas, and add up the duration of the settlement according to them, this is the result, assuming that Thorfinn Karlsefni was not among those who used the camp:

Leif	*10 months*
Thorvald	*33 months*
Freydis	*11 months*
Total	*54 months*

This represents a total of four to five years, a figure which is entirely consistent with the evidence provided by the L'Anse aux Meadows site. There is no real evidence that the settlement lasted any longer than this. As discussed above, the archaeological findings in L'Anse aux Meadows are an important validation of Leif Eiriksson's midwinter sunshine observation, reported in the Saga of the Greenlanders.

At Penobscot Bay in Maine, USA, in a region that was inhabited by Native Americans, a silver coin was found, dating from the time of King Olaf the Quiet who reigned over Norway in the late 11th century.[16] This discovery inevitably brings to mind the account in the Icelandic annals, mentioned above, that Bishop Eirik Gnupsson of Greenland sailed in search of Wineland in 1121. There is no mention of his ever returning.[17] This is another archaeological confirmation of medieval historical sources.

Spurious finds and sources

In their search for tangible proof of the Wineland voyages, some people have been tempted into excessive zeal. Birgitta Wallace has discussed some of the purported evidence which has been claimed; she regards some examples as dubious at best, others as pure fraud.[18]

At Newport, Rhode Island, there is a cylindrical tower built of natural stone and mortar, standing on eight pillars of the same material. The Dane C.C. Rafn, who carried out extensive research on Wineland with Icelander Finnur Magnusson in the early 19th century, was sent a rough drawing of the tower, which he declared to be a Norse church from the 11th century. Documents, however, prove that the tower was built in the 1650s on the property of Governor Benedict Arnold. Archaeological evidence supports this.

In 1898 a stone with a long runic inscription was found on the property of Olof Öhman, a Swedish immigrant, in Kensington, Minnesota. Submitted to the Department of Germanic Studies at the University of Illinois, the stone was examined, and the verdict was that it was a modern fake. An amateur of Norwegian descent, Hjalmar Holand, then set out to demonstrate that the stone proved there had been a Nordic presence in the region in olden times. Holand's persuasive writing style has served to convince many people, although scholars dismiss his arguments entirely. It is regarded as probable that the Swedish-American farmer and his Norwegian-American neighbour carved the runes, which are written in a bizarre Norwegian-Swedish dialect, known only in the American Midwest in the 19th century.[19]

The same applies to a number of Viking-Age iron items found in Ontario. These appear to have been brought from Norway and then buried in the New World before being "discovered."

Near Halifax, Nova Scotia, periwinkle shells have been found, which may be 500 to 900 years old. These are of the species *Littorina littorea*, and they are more recent than any other relics of the species in North America. These periwinkles live on rocky shores, and it is regarded as probable that they were brought from Europe. They have not, however, been found in Iceland, according to zoologist Agnar Ingolfsson.[20] On the basis of dating, it is entirely possible that they were taken to America after the later European discovery of the continent. It has also been suggested that yarrow, *Achilea millefolium*, which is common in Iceland and also on the eastern seaboard of North America, may have been introduced by the Wineland settlers, but such a hypothesis is hard to prove.

The *Vínland Map*, which "appeared" in 1957, may not be a fake, although it naturally gave rise to suspicion when the discoverers of the map were not willing to disclose its provenance. They maintained that the map dated from about 1440, and thus could only be based upon the explorations of the Wineland voyages. No convincing proof seems to have been produced that the map is as old as this. Cartographer Haraldur Sigurdsson believes that this "poor map" may have been drawn in the 16th century, based upon Portuguese maps mixed with confused information derived from the Wineland sagas, or else it may be a simple forgery.[21] In my view, there is so much convincing evidence for the Wineland voyages about a thousand years ago that the dubious evidence of the Vínland Map and suchlike is of little significance.

1	Olafur Halldorsson 1978.
2	Helge Ingstad 1985.
3	Jørgen Meldgaard 1977.
4	Joel Berglund 1982.
5	Olafur Halldorsson 1978.
6	Helge Ingstad 1985.
7	Birgitta Wallace 1991b.
8	Birgitta Wallace 1986. Birgitta Wallace 1991a.
9	*King's Mirror* 1917.
10	Gunnar Marel Eggertsson, oral communication.
11	Birgitta Wallace 1991a.
12	Helge Ingstad 1969.
13	Helge Ingstad 1969.
14	Anne-Stine Ingstad 1985.
15	Birgitta Wallace 1991a.
16	Kolbjørn Skaare 1979.
17	Gustav Storm 1888.
18	Birgitta Wallace 1991b.
19	Birgitta Wallace 1991b.
20	Agnar Ingolfsson, oral communication.
21	Haraldur Sigurdsson 1971.

LOCAL EVIDENCE FROM WINELAND

Climate at the time of the Wineland voyages

It is hardly possible to argue for or against the Wineland sagas without having some idea of the climate of the time. The sea route from Greenland to Labrador and the Gulf of St. Lawrence is blocked by sea ice throughout the winter and into the spring, but variations in temperature mean that the sea ice sometimes persists for a longer period, and sometimes shorter. By the same token, variations in climatic conditions mean that it may sometimes be possible to sail to Greenland in late autumn, while in other years the route is soon blocked by ice. Climatic fluctuations may also mean that plants mentioned in the sagas, such as vines and wild cereal plants, spread farther north, or retreat farther south. Such changes in distribution of vegetation take place, however, over much longer periods than simple climatic changes.

About ten thousand years ago, at the end of the Ice Age (Pleistocene Epoch), the climate underwent rapid warming.[1] During this warm period temperatures are believed to have risen 2–3°C higher than we are accustomed to, even in the warmest period of the 20th century. About 2,500 years ago, the climate cooled once more, introducing a colder period which continues today. This extended climatic period appears to have affected the northern parts of the globe fairly evenly, although short-term temperature fluctuations have had variable effects upon different regions and continents. The climate has, however, been far from constant during this 2,500-year period.

For the first three centuries after Iceland was settled (i.e. from the 9th to the 12th century), the climate is generally believed to have been fairly mild. This may be inferred, for instance, from historical sources in Iceland. Detailed accounts of the Age of Settlement (around 900), especially in the Book of the Settlements, scarcely mention sea ice being an obstacle to navigation. Journeys between Iceland and Norway were frequent, and the previously uninhabited island was settled rapidly over a period of sixty years. Had the climate been as cold in the Settlement Age as it was in the 19th century (when sea ice was frequently found around Iceland, even in summer), or even in the 1960s, known in Iceland as the "sea-ice years," the settlement of Iceland would not have been such an easy matter.

Iceland's glaciers, which today cover 11% of Iceland, were clearly smaller at the time of the settlement of the country. They spread in later centuries, as witness the fact that in the period around 1700 many farms had to be abandoned as the Drangajökull and Breidamerkurjökull glaciers spread themselves. One of the farms that disappeared under the growing glacier was Breida, which according to the Saga of Njall was the home of Kari Sölmundarson, one of the heroes of the saga. Since Kari was a wealthy magnate, this was presumably a valuable and extensive estate. The Saga of Thorgils and Haflidi, which is believed to have been written around 1237, says that in the first half of the 12th century "at that time the land was so good at Reykjaholar that the grain fields were never unfruitful." Perhaps the emphasis is upon the words "at that time" which sounds like the author looking back with nostalgia for better times, as Magnus Mar Larusson has suggested.[2] In harmony with this, placenames, legends and archaeological finds from the early years of Iceland's history indicate that cereal crops were cultivated in many places. This form of agriculture subsequently died out; in the eighteenth century, the Danes made an attempt to teach the Icelanders how to grow grain crops, but the experiment failed, apparently because the climate was too cold. During the mildest periods of the 20th century, successful experiments have been made with cereal cultivation in Iceland. This may perhaps be an indication that in the Saga Age weather conditions were similar to the warmest periods of the 20th century.

It is probable that during the three centuries after Iceland was first settled in 870 AD, the climate of Greenland and North America was similarly mild. Since the distribution of vegetation changes only slowly, it may thus be inferred that the distribution of plant species was similar to what we know today.

But this does not mean that brief, harsh periods may not have occurred during the relatively warm era, and sources confirm this. An appendix to the Book of Settlements contains what may be regarded as a summary of weather conditions during the first two centuries of Iceland's history.[3] This tells of a disastrous winter, the worst that had been experienced in Iceland; some people starved to death, while others resorted to theft. No doubt a period of cold and harsh weather had preceded this tragedy. Eighty years later, another harsh spell followed, with mass starvation, in the first year that Isleifur Gissurarson was Bishop, i.e. in 1056. The previous harsh winter may thus be dated to about 970–980.

When a brief period of harsh conditions occurs, the same may not be experienced in neighbouring countries, for instance in Greenland or on the east coast of America. Commonly, a similar pattern occurs there, but some years later. There is thus no reason to doubt the account of the hard winter experienced in Greenland, when Thorbjörg the "little prophetess" was asked to read people's fortunes, the first winter that Gudrid Thorbjarnardottir spent in Greenland, shortly after AD 1000. According to the Saga of the Greenlanders, fishing trips had been difficult, and some fishermen had not returned. This is reminiscent of failing fish catches off Iceland in recent years, and even worse conditions off Greenland, which may be largely attributable to low sea temperatures. This may be an indication that the end of the 10th century was relatively cold both in Iceland and in Greenland, perhaps as cool as the cold period from 1960–1990, although it was preceded and followed by milder conditions, similar to those experienced in Iceland in 1925–65 (about 0.7°C warmer).

Readings of layers in glacial ice give some indication of climatic change in Greenland and elsewhere. By comparison with modern temperature readings, temperatures experienced in former times may be deduced. A core of glacial ice drilled from the top of the Greenland Glacier at a latitude of 70°N shows relatively mild conditions from the late 9th century onwards. After the mid-tenth century a cooler period is indicated, with temperatures approximately one degree lower. Although the comparison should not be over-interpreted, it is broadly consistent with the tale told by Icelandic historical sources.

At L'Anse aux Meadows in Newfoundland, where ruins of buildings have been discovered, similar to the Icelandic buildings of the time, Kari E. Henningsmoen and others have made studies of pollen, that reveal no significant difference between present-day vegetation and that of a thousand years ago.[4]

My conclusion is that temperature, drift ice and vegetation at the time of the Wineland voyages were broadly similar to those we have experienced in the years 1920–1990 or so, although the weather conditions of any specific decade may have varied considerably from the mean.

Sea level

When present-day topography is compared with the descriptions of the Wineland sagas, sea level is an important factor.

In New York land has been subsiding fairly rapidly during the 20th century, by 60cm in 100 years. Hence it is probable that sea levels were lower a thousand years ago, perhaps by as much as six metres. In New Brunswick and Nova Scotia, land subsidence has been less, perhaps three metres over a thousand years.[5] But at the northernmost point of Newfoundland, at L'Anse aux Meadows, there has been little change in sea level, probably less than one metre in a thousand years.

The vegetation of Wineland

Let us now consider some of Wineland's most famous resources, the *mösur* wood, the self-sown wheat and vines. If none of these existed, it would seriously undermine the credibility of the sagas. But this is not the case.

Mösur

Eirik the Red's Saga says of the *mösur* wood found in Greenland by Leif Eiriksson's men:

> Fields of self-sown wheat and vines were growing there; also there were trees known as maple [*mösur*], and they took specimens of all of these.

Mösur was also mentioned in the Saga of the Greenlanders, when a southerner from Bremen in Saxony is said to have bought Thorfinn Karlsefni's *húsasnotra:*

> the Southerner took the decoration [*húsasnotra*] and departed. Karlsefni did not know of what wood it was made, but it was of maple [*mösur*] which had been brought from Vinland.

There is no consensus on what tree species this was. The word *mösur* can refer to a burl, as was mentioned above. A species which often grows such burls is called *masurbjörk* in Swedish. Burls occur most commonly on such tree genera as birch (*Betula*), maple (*Acer*), ash (*Fraxinus*) and walnut (*Juglans*).

Sugar maple (*Acer saccharophorum*) grows no farther north than the south of the Gulf of St. Lawrence. One of the most important commercial tree species in Canada, the sugar maple yields syrup, and also excellent hardwood which can be used e.g. for wooden floors, and also in musical instruments and other high-quality work.

Some people have believed that *mösur* may be the paper birch (*Betula papyrifera*), which grows all the way from Labrador in the north down to Long Island on the east coast of the USA.[6]

The walnut tree often forms burls, and hence the *mösur* may be the butternut tree (*Juglans cinerea*), a walnut species that grows as far north as New Brunswick and the St. Lawrence valley. The butternut tree is used in furniture making, and would thus have been a valuable resource in the eyes of the Wineland voyagers, as would the fruit, the butternut itself, which is used today in confectionery and cakes. The members of the Wineland expeditions clearly took an interest in this tree, as three butternuts were unearthed at the L'Anse aux Meadows site; these are believed to have been brought there from warmer and more southerly climes.[7] The species does not grow in Newfoundland or Nova Scotia, and on the coast of New Brunswick it is only recorded in one place. But it is found farther west in Québec, and along the St. Lawrence River, where it is common. And these areas are easily accessible by sea from Newfoundland.[8]

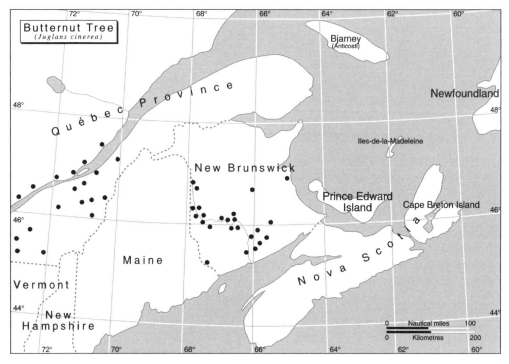

Distribution of the butternut tree.

An interesting factor in this debate is a small burl from a butternut tree, unearthed in the ruins of L'Anse aux Meadows, together with the three butternuts. This is more tangible proof that the Wineland voyagers knew this species. It is also not unlikely that Thorfinn Karlsefni's *húsasnotra* was made of a butternut burl.

Self-sown wheat
The hypothesis was first put forward in 1764 that the "self-sown wheat" of Eirik the Red's Saga was an American species of grain, the northerly species of wild rice, *Zizania palustris*.[9] By that time the Wineland sagas were well known, partly due to the work of Icelander Thormodur Torfason.[10] M.L. Fernald, an influential American botanist, rejected this theory, pointing out that the plant bears no resemblance to wheat, and this is quite true.[11] But it had to be called by some name; the name "wild oats" used by some, including Fernald himself in his botanical book,[12] is no more apt to

the appearance of the plant than "self-sown wheat." It has also been called "Indian rice," "Canada rice" and "Tuscarora rice." The botanical name *Zizania*, from the Greek, refers to weeds growing in wheatfields. Hence the Wineland voyagers were not alone in connecting the plant to wheat. Icelanders and Greenlanders were quite familiar with such grains as barley, oats and even rye, so they would have been reluctant to call this unfamiliar grain plant by the name of a completely different grain to which they were accustomed. But wheat grows only in milder climates: not in Iceland, and hardly in Norway. Since they were less familiar with the appearance of wheat, while knowing of it, they may have been more comfortable calling the exotic American grain "self-sown wheat." Although the actual grain of wild rice is dark, the husk is lighter in colour, and this colour is more noticeable in expanses of the plant. Just before fertilisation takes place, each style bears small pairs of white leaflets, which then wither and disappear; this may have played a part in the naming of the plant. Askell Löve, who was Professor of Botany at the University of Manitoba in 1951, also believed that the "self-sown wheat" must have been wild rice.[13] There is no reason to suppose that lymegrass (*Elymus arenaria*) would have been called "self-sown wheat" by the Wineland voyagers, as Fernald maintained; Icelanders were too familiar with this plant from their home territory.

Other theories have been put forward about the identity of the self-sown wheat. Mats G. Larsson (1992) has theorised that it may have been wild rye, one of the Elymus genus (*Elymus virginicus*), because he as a layman thinks it resembles the wheat plant. This view has recently been echoed by others.[14] But it is unlikely to have been primarily the external appearance of the plant that led to the self-sown wheat being rated as one of the valuable resources of Wineland; it was far more probably its value as a food. Wild rye has not been discussed from this point of view. Without making any firm assertions on the subject, according to a book on edible plants,[15] the seeds of only two species of wild rye, *Elymus condensatus* and *Elymus triticoides*, were said to have been consumed by the Native Americans. These species grow only in the midwest and southern states, south to Mexico. *Elymus virginicus* is not mentioned in the book.

It is worth mentioning here that one cannot reasonably expect settlers in unknown lands to bestow logical names on the natural phenomena they see around them. David Attenborough mentions an example of this in his book *The Private Life of Plants*:

> British colonialists, settling in lands far away from Europe, had a cheerful disregard for any kind of biological accuracy when it came to bestowing names on the animals and plants they encountered in their new homes. They simply gave them the name of the European animal or plant to which they had some superficial resemblance. If a bird had a red breast they called it a robin, even though it was a flycatcher. And the gigantic, noble tree that formed great forests in the hills of the newly founded states of Victoria and Tasmania, they called an ash even though it is obviously a member of that widespread, abundant and typically Australian family, the eucalypts.[16]

The southern species of wild rice (*Zizania aquatica*) is a large plant that reaches a height of 1–3 metres, and grows as far north as southern Maine in the USA and as far south as Florida. Smaller species of *aquatica* are found farther north. The smallest of this wild rice species, that bears small grains, grows at the innermost end of the Gulf of St. Lawrence.

The northern species *Zizania palustris* has been an important food source for Native Americans for thousands of years. By the time of the European settlement of America, many Native American tribes had long given up their nomadic way of life and settled in areas where wild rice was a reliable food source. This species grows throughout the St. Lawrence valley, east to New Brunswick and also in Nova Scotia.[17] European settlers also made use of wild rice. Einar Ingi Siggeirsson told the present author that he ate wild rice in North Dakota; among other things, it was ground into flour and used to bake bread.[18] Wild rice tends to grow in hollows, as described in Eirik the Red's Saga, since it thrives in marshy ground or shallow water.

In recent years wild rice has become a popular, and high-priced, gourmet dish. It is also offered as food to ducks – in some cases in the cause of protecting them, and in other cases in order to hunt

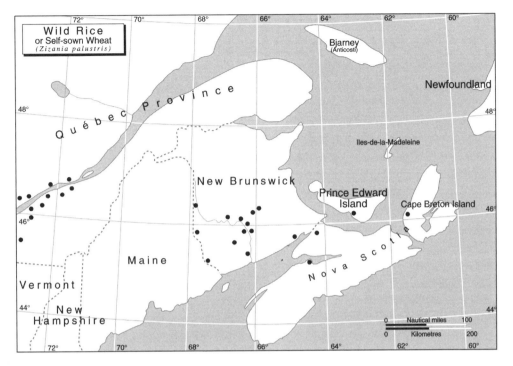

Distribution of self-sown wheat (wild rice).

them. Wild rice is increasingly being cultivated where conditions are favourable. It grows best in water about 30–60 centimetres deep, on a muddy bottom, with no more than a trace of salt in the water. Wild rice is an annual plant, i.e. it is "self-sown" as the Wineland travellers said. The actual grain is dark purple in colour, about a centimetre long, narrow and cylindrical. It requires longer cooking than ordinary rice.

On Friday 16 August 1996, Baldur and I visited Ducks Unlimited Canada in Amherst near the border of New Brunswick. Wild rice (the species Zizania palustris*) is cultivated here. We met biologist John Wile, who showed us around. In olden times, there were huge expanses of "self-sown wheat" in the region, but this has largely been wiped out by the draining of land for pasture. In the modern spirit of environmentalism,* *this process is now being reversed, the drainage ditches filled, the land watered once more, and wild rice sown. The intention was to restore the birdlife of the region; ducks have a taste for wild rice, and we saw flocks of them in search of food. A total of 4,000 hectares has been devoted to cultivating wild rice, which is not only grown for the benefit of the ducks, but also gathered and sold for human consumption. John had a boat ready on the roof of his car, prepared to start the harvest. When he examined the plants along the edge of the lake, he said that the crop would probably be ripe in another week. He told us that wild rice is a rather sensitive plant, with a low tolerance for changes in water level. Ideally, it should grow in 30–60 centimetres of water, preferably growing shallower as the summer progresses. Preferably, there should be some flow of water through the fields. There must hardly be any salt in the water, and the soil must be good, and not acid as it commonly is in Nova Scotia. The sensitivity of the plant, together with farmers' passion for draining land in past centuries, to create more grassland, has no doubt contributed to the extinction of wild rice in Nova Scotia. Baldur photographed these remarkable fields of "self-sown wheat," and we said farewell to John Wile, and this place where the old resources of Wineland are being recreated (see photo on page iii.)*

A certain Jesuit is said to have given the first description of how the Native Americans harvested wild rice, in the seventeenth century. They cleared narrow channels for their boats by tying the stalks together on either side. When the grain was ripe, they bent the stalks over the boat, knocked off the grain, transported it to shore and stored it in holes on the riverbank. It was subsequently dried on skins or smooth rocks. It was then heated in a pan over a fire, and the husks were loosened by treading. The grain was winnowed by tossing it up in the air and letting it fall into a large vessel; the wind blew the husks away. Finally the grain was placed in bark chests for storage.

This was the account given by the Jesuit, but according to other sources the Native Americans did not all handle the wild rice in the same way.[19] Hence some tribes may have used containers made of wood, as discussed in the section on Thorvald Eiriksson's journey (p. 40).

This description is included here because it is clear from the Saga of the Greenlanders that the Wineland voyagers need not ever have seen Native Americans in order to know about their use of wild rice: the saga tells that Thorvald Eiriksson's men found a grain cover, although they saw no other man-made structure or sign of human habitation.

Wild vines

In the region where the Wineland travellers may have been, two species of wild grapes are found, which they may have been interested in using, i.e. fox grapes and riverbank grapes.

The fox grape (*Vitis labrusca*) is found over a large region of eastern North America. The area of distribution stretches almost as far north as the regions where viticulture has been practised.[20] Its northern limits run from southern Maine westward to Michigan, then southeast to Georgia. In 1606 the explorer Lescarbot found quantities of large, tasty grapes at Saco, at a latitude of 43.5°N.[21] The vines grew three to four feet tall (90–120 centimetres) and grew as thick in places as a fist, with beautiful black grapes, some of which were as big as plums. Farther north, he found smaller grapes in 1607 on his journey along the Saint John River in New Brunswick; this was probably another species, the riverbank grape. At Cape Cod, close to 40°N, Henry Hudson found large, tasty grapes which were undoubtedly fox grapes.

Many cultivated species of fox grapes exist, such as Cotawba. They are used to make such wines as Concord, Champion, Chautaqua, Moore's Early and others. These wild grapes are dark purple or brown in colour, 1.5–2 cm across, and sweet-tasting. Each bunch contains 20 grapes or fewer. The wines have an unusual, so-called "foxy" flavour, which is said to be an acquired taste.[22] The vines climb up tree trunks in coppices and at the edge of woodlands, and are hence found mainly in hilly ground above marshy areas, just as Eirik the Red's Saga describes.

But the grape that the Wineland explorers probably found first is the riverbank grape (*Vitis riparia*). These are smaller, about 1 cm

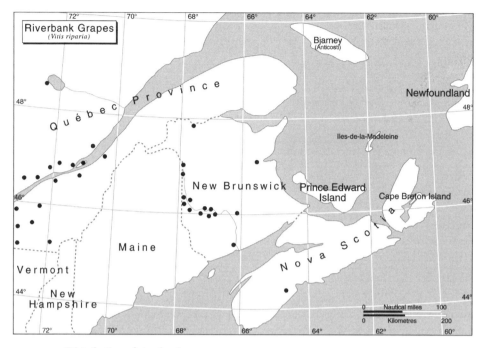

Distribution of riverbank grapes.

in diameter and with a tart taste. They do not require such warm temperatures as the fox grape, and hence grow farther north. These vines were found in a few places in Nova Scotia in the seventeenth century, and also along the Saint John river, far inland from the town of Saint John in New Brunswick. The most northerly location is a short distance northeast of Québec city, near the Montmorency Falls.[23] South of Québec in the St. Lawrence valley, the wild grape is still widespread today, as demonstrated by a map of the flora of the province of Québec (see map above). According to Professor Joseph O. Vandal at Laval University in Québec, the Jesuits soon attempted to make communion wine from the grapes, but the resulting wine was very sour and unpleasant to the taste.[24] An unusual feature of the riverbank grapevine is that it climbs high up into trees. This may explain the statement in the Saga of the Greenlanders that trees were felled in order to gather the grapes, as mentioned before.

Details of the locations in Nova Scotia where fox grapes are known to have grown are shown in the following table:[25]

17*th*-century sources	19*th*-century sources
An island in the East river, near Stellarton, Pictou county (Denys).	*Woods near Stellarton and some miles farther up the East river (Lawson).*
Upper reaches of the Annapolis river, Bear river and Allen's river, Annapolis County (Denys).	*Between Annapolis and Bear river and the other side of Allen's river (Lawson).*
The site of Annapolis, before the forests were cleared (Champlain).	*Near Annapolis and another site less than a mile from Annapolis (Lawson).*

The species of vine is not specified in these cases.

In 1924, riverbank grapes were found near Bridgewater in southwestern Nova Scotia. On my visit to Nova Scotia, I was shown riverbank grapes at an old carding mill in Bridgewater. Riverbanks offer a favourable habitat for the vine, as it requires sunlight, and light conditions are good at the edge of the woods along the riverbank, where reflection from the river provides more light and heat than in the shady woods.

The vines along the St. Lawrence river are known from the time of the second settlement of North America. In 1535 French explorer Jacques Cartier travelled there, and recorded his impressions.[26] His description is consistent with "Wineland the Good," where I believe Leif Eiriksson made his temporary camp:

On both sides of it we found the fairest and best lands to look at that it may be possible to behold – full of the goodiest trees in the world, and so many vines loaded with grapes along the said river that it seems they may rather have been planted there by the hand of man than otherwise: but because they are not cultivated nor pruned, the grapes are not so big and sweet as ours […]

Finest trees in the world: to wit, oaks, elms, &c, and what are better, a great many vines, which had so great abundance of grapes that the crew came aboard all loaded down with them.

Vines were even found on the Île d'Orléans outside Québec, and hence Cartier called the island Île de Bacchus. His description of the size and taste of the grapes seems consistent with the sour riverbank grape *Vitis riparia*, which is still abundant in the St. Lawrence valley. Conditions for viticulture in the Québec area are favourable enough that during the Prohibition years in the USA, the people of Québec cultivated vineyards in order to provide refreshment to their neighbours in the south, supplied via enterprising smugglers. Even if Leif named Wineland for the small, sour riverbank grape, this fruit could have been exotic enough to impress him, just as it did Cartier.

As mentioned above, viticulture is practised to some degree in Nova Scotia, and with success. This is an indication that riverbank grapes could have flourished there in past times.

It was on Friday 16 August 1996 that Baldur and I had seen fields of wild rice (self-sown wheat) near Amherst, Nova Scotia. We travelled on eastwards along the north coast to Malagash, where a vineyard was planted by a German, Hans Jost, who immigrated to Canada in 1970. His family had cultivated grapes in the Rhine valley for more than a century. He settled on a small headland on Northumberland Strait where the sea grows warm in summer and retains its heat into the autumn. This area is also sunnier than southern Nova Scotia, which experiences frequent low-pressure areas and rain in summer. We looked around the vineyards, and saw a presentation on the business; sophisticated equipment and methods are used in pressing and fermenting wines in the cellar. Many different species of grape are used, but the species used most is a hybrid of European grapes (Vitis vinifera), *which gives flavour, and wild American grapes, which are resistant to the American root-pest phylloxera and tolerate cooler conditions than in the wine-growing regions of Europe. This vineyard has recently started producing a variety of Eiswein, in which the grapes are pressed half-frozen; they retain the frozen water, yielding a sweet juice. This ice-wine is named after Matina, the viticulturist's younger daughter. Now deceased, he received many awards for his wines. No doubt this achievement may be attributed to old family traditions, precision and care, but it also confirms that this sunny coast can be regarded as part of Wineland.*

Butternut trees, grapes and wild rice on the Gulf of St. Lawrence

If we assume that those who resided at L'Anse aux Meadows sailed along the coast of the Gulf of St. Lawrence to gather the resources of Wineland, it is highly improbable that they would have found them all together until they had travelled as far west as the present Québec city; at this point, they were all present in abundance.[27] Wild grapes are not present today anywhere else along the shore of the Gulf, and the butternut tree is known only in the Kouchibouguac National Park on the east coast of New Brunswick – but no wild rice is found there. Wild rice is said to exist on Prince Edward Island, and on the west coast of Cape Breton Island, but this is nowhere near any butternut trees or wild vines. This constitutes a strong indication that, along the St. Lawrence, the fruits of Wineland are likely to have been gathered near Québec city. And this is consistent with the accounts of the journeys of Leif the Lucky and his brother Thorvald, which both indicate that they travelled this way. Thorfinn too travelled towards Québec city, when he went in search of Thorhall the Huntsman, who had gone in search of Leif's Wineland.

Skrælings

The Wineland sagas, especially Eirik the Red's Saga, tell of various contacts between Thorfinn Karlsefni's expedition and Native Americans or *skrælings*. Most of these stories are quite believable when compared with other information on the Native Americans. Gathorne-Hardy considered these factors in detail, and his findings include the following:[28]

The skrælings are said to have waved "sticks" ("poles" in *Hauksbók*) on their ships, which made a swishing noise like the flails used in the Nordic countries for threshing grain [*lét því líkast í sem í hálmþústum*]. These Nordic flails consisted of a rod up to a metre in length, with another, shorter piece of wood attached to the end. The saga recounts that the Native Americans' sticks were waved clockwise ("sunwise") when they came in peace, otherwise anti-clockwise ("countersunwise"). It has also been maintained that the Native Americans used a kind of "rattle-stick," as Gathorne-Hardy calls it, in some of their ceremonies. But these may have been simply an early form of the tomahawk or battle-axe; these could bear some resemblance to a flail, with a stone tied to the handle instead of a piece of wood. When waved, they would also make a similar whistling sound to that of flails.[29] Waving the weapons in a certain manner may well have been a sign of whether the Native Americans came in peace or with warlike intentions.

At the battle at Hop, the skrælings raised a large blue sphere on sticks, which flew over the men and made a commotion where it landed. A source from the mid-19th century tells of a primitive weapon used once by the Algonquins.[30] A large boulder was sewn into a covering of fresh hide, and tied to a long pole. The hide tightened around the rock as it dried, and it was then painted with devices. Several warriors carried the weapon, which was then thrown as a missile. As Matthias Thordarson remarked, it would be "unpleasant" to be hit by such a projectile.[31] This weapon appears to have been essentially a giant version of a primitive tomahawk.

The tomahawk was the Native American battle axe. In the most primitive form, a groove was cut into a stone as shown in the picture, and this was then tied to a wooden handle. In the Nordic world, flails for winnowing grain were similarly constructed, but the head was made of wood and not stone.

Eirik the Red's Saga tells of the skrælings' skin boats. This has usually been regarded as a misnomer for the bark boats which were used there. But it transpires that some tribes of Native Americans in New England used boats covered with moose hides in olden times.[32] Moose were common in larch woods, which stretch as far south as New York. The skin boats were regarded as useful on routes where they could be carried from one river to another, and for use during the spring migration of Native Americans from inland areas to the sea. The boats were propelled by paddles.[33] Frank G. Speck describes as follows a hide-covered boat of the 20th century:

> Two or three skins were sewed together head to tail, and the seams were covered with moose tallow boiled with pitch. About a dozen ribs, the keel, thwarts and gunwales, over which the skin covering was stretched, completed the framework.[34]

When Freydis Eiriksdottir beat her bare breast with a sword and prepared to defend herself against the skrælings, they were terrified and ran away. According to Farley Mowat,[35] fighting with women was taboo among the Beothuk, and such a taboo may well have applied in other tribes. It is even possible that Freydis knew of the taboo, and that she acted deliberately to scare off the attacking braves, rather than simply being lucky.

The skrælings are said to have been keen to purchase red cloth from the settlers in return for animal pelts. Henry Hudson said the same in 1609.[36]

On their way from Hop to Straumsfjord, the travellers came across skrælings asleep "in skin sacks" [í skinnhjúpum] near the sea. They had skrokkar ("containers") or according to Hauksbók, stokkar ("vessels") containing marrow and blood of animals. They believed the skrælings were outlaws and killed them. The "skin sacks" may have been their hide cloaks. This event was discussed on pp. 90–91, in connection with Thorfinn Karlsefni's journey. Sven B.F. Jansson believed that the "containers" or "vessels" carried by the skrælings were made of bark or wicker. Other interpretations are possible; for instance, in Faroese, closely related to Old

Norse and Icelandic, the word *skrokkur* means skull.[37] The word *skrokkur* is probably related to *skrukka* (= something shrunken, wrinkled) and so it might refer to a pouch of hide. Gathorne-Hardy quotes the explorer Denys in his work on Nova Scotia as saying that when the Native Americans went on hunting trips they took only *pemmican* – cakes of hardened fat from the bones of moose – for food. Leclerq too mentions pemmican in his book on Gaspésie. The Encyclopaedia Britannica describes pemmican as follows: "Thin slices of lean bison or venison were dried in the sun and then pounded to a powder, seasoned, blended with equal parts of melted fat and packed in raw-hide bags."[38] This food kept well, and was eaten raw. It could also be cooked in a broth of grain, to which berries or dried fruit might be added. The European settlers, especially French settlers in Canada, learned from the Native Americans how to make pemmican, and a variant of pemmican made from beef was used by explorers until the 20th century.

The description in Eirik the Red's saga, however, is more consistent with the account given by Arctic explorer Vilhjalmur Stefansson, who informed Gathorne-Hardy that the Inuit, from the Bering Strait to Hudson Bay, commonly stored reindeer marrow in pouches for later use. In marrow stored in this way, blood separates out.[39] Helge Ingstad confirmed this with a member of the Naskapi tribe in Labrador, who told him that this was a common food, called *monapon*.[40] These foods all appear to be similar in nature, and support the credibility of Eirik the Red's Saga.

Eirik's Saga implies that the skrælings understood the significance of a white shield for peace, and a red symbol for war. Gathorne-Hardy quotes Wood in his Natural History of Man as saying that these colours had the same meaning for the Native Americans, and that their chiefs commonly carried two small banners, one of white bison hide, the other of reddened leather.

When the skrælings attacked, the saga says that they gave a howling cry. The ululating Native American war-cry is well-known, and the saga describes it perfectly.

The skrælings on the Gaspé peninsula and in Labrador were mentioned above. Eirik's Saga gives the following description of the skrælings at Hop.

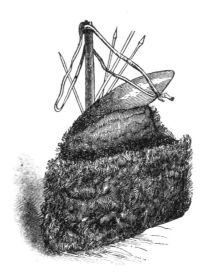

Drawing of a Native American pouch, made of animal skin and used for storing, among other things, food on journeys. The five skrælings killed by Thorfinn's company may have stored their supplies in such pouches.

They were short in height [*Hauksbók*: black-haired] with threatening features and tangled hair on their heads. Their eyes were large and their cheeks broad. They stayed there awhile, marvelling, then rowed away again to the south around the point.

The inference is that the headland was on one side of the narrow place where the river flowed into the sea. This may be consistent with the river flowing from the north, like the Hudson river in New York, since they rowed south round the headland. This is also consistent with the hypothesis that Thorfinn settled at Gowanus Bay in Brooklyn, discussed above (p. 88).

Gathorne-Hardy wrote of the descriptions of skrælings in the Wineland Sagas:

The descriptions are accurate and lifelike, and show no clear traces of features borrowed from Celtic or other romantic sources. On the whole, then, we may assert confidently that the sagas contain accurate descriptions of American Indians,

A Native American, captured by a hostile tribe, is cast on a fire, but waves his tomahawk and is unscathed by the flames. From Nine Micmac Legends by Alden Nowlan. Drawing Shirley Bear.

and that these, made at a time when savages were otherwise unknown to the Norsemen, constitute an unimpeachable confirmation of the essential historic accuracy of the story.[41]

The first day that Baldur and I were in Halifax, 14 August 1996, we set out to find out what we could about the Micmac tribe of Native Americans. We went to the Micmac Heritage Gallery. Only one of the two assistants said she had a little Micmac blood in her veins – not the one I would have expected. Various souvenirs were offered for sale, and I noticed a collection of stories by a well-known Canadian writer, Alden Nowlan, illustrated by Shirley Bear. These are retellings of traditional Micmac tales collected by a Baptist missionary in Nova Scotia in the 19th century. Nowlan has aimed to approach the original stories as far as possible, excluding anything that the Native Americans could not have known before the arrival of the white man. But he says that the stories undoubtedly reflect considerable European influence, nonetheless. And perhaps they may contain some thousand-year-old memories of Icelanders and Greenlanders, together with horrors and dreams on how to defeat the enemy and drive him out of the land he claimed, although he had no right to it?

We went on to the Micmac Friendship Center in Göttingen Street, where we were warmly welcomed, and shown this very modest social centre; the chairs, for instance, were a random collection. But this was the Micmacs' own haven, where the aim was to help people to be self-reliant and gain confidence.

Six days later we visited a Native American area in Millbrook just south of Truro on the west coast of Nova Scotia. We happened upon a group of Native Americans who were marching to raise money for Native American children. Their leader had walked all the way from British Columbia, on the other side of the continent. It was a special experience for Baldur and me to come face to face with this group. Shortly afterwards we went into a souvenir shop, where I bought a figure I call the "Native American widow" holding her baby. It reminds me of the skrælings slain by Thorvald and his men at Krossanes for no reason at all. But their companions gathered forces, killed Thorvald, and drove off his followers. No doubt this event was remembered for a long time among the Ellena tribe, as Nowland says they called themselves.

Scandinavian wildcats

The interpretation of Eirik the Red's Saga put forward in this book supposes that Thorfinn Karlsefni travelled south by way of New York, and so it may be regarded as likely that he and his company explored the coast from the Bay of Fundy to New York, including Boston and its environs. Interestingly enough, statistical studies by zoologists Stefan Adalsteinsson and B. Blumenberg indicate that, unlike other North American cats, the cats of New York and

Boston are closely related to the feline population of islands colonised by Scandinavians, including Iceland.[42] In past centuries, cats were commonly kept on board ship to protect the cargo from rats and mice. The unusual characteristics of the New York and Boston cats could be due to cats or kittens being released, or escaping, from the ships of the Norse explorers a thousand years ago. Since the climate was mild enough to enable them to hunt and fend for themselves, the cats turned feral and bred in the wild. When the second European influx began five centuries later, the feral cats were reunited with their European cousins. Since the feral cats were far more numerous, they dominated the gene pool of cats in the region. The feral cats keep a low profile and avoid contact with man. Even if the settlers of the sixteenth century were aware of the wild cat population, this need not have surprised them, as domestic cats can easily turn feral.

At Blue Hills in south Boston, the lowest winter temperatures at sea level are -2°C. Farther north the winters are harsher. At the mouth of the Bay of Fundy, which I believe to be Straumsfjord, average January temperatures sink as low as -8°C with heavy snow.[43] Icelandic cats would have had difficulty surviving such chilly conditions if they had attempted to live in the wild in this area, and indeed there is no similarity between the cats of Saint John on the Bay of Fundy and the cats of Iceland.

This feline study provides yet more support for the hypothesis proposed here on Thorfinn Karlsefni's journeys, and no scholarly arguments have been put forward to refute this theory of the feline colonisation of North America from the Scandinavian world.

1 Pall Bergthorsson 1987.
2 Magnus Mar Larusson 1969.
3 *Book of Settlements* 1986.
4 Helge Ingstad 1985.
5 D.R. Grant 1975.
6 Askell Löve 1951.
7 Birgitta Wallace 1991a.

8 H.J. Scoggan 1978–79.
9 Askell Löve 1951.
10 Thormodur Torfason 1715.
11 M.L. Fernald 1910.
12 M.L. Fernald et. al. 1950.
13 Askell Löve 1951.
14 *Vikings. The North Atlantic Saga.* 2000.
15 George Usher, 1974.
16 David Attenborough 1995.
17 S.G. Aiken et. al. 1988.
18 Einar Ingi Siggeirsson, personal communication.
19 S.G. Aiken et. al. 1988.
20 Hugh Johnson 1985.
21 Marc Lescarbot 1911.
22 Hugh Johnson 1985.
23 H.J. Scoggan 1978–79.
24 Joseph O. Vandal 1986.
25 Mats G. Larsson 1992.
26 William Hovgaard 1914.
27 H.J. Scoggan 1978–79.
28 G.M. Gathorne-Hardy 1921.
29 *Norsk Landbruksordbok* 1979.
30 Henry R. Schoolcraft 1851.
31 Matthias Thordarson 1929.
32 Frank G. Speck 1940.
33 Mats G. Larsson 1992.
34 Edward Reman 1990.
35 Farley Mowat 1966.
36 G.M. Gathorne-Hardy 1921.
37 Asgeir Blöndal Magnusson 1989.
38 *Encyclopaedia Britannica.*
39 Olafur Halldorsson 1978.
40 Helge Ingstad 1969.
41 G.M. Gathorne-Hardy 1921.
42 Stefan Adalsteinsson and B. Blumenberg 1983.
43 *Canadian Climate Normals* 1961–1990.

PRINCIPAL CONCLUSIONS

Bjarni Herjolfsson was carried off course at sea shortly before AD 999, and as a result became the first European to find the North American continent. He studied the land from the sea, so that he was able to provide useful directions to subsequent expeditions. His first landfall was probably in Labrador, south of Hamilton Inlet, after which he sailed northwards over a period of two half-days (about 24 hours), to Davis Inlet or Nain. He then sailed on northwards to Resolution Island in three half-days (about 36 hours), whence he could see the Grinnel and Hall glaciers on Baffin Island, and sailed eastwards to Greenland in four half-days (about 48 hours). The account of Bjarni's journey includes very convincing descriptions of the sea passage.

The account of Leif Eiriksson's journey to Wineland given in the Saga of the Greenlanders is more detailed, and also more credible, than the version in Eirik the Red's Saga. Leif probably set off from Greenland in AD1001, retracing Bjarni's journey; he arrived first at Baffin Island, which he called Helluland (Stone-slab Land), then crossed the Hudson Strait to Labrador, which he named Markland (Forest Land). Sailing between Labrador and Newfoundland, he may have made landfall on the small Cybele Bay, south of the easternmost point of Anticosti. He then went on westwards along the Gulf of St. Lawrence, to where Québec city now stands; here he found grapes. In the autumn he probably went to Newfoundland, where he built "large houses," Leif's Camp, at the place now called L'Anse aux Meadows. He returned to Greenland the following summer.

The next expedition was led by Thorvald Eiriksson, Leif's brother. He set off probably in AD 1002, and wintered at Leif's Camp. During the first summer he explored the south shore of the Gulf of St. Lawrence, starting in the west, where a grain cover was found on an island, probably the Île d'Orléans. In the autumn he returned to Leif's Camp. The following summer he explored the south coast of the Gulf farther east. The keel of his ship was damaged at Kjalarnes (Keel Point), probably Cape North on Cape Breton Island, the northern part of Nova Scotia. He was delayed there while the ship was repaired. He then sailed on southwards along the east coast of Nova Scotia, where he reached a wooded headland, Krossanes (Cross Point), probably Kelly's Point at New Campbellton on Big Bras D'Or. He thought of making his home here, but was killed in a hail of Native American arrows. He was probably buried at Krossanes, while the rest of his company gathered the resources of Wineland and returned home to Greenland in the spring.

The next expedition bound for Wineland was led by Thorstein Eiriksson, another son of Eirik the Red. He set off probably in 1006, was carried off course and did not reach Wineland. After being caught in storms at sea, the travellers reached the Western Settlement, where Thorstein and many of his ship's company died of a fever. Their bodies were taken back to Eiriksfjord for burial, and may lie buried at the south wall of Thjodhild's church.

Thorfinn Karlsefni was the leader of the fifth expedition. The account of his journey in Eirik the Red's Saga is far more detailed than in the Saga of the Greenlanders, and probably more reliable. The expedition comprised three ships and 140 or 160 people. Thorfinn appears to have sailed from Eirik the Red's farmstead at Brattahlid in the summer of AD 1008. He set off northwards along the west coast of Greenland to the Bear Islands, then in two half-days (24 hours) across to Baffin Island, at the narrowest point of the Davis Strait. He then sailed southwards along the coast of Baffin Island, which he called Helluland (Stone-slab Land) because of the peculiar stone slabs he saw there. Then he crossed the Hudson Strait in two half-days (24 hours). This brought him to Labrador, which he called Markland (Forest Land), and sailed on to the island of Anticosti which he called Bjarney (Bear Island). From here he crossed the Gulf of St. Lawrence in two half-days (24 hours), and sailed around Kjalarnes (Keel Point, now Cape North), with the land on the starboard side. He then sailed along Furdustrandir, the east and southeast coast of Nova Scotia, where Haki and Hekja found grapes and self-sown wheat. In the autumn

Thorfinn settled on the Bay of Fundy, which he called Straums-fjord – possibly where the town of Saint John now stands. This is the birthplace of the first Nordic child born in America: Snorri, son of Thorfinn Karlsefni and his wife Gudrid Thorbjarnardottir. During the first winter, food and fodder ran out, and the settlers moved out to Grand Manan Island, which they called Straumsey. The following summer some of the company travelled south to Hop; the description of the environment is consistent with New York; more precisely, Gowanus Bay in Brooklyn. The settlers traded with Native Americans, but soon found themselves in conflict with them, and withdrew northwards into Straumsfjord the following spring. They travelled with only one vessel northwards past Furdustrandir and Kjalarnes, west of the Gaspé peninsula, to the region they called the Land of the One-Legged, in search of Thorhall the Huntsman and his party. They made excellent geographical observations, described the position of mountain ranges, and the relative distance between Hop, Straumsfjord and the Land of the One-Legged. They probably intended to search for Thorhall in Leif's Wineland, where Québec city now stands, but had to retreat, and spent the winter at Straumsfjord. Disputes arose among the members of the party; Thorfinn abandoned the idea of settling in Wineland and returned to Greenland. On their way, probably in Labrador, they seized two Inuit boys, baptised them and taught them their language.

Freydis Eiriksdottir, daughter of Eirik the Red, led the sixth Wineland expedition; she commanded one ship, while two Icelanders captained the other. They set off around AD1012. They spent the winter at Leif's Camp, where Freydis had all the Icelanders slain, and returned to Greenland with their ship the following spring.

The seventh Wineland voyage was made by Bishop Eirik Gnupsson of Greenland in 1121.

The sources
The Saga of the Greenlanders and Eirik the Red's Saga were probably recorded independently, based on traditional tales; these may be to some extent common to both sagas. In the Saga of the Greenlanders, the intention would appear to be to tell of all the known Wineland voyages. Eirik the Red's Saga, on the contrary,

focuses on Gudrid Thorbjarnardottir and her husband Thorfinn Karlsefni, and their Wineland journey, while devoting less space to other expeditions, except where they are relevant to the story of Gudrid and Thorfinn.

Genealogical details given at the end of both sagas may perhaps provide a clue to the provenance and age of the sagas: in the Saga of the Greenlanders, the emphasis is placed upon Gudrid's descendant Bishop Brand Sæmundarson (1162–1201), while in Eirik the Red's saga, Bishop Thorlak Runolfsson (1086–1133) is given more prominence. The original version of Eirik the Red's Saga may have been written early in the 12th century in the days of Bishop Thorlak, who was a great-grandson of Gudrid and Thorfinn. If Bishop Brand, also a descendant of Gudrid and Thorfinn, contributed to the writing of the Saga of the Greenlanders, this was probably in the late 12th century.

My policy has been to regard both sagas as credible as far as possible. Where they are not consistent, I have generally taken the more detailed account to be the more reliable.

Sailing speeds
Experiments with replicas of Viking vessels – longship and *knörr* – have demonstrated that they could achieve higher sailing speeds than has generally been believed until the 20th century. In average summer wind conditions, a longship can sail at 10 knots (10 nautical miles per hour) with a following wind, while a *knörr* can reach 8 knots. They can sail at a considerable angle to the wind, so they make some way even in a headwind, and with a sidewind they sail at almost full speed. If winds are experienced equally from all directions, at average wind speeds, a *knörr* would thus achieve an average speed of 75–80 nautical miles over 12 hours (one half-day), while a longship should sail nearly 90 nautical miles in the same conditions. This is entirely consistent with the information given in many old sources, that it took seven half-days (three-and-a-half days) to sail between Stad in Norway and Horn on the East Fjords of Iceland.

Navigational aids
Adjustments made to the Icelandic almanac by Thorstein Surt in

the 10th century indicate that the movements of the sun were well understood. And evidence of sophisticated knowledge of astronomy is provided by Star-Oddi's observations of solar altitude and the azimuth of the sun at dawn and dusk.

Various simpler methods which were used to measure solar altitude, such as observation of when the sun was "shaft-high" and a method of finding the altitude of the Pole Star south in Palestine, are interesting.

Credible accounts of observed solar altitude on Kroksfjardarheidi and in Gardar, in Greenland, indicate that observations of the sun's altitude were also made in Greenland, for practical purposes.

The old Icelandic encyclopaedia *Rím II* gives a detailed description of a quadrant, used for measuring the altitude of the sun on sea and land, but it is not clear when this instrument was first used.

An early nineteenth-century Faroese source tells of a simple but practical instrument for measuring the altitude of the sun, a gnomon, which is similar to instruments used as long ago as in Ancient Greece. This enabled the navigator to tell whether the ship was being carried northwards or southwards, off a course along a line of latitude. This would have been even more useful if Star-Oddi's knowledge of the seasonal variations in the sun's path were generally known. Circular patterns on the Gokstad ship, and archaeological finds from Greenland and Iceland, may indicate that gnomons were used in navigation in the Saga Age.

The Saga of the Greenlanders states that the sun was visible from *eyktarstaður* to *dagmálastaður* at the darkest season of the year at Leif's Camp. *Eyktarstaður* was 52.5° west of south, and was used as a yardstick for when the hour of nones (3 p.m.) had arrived, in summer. The observation that the sun was visible from 52.5° east of south to 52.5° west of south at the darkest time of the year is consistent with the latitude of the ruins of Leif's Camp at L'Anse aux Meadows.

A copper disc from Storaborg, south Iceland, which probably dates from the 13th century, appears to have been a sundial that showed the correct hours in midsummer. It indicates that fairly accurate methods of measuring time were available in olden times.

A water-clock existed at Krysuvik, and another at Hvamm in Kjos, in southwest Iceland, around 1570. These indicate that this method of measuring time, used by the ancient Egyptians and the Romans, was known in Iceland in the medieval period.

Old writings mention a "sun stone" which was said to enable the observer to pinpoint the sun, even in cloudy weather. This is unlikely to have been a useful navigational instrument.

The theory is proposed here that the *húsasnotra* was not an ornament, as has generally been assumed, but some form of astrolabe, a valuable navigational aid, known in ancient Greece more than 2,000 years ago. The archaeological find of what appears to be a navigational instrument at the Île de Groix in France supports this conclusion. A piece of oak found in Greenland may also have been a primitive astrolabe.

Seafarers found themselves in difficulties when they did not see the sun for days at a time. Under these circumstances, their knowledge of the kind of weather conditions that tend to accompany certain wind directions would have been a useful guide.

Many other indications could provide clues to seafarers, such as sightings of birds and whales, their behaviour, variations in the colour and temperature of the sea, the sound of crashing surf and the cacophony of birdcliffs, odours from land such as the scent of new-mown hay and forests, sightings of familiar landmarks such as mountains, mirages, cloud formations over land masses and mountains, the blink of sea ice, the direction of swell and wind-driven waves, and depth measurements by a sounding line.

   Another important factor was to choose the safest sailing route, keeping land masses and islands in sight for as much of the route as possible.

Archaeological evidence

Greenland abounds in archaeological sites which serve to confirm the evidence of the Wineland sagas with regard to Greenland and the Nordic settlement there. From this it may be inferred that the Wineland passages of the sagas are also, broadly speaking, reliable.

A lump of anthracite found in the Western Settlement in Greenland may have been brought there from Rhode Island in the USA. A quartzite arrowhead found nearby is believed to be of Native American type. And larch coffins from the cemetery at Herjolfsnes are probably made of timber brought from the New World.

By far the most important archaeological evidence is that of the L'Anse aux Meadows site in Newfoundland, which is in all probability Leif's Camp. This hypothesis is supported by the fact that the observations of the position of the sun made by Leif's company are consistent with the Newfoundland site. This provides a strong indication that the Wineland explorers travelled along the Gulf of St. Lawrence, rather than southwards along the east coast of Newfoundland. This facilitates the search for other places connected with the Wineland voyages.

A silver coin found in Maine, USA, may have been brought to America by Eirik Gnupsson, Bishop of Greenland.

Various archaeological evidence that was supposed to prove the truth of the Wineland voyages turned out to be falsified, and the same may apply to the so-called Vínland Map, especially because of the continuing mystery surrounding its provenance.

Conditions in Wineland

In all probability, the climate of the time of the Wineland voyages was broadly similar to that experienced in northern regions in the warm period from 1930 to 1960. Colder periods probably occurred from time to time, however, similar to those experienced in 1960-1990. Vegetation patterns are likely to have been similar to those of the present day, taking into account man-made changes. Grapes, "self-sown wheat" (wild rice) and butternuts, as found in the ruins at L'Anse aux Meadows, still grow on the Gulf of St. Lawrence. But only at one point in the Gulf, along the St. Lawrence valley, are all these species found in the same place. Thus the probability is that this was where the travellers found the resources of Wineland, except for Thorfinn Karlsefni, who went on south to Hop. This was probably New York, where superior species of grapes and wild rice were to be found.

The descriptions of indigenous peoples in the Wineland sagas are credible in light of modern knowledge of their history and culture.

AFTERWORD

Interpreting saga literature as history has tended to meet with disapproval in recent years, and no doubt the sagas are far from fulfilling modern standards of history writing. However, in this study of the topography of the Wineland sagas, it was surprising to find how easily the Wineland voyages could be traced, one after the other, step by step, and how the account was backed up by modern knowledge of the nature and people of the areas. This applies both to individual events, and to the overall picture depicted. It would of course be unreasonable to expect every word of the sagas to be true; no doubt oral accounts were passed from person to person for at least a hundred years, until the sagas were written down – and perhaps much longer. The copying and recopying of manuscripts may also have led to corruptions.

It is hardly necessary to state that the enigma of Wineland has not been fully solved. No doubt some of the hypotheses put forward here will require revision, or may even be wrong. The task requires the participation not only of historians, but also various other specialists, in such fields as natural sciences, archaeology, navigation and anthropology. In this book I have focussed largely on Québec, the Bay of Fundy and New York as possible places where the Wineland voyagers may have been, in addition to Leif's Camp at L'Anse aux Meadows. But other places, of course, should be considered, without allowing preconceived ideas to have too much influence on the study. In most of these places, the search for archaeological evidence is difficult because of urban development and other disruption of the natural environment, but other topographical evidence can still provide many clues to the credibility of the sagas. To some degree, such studies may be as good as archaeological evidence.

But, in spite of many unanswered questions, I hope that I have succeeded in demonstrating that much of the content of the sagas can be supported by evidence now available to us, on the natural environment and folkways of the New World, ancient and modern.

Acknowledgements

Finally, I wish to thank the many men and women who have contributed to the writing of this book. President Olafur Ragnar Grimsson and his late wife Gudrun Katrin Thorbergsdottir took a keen interest in the project, as witness the president's foreword. I thank Dr. Olafur Halldorsson for his advice and encouragement. Translator Anna Yates has worked with meticulous care, and been very patient with me and my methods of work. I thank the Leifur Eiriksson publishing company, Penguin Books, and translator Keneva Kunz for their kind permission to use their translations of the Saga of the Greenlanders and Eirik the Red's Saga. And my publisher, Mál og menning, has spared no effort in the publication of the book. The Icelandic Research Council contributed to the costs of my travels to areas probably visited by the Wineland voyagers.

EIRIK THE RED'S SAGA

1   There was a warrior king named Oleif who was called Oleif the White.

He was the son of King Ingjald, who was the son of Helgi, who was son of Olaf, who was son of Gudrod, who was son of Halfdan White-leg, king of the people of Oppland.

Oleif went on Viking expeditions around Britain, conquering the shire of Dublin, over which he declared himself king. As his wife he took Aud the Deep-minded, the daughter of Ketil Flat-nose, son of Bjorn Buna, an excellent man from Norway. Their son was named Thorstein the Red.

After Oleif was killed in battle in Ireland, Aud and Thorstein went to the Hebrides. There Thorstein married Thurid, the daughter of Eyvind the Easterner and sister of Helgi the Lean. They had a large number of children.

Thorstein became a warrior king, throwing in his lot with Earl Sigurd the Powerful, the son of Eystein Glumra. They conquered Caithness and Sutherland, Ross and Moray, and more than half of Scotland. Thorstein became king there until the Scots betrayed him and he was killed in battle.

Aud was at Caithness when she learned of the death of Thorstein. She had a knorr built secretly in the forest and, when it was finished, set out for the Orkneys. There she arranged the marriage of Groa, Thorstein the Red's daughter. Groa was the mother of Grelod, who was married to Earl Thorfinn the Skull-splitter.

After this Aud set out for Iceland. On her ship she had a crew of twenty free-born men. Aud reached Iceland and spent the first winter in Bjarnarhofn with her brother Bjorn. Afterwards Aud claimed all the land in the Dales between the Dagverdara and Skraumuhlaupsa rivers and settled at Hvamm.

She used to pray on the Krossholar hill, where she had crosses erected, for she was baptized and a devout Christian. Accompanying her on her journey to Iceland were many men of good family who had been taken prisoner by Vikings raiding around Britain and were called bondsmen. One of them was named Vifil. He was a man of very good family who had been taken prisoner in Britain and was called a bondsman until Aud gave him his freedom. When Aud gave her crew farm sites, Vifil asked her why she had not given him one like the others. Aud replied that it made no difference [whether he owned land or not], he would be considered just as fine a man wherever he was. Aud gave him Vifilsdal and he settled there.

He had a wife and two sons, Thorgeir and Thorbjorn. They were promising men and grew up with their father.

2   There was a man named Thorvald, the son of Asvald Ulfsson, son of Ox-Thorir. His son was named Eirik the Red. Father and son left Jaeren and sailed to Iceland because [they had been involved in] slayings.

They claimed land on the coast of Hornstrandir and settled at Drangar.

There Thorvald died.

As his wife Eirik took Thjodhild, the daughter of Jorund Atlason. Her mother, Thorbjorg Ship-breast, was married to Thorbjorn of Haukadal then.

Eirik then moved south, cleared land in Haukadal and built a farm at Eiriksstadir by Vatnshorn.

Eirik's slaves then caused a landslide to fall on the farm of Valthjof at Valthjofsstadir. His kinsman Filth-Eyjolf killed the slaves near Skeidsbrekkur above Vatnshorn. For this, Eirik slew Filth-Eyjolf. He also killed Hrafn the Dueller at Leikskalar. Geirstein and Odd of Jorvi, Eyjolf's kinsmen, sought redress for his killing.

After this Eirik was outlawed from Haukadal. He claimed the islands Brokey and Oxney and farmed at Tradir on Sudurey island the first winter.

It was then Eirik lent Thorgest bedstead boards. Later he moved to Oxney where he farmed at Eiriksstadir. He then asked for the bedstead boards back without success. Eirik went to Breidabolstad and took the boards, and Thorgest came after him. They fought not far from the farm at Drangar, where two of Thorgest's sons were killed, along with several other men.

After that both of them kept a large following. Eirik had the support of Styr and Eyjolf of Sviney, Thorbjorn Vifilsson and the sons of Thorbrand of Alftafjord, while Thord Bellower and Thorgeir of Hitardal, Aslak of Langadal and his son Illugi gave their support to Thorgest. Eirik and his companions were sentenced to outlawry at the Thorsnes Assembly. He made his ship ready in Eiriksvog and Eyjolf hid him in Dimunarvog while Thorgest and his men searched the islands for him. Thorbjorn, Eyjolf and Styr accompanied Eirik through the islands. Eirik said he intended to seek out the land that Gunnbjorn, the son of Ulf Crow, had seen when he was driven off course westward and discovered Gunnbjarnarsker (Gunnbjorn's skerry). If he found the land he promised to return to his friends and they parted with great warmth. Eirik promised to support them in any way he could if they should need his help.

Eirik sailed seaward from Snaefellsnes and approached land [in Greenland] under the glacier called Hvitserk (White shift). From there he sailed southwards, seeking suitable land for settlement.

He spent the first winter on Eiriksey island, near the middle of the eastern settlement. The following spring he travelled to Eiriksfjord where he settled. That summer he travelled around the [then] uninhabited western settlement, giving names to a number of sites. The second winter he spent in Eiriksholmar near Hvarfsgnipa, and the third summer he sailed as far north as Snaefell and into Hrafnsfjord. There he thought he had reached the head of Eiriksfjord. He then returned to spend the third winter in Eiriksey, at the mouth of Eiriksfjord.

The following summer he sailed to Iceland and made land in Breidafjord.

He spent the winter with Ingolf at Holmlatur. The following spring he fought with Thorgest and lost, after which they made their peace.

In the summer Eirik left to settle in the country he had found, which he called Greenland, as he said people would be attracted there if it had a favourable name.

3   Thorgeir Vifilsson took as his wife Arnora, the daughter of Einar of Laugarbrekka, the son of Sigmund, son of Ketil Thistle who had claimed land in Thistilfjord.

Einar had another daughter named Hallveig. She was married to Thorbjorn Vifilsson and was given land at Laugarbrekka, at Hellisvellir. Thorbjorn moved his household there and became a man of great worth. He ran a prosperous farm and lived in grand style. Gudrid was the name of Thorbjorn's daughter. She was the most attractive of women and one to be reckoned with in all her dealings.

A man named Orm farmed at Arnarstapi. His wife was named Halldis.

Orm was a good farmer and a great friend of Thorbjorn's. The couple fostered Gudrid, who spent long periods of time there.

A man named Thorgeir farmed at Thorgeirsfell. He was very rich in livestock and was a freed slave. He had a son named Einar, a handsome and capable man, with a liking for fine dress. Einar went on trading voyages abroad, at which he was quite successful, and he usually spent the winters in Iceland and Norway by turn.

It is said that one autumn, when Einar was in Iceland, he travelled with his goods out to the Snaefellsnes peninsula, intending to sell them. He came to Arnarstapi and Orm invited him to stay with them, which Einar accepted, as friendship was included in the bargain. Einar's goods were placed in a shed. He took them out to show to Orm and his household, and asked Orm to choose as much as he wished for himself. Orm accepted and praised Einar as both a merchant of good repute and man of great fortune. While they were occupied with the goods a woman passed in front of the shed doorway.

Einar asked Orm who this beautiful woman was who had passed in front of the doorway – 'I haven't seen her here before.' Orm said, 'That is Gudrid, my foster-daughter, the daughter of the farmer Thorbjorn of Laugarbrekka.' Einar spoke: 'She'd make a fine match. Or has anyone already turned up to ask for her hand?' Orm answered, 'She's been asked for right enough, my friend, but is no easy prize. As it turns out, she is choosy about her husband, as is her father as well.' 'Be that as it may,' Einar spoke, 'she's the woman I intend to propose to, and I would like you to put my proposal to her father, and if you do your best to support my suit I'll repay you with the truest of friendship. Farmer Thorbjorn should see that we'd be well connected, as he's a man of high repute and has a good farm, but I'm told his means have been much depleted.

My father and I lack neither land nor means, so we'd be a considerable support to Thorbjorn if the match were concluded.' Orm answered, 'Though I think of myself as your friend, I'm not eager to breach the question with him, for Thorbjorn is prone to take offence, and a man with no small sense of his own worth.' Einar replied he would not be satisfied unless the proposal was made, and Orm said he would have his way. Einar headed south once more until he arrived back home.

Some time later Thorbjorn held an autumn feast, as was his custom, for he lived in high style. Orm from Arnarstapi attended and many other friends of Thorbjorn's.

Orm managed to speak privately to Thorbjorn and told him of the recent visit by Einar of Thorgeirsfell, who was becoming a man of promise. Orm then put Einar's proposal to Thorbjorn and said it would be suitable on a number of accounts – 'it would be a considerable support to you as far as money is concerned'. Thorbjorn answered, 'I never expected to hear such words from you, telling me to marry my daughter to the son of a slave, as you suggest now, since you think I'm running short of money. She'll not go back with you, since you think her worthy of such a lowly match.' Orm then returned home and all the other guests went to their homes.

Gudrid stayed behind with her father and spent that winter at home. When spring came Thorbjorn invited some friends to a feast. The provisions were plentiful, and it was attended by many people who enjoyed the finest of feasts.

During the feasting Thorbjorn called for silence, then spoke: 'Here I have lived a life of some length. I have enjoyed the kindness and warmth of others, and to my mind our dealings have gone well. My financial situation, however, which has not up to now been considered an unworthy one, is on the decline. So I would rather leave my farm than live with this loss of honour, and rather leave the country than shame my family. I intend to take up the offer made to me by my friend Eirik the Red, when he took his leave of me in Breidafjord. I intend to head for Greenland this summer if things go as I wish.' These plans caused a great stir, as Thorbjorn had long been popular, but it was generally felt that once he had spoken in this way there would be little point in trying to dissuade him. Thorbjorn gave people gifts and the feast came to an end after this, with everyone returning to their homes.

Thorbjorn sold his lands and bought a ship which had been beached at the Hraunhafnaros estuary. Thirty men accompanied him on his voyage.

Among them were Orm of Arnarstapi and his wife, and other friends of Thorbjorn's who did not want to part with him.

After this they set sail but the weather, which had been favourable when they set out, changed. The favourable wind dropped and they were beset by storms, so that they made little progress during the summer. Following this, illness plagued their company, and Orm and his wife and half the company died. The sea swelled and their boat took on much water but, despite many other hardships, they made land in Greenland at Herjolfsnes during the Winter Nights.

At Herjolfsnes lived a man named Thorkel. He was a capable man and the best of farmers. He gave Thorbjorn and all his companions shelter for the winter, treating them generously. Thorbjorn and all his companions were highly pleased.

4   This was a very lean time in Greenland. Those who had gone hunting had had poor catches, and some of them had failed to return.

In the district there lived a woman named Thorbjorg, a seeress who was called the 'Little Prophetess'. She was one of ten sisters, all of whom had the gift of prophecy, and was the only one of them still alive.

It was Thorbjorg's custom to spend the winter visiting, one after another, farms to which she had been invited, mostly by people curious to learn of their own future or what was in store for the coming year. Since Thorkel was the leading farmer there, people felt it was up to him to try to find out when the hard times which had been oppressing them would let up. Thorkel invited the seeress to visit and preparations were made to entertain her well, as was the custom of the time when a woman of this type was received. A high seat was set for her, complete with cushion. This was to be stuffed with chicken feathers.

When she arrived one evening, along with the man who had been sent to fetch her, she was wearing a black mantle with a strap, which was adorned with precious stones right down to the hem. About her neck she wore a string of glass beads and on her head a hood of black lambskin lined with white catskin. She bore a staff with a knob at the top, adorned with brass set with stones on top. About her waist she had a linked charm belt with a large purse. In it she kept the charms which she needed for her predictions.

She wore calfskin boots lined with fur, with long, sturdy laces and large pewter knobs on the ends. On her hands she wore gloves of catskin, white and lined with fur.

When she entered, everyone was supposed to offer her respectful greetings, and she responded according to how the person appealed to her. Farmer Thorkel took the wise woman by the hand and led her to the seat which had been prepared for her. He then asked her to survey his flock, servants and buildings. She had little to say about all of it.

That evening tables were set up and food prepared for the seeress. A porridge of kid's milk was made for her and as meat she was given the hearts of all the animals available there. She had a spoon of brass and a knife with an ivory shaft, its two halves clasped with bronze bands, and the point of which had broken off.

Once the tables had been cleared away, Thorkel approached Thorbjorg and asked what she thought of the house there and the conduct of the household, and how soon he could expect an answer to what he had asked and everyone wished to know. She answered that she would not reveal this until the next day after having spent the night there. Late the following day she was provided with things she required to carry out her magic rites. She asked for women who knew the chants required for carrying out magic rites, which are called ward songs. But such women were not to be found. Then the people of the household were asked if there was anyone with such knowledge.

Gudrid answered, 'I have neither magical powers nor the gift of prophecy, but in Iceland my foster-mother, Halldis, taught me chants she called ward songs.' Thorbjorg answered, 'Then you know more than I expected.' Gudrid said, 'These are the sort of actions in which I intend to take no part, because I am a Christian woman.' Thorbjorg answered: 'It could be that you could help the people here by so doing, and you'd be no worse a woman for that. But I expect Thorkel to provide me with what I need.' Thorkel then urged Gudrid, who said she would do as he wished. The women formed a warding ring around the platform raised for sorcery, with Thorbjorg perched atop it. Gudrid spoke the chant so well and so beautifully that people there said they had never heard anyone recite in a fairer voice.

The seeress thanked her for her chant. She said many spirits had been attracted who thought the chant fair to hear – 'though earlier they wished to turn their backs on us and refused to do our bidding. Many things are now clear to me which were earlier concealed from both me and others.

And I can tell you that this spell of hardship will last no longer, and times will improve as the spring advances. The bout of illness which has long plagued you will also improve sooner than you expect. And you, Gudrid, I will reward on the spot for the help we have received, since your fate is now very clear to me. You will make the most honourable of matches here in Greenland, though you won't be putting down roots here, as your path leads to Iceland and from you will be descended a long and worthy line.

Over all the branches of that family a bright ray will shine. May you fare well, now, my child.' After that people approached the wise woman to learn what each of them was most curious to know. She made them good answer, and little that she predicted did not occur.

Following this an escort arrived from another farm and the seeress departed. Thorbjorn was also sent for, as he had refused to remain at home on the farm while such heathen practices were going on.

With the arrival of spring the weather soon improved, as Thorbjorg had predicted. Thorbjorn made his ship ready and sailed until he reached Brattahlid. Eirik received him with open arms and declared how good it was that he had come. Thorbjorn and his family spent the winter with him.

The following spring Eirik gave Thorbjorn land at Stokkanes, where he built an impressive farmhouse and lived from then on.

5   Eirik had a wife named Thjodhild, and two sons, Thorstein and Leif.

Both of them were promising young men. Thorstein lived at home with his father, and there was no man in Greenland who was considered as handsome as he.

Leif had sailed to Norway where he was one of King Olaf Tryggvason's men.

But when Leif sailed from Greenland that summer the ship was driven off course to land in the Hebrides. From there they failed to get a favourable wind and had to stay in the islands for much of the summer.

Leif fell in love with a woman named Thorgunna. She was of very good family, and Leif realized that she knew a thing or two.

When Leif was leaving Thorgunna asked to go with him. Leif asked whether her kinsmen were of any mind to agree to this, and she declared she did not care. Leif said he was reluctant to abduct a woman of such high birth from a foreign country – 'there are so few of us'.

Thorgunna spoke: 'I'm not sure you'll like the alternative better.' 'I'll take my chances on that,' Leif said.

'Then I will tell you,' Thorgunna said, 'that I am with child, and that this child is yours. It's my guess that I will give birth to a boy, in due course.

And even though you ignore him, I will raise the boy and send him to you in Greenland as soon as he is of an age to travel with others. But it's my guess that he will serve you as well as you have served me now with your departure. I intend to come to Greenland myself before it's all over.' He gave her a gold ring, a Greenland cape and a belt of ivory.

The boy, who was named Thorgils, did come to Greenland and Leif recognized him as his son. – Some men say that this Thorgils came to Iceland before the hauntings at Froda in the summer. – Thorgils stayed in Greenland after that, and before it was all over he was also thought to have something preternatural about him.

Leif and his men left the Hebrides and made land in Norway in the autumn.

Leif became one of the king's men, and King Olaf Tryggvason showed him much honour, as Leif appeared to him to be a man of good breeding.

On one occasion the king spoke to Leif privately and asked, 'Do you intend to sail to Greenland this summer?' Leif answered, 'I would like to do so, if it is your wish.' The king answered, 'It could well be so; you will go as my envoy and convert Greenland to Christianity.' Leif said the king should decide that, but added that he feared this message would meet with a harsh reception in Greenland. The king said he saw no man more suitable for the job than Leif – 'and you'll have the good fortune that's needed'.

'If that's so,' Leif declared, 'then only because I enjoy yours as well.' Once he had made ready, Leif set sail. After being tossed about at sea for a long time he chanced upon land where he had not expected any to be found. Fields of self-sown wheat and vines were growing there; also, there were trees known as maple [mös-ur], and they took specimens of all of them.

Leif also chanced upon men clinging to a ship's wreck, whom he brought home and found shelter for over the winter. In so doing he showed his strong character and kindness. He converted the country to Christianity. Afterwards he became known as Leif the Lucky.

Leif made land in Eiriksfjord and went home to the farm at Brattahlid.

There he was received warmly. He soon began to advocate Christianity and the true catholic faith throughout the country, revealing the messages of King Olaf Tryggvason to the people, and telling them how excellent and glorious this faith was.

Eirik was reluctant to give up his faith, but Thjodhild was quick to convert and had a church built a fair distance from the house. It was called Thjodhild's church and there she prayed, along with those other people who converted to Christianity, of whom there were many. After her conversion, Thjodhild refused to sleep with Eirik, much to his displeasure.

The suggestion that men go to seek out the land which Leif had found soon gained wide support. The leading proponent was Eirik's son, Thorstein, a good, wise and popular man. Eirik was also urged to go, as people valued most his good fortune and leadership. For a long time he was against going, but when his friends urged him he did not refuse.

They made ready the ship on which Thorbjorn had sailed to Greenland, with twenty men to go on the journey. They took few trading goods, but all the more weapons and provisions.

The morning that he left, Eirik took a small chest containing gold and silver. He hid the money and then went on his way. After going only a short way he fell from his horse, breaking several ribs and injuring his shoulder, so that he cried out, 'Ow, ow!' Because of his mishap he sent word to his wife to retrieve the money he had hidden, saying he had been punished for having hidden it.

They then sailed out of Eiriksfjord in fine spirits, pleased with their prospects.

They were tossed about at sea for a long time and failed to reach their intended destination. They came in sight of Iceland and noticed birds from Ireland. Their ship was driven to and fro across the sea until they returned to Greenland in the autumn, worn out and in poor shape, and made land when it was almost winter in Eiriksfjord.

Eirik then spoke: 'More cheerful we were in the summer to leave this fjord than now to return to it, though we have much to welcome us.' Thorstein spoke: 'We'd be doing the generous thing by seeing to those men who have no house to go to and providing for them over the winter.' Eirik answered, 'It's usually true, as they say, that you can't know a good question until you have the answer, and so it'll turn out here. We'll do as you say.' All those men who had no other house to go to were taken in by father and son for the winter. They went home to Brattahlid then and spent the winter there.

6   The next thing to be told of is the proposal made by Thorstein Eiriksson to Gudrid Thorbjarnardottir. He was given a favourable answer by both Gudrid and her father, and so Thorstein married Gudrid and their wedding was held at Brattahlid that autumn. The wedding feast was a grand one and the guests were many.

Thorstein had a farm and livestock in the western settlement at a place called Lysufjord. A man there named Thorstein owned a half-share in this farm; his wife was named Sigrid. Thorstein and Gudrid went to his namesake in Lysufjord that autumn where they were received warmly. They spent the winter there.

It then happened that sickness struck the farm shortly after the beginning of winter. The foreman, named Gardi, was an unpopular man. He was the first to fall ill and die. It was not long until the inhabitants caught the sickness, one after the other and died, until Thorstein Eiriksson and Sigrid, the farmer's wife, fell ill, too.

One evening Sigrid wanted to go to the outhouse which stood opposite the door of the farmhouse. Gudrid went with her and as they looked at the doorway Sigrid cried, 'Oh!' Gudrid spoke: 'We have acted carelessly, you shouldn't be exposed to the cold at all; we must get back inside as quickly as we can!' Sigrid answered, 'I won't go out with things as they are! All of those who are dead are standing there before the door; among them I recognize your husband Thorstein and myself as well. How horrible to see it!' When it had passed, she spoke: 'I don't see them now.' The foreman, whom she had seen with a whip in his hand, ready to strike the dead, had also disappeared. They then entered the house.

Before morning came she was dead and a coffin was made for her body.

That same day men were going fishing and Thorstein accompanied them down to where the boats were beached. Towards dusk he went again to check on their catch. Then Thorstein Eiriksson sent him word to come to him, saying there was no peace at home as the farmer's wife was trying to rise up and get into the bed with him. When he entered she had reached the sideboards of the bed. He took hold of her and drove an axe into her breast.

Thorstein Eiriksson died near sundown. Thorstein told Gudrid to lie down and sleep; he would keep watch over the bodies that night, he said.

Gudrid did so and soon fell asleep.

Only a little of the night had passed when Thorstein rose up, saying that he wished Gudrid to be summoned and wanted to speak to her: 'It is God's will that I be granted an exception for this brief time to improve my prospects.' Thorstein went to Gudrid, woke her and told her to cross herself and ask the Lord for help – 'Thorstein Eiriksson has spoken to me and said he wanted to see you. It is your decision; I will not advise you either way.' She answered, 'It may be that there is a purpose for this strange occurrence, and it will have consequences long to be remembered. I expect that God will grant me his protection. I will take the chance, with God's mercy, of speaking to him, as I cannot escape any threat to myself. I would rather he need not look farther, and I suspect that would be the alternative.' Gudrid then went to see Thorstein, and he seemed to her to shed tears.

He spoke several words in her ear in a low voice, so that she alone heard, and said that those men rejoiced who kept their faith well and it brought mercy and salvation. Yet he said many kept their faith poorly.

'These practices will not do which have been followed here in Greenland after the coming of Christianity: burying people in unconsecrated ground with little if any service said over them. I want to have my corpse taken to a church, along with those of the other people who have died here. But Gardi should be burned on a pyre straight away, as he has caused all the hauntings which have occurred here this winter.' He also spoke of his situation and declared that her future held great things in store, but he warned her against marrying a Greenlander. He also asked her to donate their money to a church or to poor people, and then he sank down for the second time.

It had been common practice in Greenland, since Christianity had been adopted, to bury people in unconsecrated ground on the farms where they died. A pole was set up on the breast of each corpse until a priest came, then the pole was pulled out and consecrated water poured into the hole and a burial service performed, even though this was only done much later.

The bodies were taken to the church in Eiriksfjord, and priests held burial services for them.

After this Thorbjorn died. All of his money went to Gudrid. Eirik invited her to live with them and saw that she was well provided for.

7   There was a man named Thorfinn Karlsefni, the son of Thord Horse head who lived in north Iceland, at the place now called Reynines in Skagafjord. Karlsefni was a man of good family and good means. His mother was named Thorunn. He went on trading voyages and was a merchant of good repute.

One summer Karlsefni made his ship ready for a voyage to Greenland.

Snorri Thorbrandsson of Alftafjord was to accompany him and they took a party of forty men with them.

A man named Bjarni Grimolfsson, from Breidafjord, and another named Thorhall Gamlason, from the East Fjords, made their ship ready the same summer as Karlsefni and were also heading for Greenland. There were forty men on their ship. The two ships set sail once they had made ready.

There is no mention of how long they were at sea. But it is said that both these ships sailed into Eiriksfjord that autumn.

Eirik rode to the ships, along with other Greenlanders, and busy trading commenced. The skippers of the vessels invited Eirik to take his pick of their wares, and Eirik repaid them generously, as he invited both crews home to stay the winter with him in Brattahlid. This the merchants accepted and went home with him. Their goods were later transported to Brattahlid, where there was no lack of good and ample outbuildings to store them in.

The merchants were highly pleased with their winter stay with Eirik.

But as Yule approached, Eirik grew sadder than was his wont. On one occasion Karlsefni spoke to him privately and asked, 'Is something troubling you, Eirik? You seem to me to be more silent than before. You have treated us very generously, and we owe it to you to repay you by any means we can. Tell me what is causing your sadness.' Eirik answered, 'You have also accepted with gratitude and respect, and I don't feel that your contribution to our exchange has been lacking in any way. But I'll regret it if word gets round that you've spent here a Yuletide as lean as the one now approaching.' Karlsefni answered, 'It won't be that at all. We've malt and flour and grain aboard our ships, and you may help yourself to them as you will, to prepare a feast worthy of your generous hospitality.' Eirik accepted this. Preparations for a Yule feast began, which proved to be so bountiful that men could scarcely recall having seen its like.

After Yule Karlsefni approached Eirik to ask for Gudrid's hand, as it seemed to him that she was under Eirik's protection, and both an attractive and knowledgeable woman. Eirik answered that he would support his suit, and that she was a fine match – 'and it's likely that her fate will turn out as prophesied,' he added, even if she did marry Karlsefni, whom he knew to be a worthy man. The subject was broached with Gudrid and she allowed herself to be guided by Eirik's advice. No more needs to be said on that point, except that the match was agreed and the celebrations extended to include the wedding which took place.

That winter there was much merrymaking in Brattahlid; many board games were played, there was storytelling and plenty of other entertainment to brighten the life of the household.

8   There were great discussions that winter in Brattahlid of Snorri and Karlsefni setting sail for Vinland, and people talked at length about it. In the end Snorri and Karlsefni made their vessel ready, intending to sail in search of Vinland that summer. Bjarni and Thorhall decided to accompany them on the voyage, taking their own ship and their companions who had sailed with them on the voyage out.

A man named Thorvard was married to Freydis, who was an illegitimate daughter of Eirik the Red. He went with them, along with Thorvald, Eirik's son, and Thorhall who was called the Huntsman. For years he had accompanied Eirik on hunting trips in the summers, and was entrusted with many tasks. Thorhall was a large man, dark and coarse-featured; he was getting on in years and difficult to handle. He was a silent man, who was not generally given to conversation, devious and yet insulting in his speech, and who usually did his best to make trouble. He had paid scant heed to the faith since it had come to Greenland. Thorhall was not popular with most people but he had long been in Eirik's confidence. He was among those on the ship with Thorvald and Thorvard, as he had a wide knowledge of the uninhabited regions. They had the ship which Thorbjorn had brought to Greenland and set sail with Karlsefni and his group. Most of the men aboard were from Greenland. The crews of the three ships made a hundred plus forty men.

They sailed along the coast to the western settlement, then to the Bear islands and from there with a northerly wind. After two days [*dægur*] at sea they sighted land and rowed over in boats to explore it. There they found many flat slabs of stone, so large that two men could lie foot-to-foot across them. There were many foxes there. They gave the land the name Helluland (Stone-slab land).

After that they sailed with a northerly wind for two days [*dægur*], and again sighted land, with large forests and many animals. An island lay to the south-east, off the coast, where they discovered a bear, and they called it Bjarney (Bear Island), and the forested land itself Markland.

After another two days [*dægur*] passed they again sighted land and approached the shore where a peninsula jutted out. They sailed upwind along the coast, keeping the land on the starboard. The country was wild with a long shoreline and sand flats. They rowed ashore in boats and, discovering the keel of a ship there, named this point Kjalarnes (Keel point). They also gave the beaches the name Furdustrandir (Wonder beaches) for their surprising length. After this the coastline was indented with numerous inlets which they skirted in their ships. When Leif had served King Olaf Tryggvason and was told by him to convert Greenland to Christianity, the king had given him two Scots, a man named Haki and a woman called Hekja. The king told him to call upon them whenever he needed someone with speed, as they were fleeter of foot than any deer. Leif and Eirik had sent them to accompany Karlsefni.

After sailing the length of the Furdustrandir, they put the two Scots ashore and told them to run southwards to explore the country and return before three days' [*dægur*] time had elapsed. They were dressed in a garment known as a kjafal, which had a hood at the top but no arms, and was open at the sides and fastened between the legs with a button and loop; they wore nothing else.

The ships cast anchor and lay to during this time.

After three days had passed the two returned to the shore, one of them with grapes in hand and the other with self-sown wheat. Karlsefni said that they had found good land. After taking them on board once more, they sailed onwards, until they reached a fjord cutting into the coast. They steered the ships into the fjord with an island near its mouth, where there were strong currents, and called the island Straumsey (Stream island). There were so many birds there that they could hardly walk without stepping on eggs. They sailed up into the fjord, which they called Straumsfjord, unloaded the cargo from the ships and began settling in.

They had brought all sorts of livestock with them and explored the land and its resources. There were mountains there, and a pleasant landscape.

They paid little attention to things other than exploring the land. The grass there grew tall.

They spent the winter there, and it was a harsh winter, for which they had made little preparation, and they grew short of food and caught nothing when hunting or fishing. They went out to the island, expecting to find some prey to hunt or food on the beaches. They found little food, but their livestock improved there. After this they entreated God to send them something to eat, but the response was not as quick in coming as their need was urgent. Thorhall disappeared and men went to look for him. They searched for three days, and on the fourth Karlsefni and Bjarni found him at the edge of a cliff. He was staring skywards, with his mouth, nostrils and eyes wide open, scratching and pinching himself and mumbling something.

They asked what he was doing there, and he replied that it made no difference. He said they need not look so surprised and said for most of his life he had got along without their advice. They told him to come back with them and he did so.

Shortly afterwards they found a beached whale and flocked to the site to carve it up, although they failed to recognize what type it was. Karlsefni had a wide knowledge of whales, but even he did not recognize it. The cooks boiled the meat and they ate it, but it made everyone ill.

Thorhall then came up and spoke: 'Didn't Old Redbeard prove to be more help than your Christ? This was my payment for the poem I composed about Thor, my guardian, who's seldom disappointed me.' Once they heard this no one wanted to eat the whale meat, they cast it off a cliff and threw themselves on God's mercy. The weather improved so they could go fishing, and from then on they had supplies in plenty.

In the spring they moved further into Straumsfjord and lived on the produce of both shores of the fjord: hunting game inland, gathering eggs on the island and fishing at sea.

9 They then began to discuss and plan the continuation of their journey.

Thorhall wanted to head north, past Furdustrandir and around Kjalarnes to seek Vinland. Karlsefni wished to sail south along the east shore, feeling the land would be more substantial the farther south it was, and he felt it was advisable to explore both.

Thorhall then made his ship ready close to the island, with no more than nine men to accompany him. The rest of their company went with Karlsefni.

One day as Thorhall was carrying water aboard his ship he drank of it and spoke this verse:

1. With promises of fine drinks the war-trees wheedled, spurring me to journey to these scanty shores.

War-oak of the helmet god, I now wield but a bucket, no sweet wine do I sup stooping at the spring.

After that they set out, and Karlsefni followed them as far as the island.

Before hoisting the sail Thorhall spoke this verse:

2. We'll return to where our countrymen await us, head our sand-heaven's horse, to scout the ship's wide plains. Let the wielders of sword storms laud the land, unwearied, settle Wonder Beaches and serve up their whale.

They then separated and Thorhall and his crew sailed north past Furdustrandir and Kjalarnes, and from there attempted to sail to the west of it.

But they ran into storms and were driven ashore in Ireland, where they were beaten and enslaved. There Thorhall died.

10 Karlsefni headed south around the coast, with Snorri and Bjarni and the rest of their company. They sailed a long time, until they came to a river which flowed into a lake and from there into the sea. There were wide sandbars beyond the mouth of the river, and they could only sail into the river at high tide. Karlsefni and his company sailed into the lagoon and called the land Hop (Tidal pool). There they found fields of self-sown wheat in the low-lying areas and vines growing on the hills. Every stream was teeming with fish. They dug trenches along the high-water mark and when the tide ebbed there were halibut [*helgir fiskar*] in them. There were a great number of deer of all kinds in the forest.

They stayed there for a fortnight, enjoying themselves and finding nothing unusual. They had taken their livestock with them.

Early one morning they noticed nine hide-covered boats, and the people in them waved wooden poles that made a swishing sound [*sem í hálmþústum*] as they turned them around sunwise.

Karlsefni then spoke: 'What can this mean?' Snorri replied: 'It may be a sign of peace; we should take a white shield and lift it up in return.' This they did.

The others then rowed towards them and were astonished at the sight of them as they landed on the shore. They were short in height with threatening features and tangled hair on their heads. Their eyes were large and their cheeks broad. They stayed there awhile, marvelling, then rowed away again to the south around the point.

The group had built their booths up above the lake, with some of the huts farther inland, and others close to the shore.

They remained there that winter. There was no snow at all and the livestock could fend for themselves out of doors.

11 One morning, as spring advanced, they noticed a large number of hide-covered boats rowing up from the south around the point. There were so many of them that it looked as if bits of coal had been tossed over the water, and there was a pole waving from each boat. They signalled with their shields and began trading with the visitors, who mostly wished to trade for red cloth. They also wanted to purchase swords and spears, but Karlsefni and Snorri forbade this. They traded dark pelts for the cloth, and for each pelt they took cloth a hand in length, which they bound about their heads.

This went on for some time, until there was little cloth left. They then cut the cloth into smaller pieces, each no wider than a finger's width, but the natives gave just as much for it or more.

At this point a bull, owned by Karlsefni and his companions, ran out of the forest and bellowed loudly. The natives took fright at this, ran to their boats and rowed off to the south. Three weeks passed and there was no sign of them.

After that they saw a large group of native boats approach from the south, as thick as a steady stream. They were waving poles counter-sunwise now and all of them were shrieking loudly. The men took up their red shields and went towards them. They met and began fighting. A hard barrage rained down and the natives also had catapults. Karlsefni and Snorri then saw the natives lift up on poles a large round object, about the size of a sheep's gut and black in colour, which came flying up on the land and made a threatening noise when it landed. It struck great fear into Karlsefni and his men, who decided their best course was to flee upriver, since the native party seemed to be attacking from all sides, until they reached a cliff wall where they could put up a good fight.

Freydis came out of the camp as they were fleeing. She called, 'Why do you flee such miserable opponents, men like you who look to me to be capable of killing them off like sheep? Had I a weapon I'm sure I would fight better than any of you.' They paid no attention to what she said. Freydis wanted to go with them, but moved somewhat slowly, as she was with child.

She followed them into the forest, but the natives reached her. She came across a slain man, Thorbrand Snorrason, who had been struck in the head by a slab of stone. His sword lay beside him, and this she snatched up and prepared to defend herself with it as the natives approached her. Freeing one of her breasts from her shift, she smacked the sword with it. This frightened the natives, who turned and ran back to their boats and rowed away.

Karlsefni and his men came back to her and praised her luck.

Two of Karlsefni's men were killed and many of the natives were slain, yet Karlsefni and his men were outnumbered. They returned to the booths wondering who these numerous people were who had attacked them on land. But it now looked to them as if the company in the boats had been the sole attackers, and any other attackers had only been an illusion.

The natives also found one of the dead men, whose axe lay beside him.

One of them picked up the axe and chopped at a tree, and then each took his turn at it. They thought this thing which cut so well a real treasure. One of them struck a stone and the axe broke. He thought a thing which could not withstand stone to be of little worth, and tossed it away.

The party then realized that, despite everything the land had to offer there, they would be under constant threat of attack from its prior inhabitants.

They made ready to depart for their own country. Sailing north along the shore, they discovered five natives sleeping in skin sacks near the shore.

Beside them they had vessels filled with deer marrow blended with blood.

They assumed these men to be outlaws and killed them.

They then came to a headland thick with deer. The point looked like a huge dunghill, as the deer gathered there at night to sleep. They then entered Straumsfjord, where they found food in plenty. Some people say that Bjarni and Gudrid had remained behind there with a hundred [*tíu tigir*] others and gone no farther, and that it was Karlsefni and Snorri who went further south with some forty men, stayed no more than two months at Hop and returned the same summer.

The group stayed there while Karlsefni went on one ship to look for Thorhall. They sailed north around Kjalarnes Point and then westwards of it, keeping the land on their port side. They saw nothing but wild forest.

When they had sailed for a long time they reached a river flowing from east to west. They sailed into the mouth of the river and lay to near the south bank.

12 One morning Karlsefni's men saw something shiny above a clearing in the trees, and they called out. It moved and proved to be a one-legged creature which darted down to where the ship lay tied. Thorvald, Eirik the Red's son, was at the helm, and the one-legged man shot an arrow into his intestine. Thorvald drew the arrow out and spoke: 'Fat paunch that was. We've found a land of fine resources, though we'll hardly enjoy much of them.' Thorvald died from the wound shortly after. The one-legged man then ran off back north. They pursued him and caught glimpses of him now and again. He then fled into a cove and they turned back.

One of the men then spoke this verse:

3. True it was that our men tracked a one-legged creature down to the shore.

The uncanny fellow fled in a flash, though rough was his way, hear us, Karlsefni!

They soon left to head northwards where they thought they sighted the Land of the One-Legged, but did not want to put their lives in further danger. They saw mountains which they felt to be the same as those near Hop, and both these places seemed to be equally far away from Straumsfjord.

They returned to spend their third winter in Straumsfjord. Many quarrels arose, as the men who had no wives sought to take those of the married men. Karlsefni's son Snorri was born there the first autumn and was three years old when they left.

They had southerly winds and reached Markland, where they met five natives. One was bearded, two were women and two of them children.

Karlsefni and his men caught the boys but the others escaped and disappeared into the earth. They took the boys with them and taught them their language and had them baptized. They called their mother Vethild and their father Ovaegi. They said that kings ruled the land of the natives; one of them was called Avaldamon and the other Valdidida. No houses were there, they said, but people slept in caves or holes. They spoke of another land, across from their own. There people dressed in white clothing, shouted loudly and bore poles and waved banners. This people assumed to be the land of the white men. They then came to Greenland and spent the winter with Eirik the Red.

13 Bjarni Grimolfsson and his group were borne into the Greenland Straits and entered Madkasjo (Sea of Worms), although they
failed to realize it until the ship under them had become infested
with shipworms.

They then discussed what to do. They had a ship's boat in tow
which had been smeared with tar made of seal blubber. It is said
that shell maggots cannot infest wood smeared with such tar. The
majority proposed to set as many men into the boat as it could
carry. When this was tried, it turned out to have room for no more
than half of them.

Bjarni then said they should decide by lot who should go in the
boat, and not decide by status. Although all of the people there
wanted to go into the boat, it couldn't take them all. So they decided to draw lots to decide who would board the boat and who
would remain aboard the trading vessel. The outcome was that it
fell to Bjarni and almost half of those on board to go in the boat.

Those who had been selected left the ship and boarded the boat.

Once they were aboard the boat one young Icelander, who had
sailed with Bjarni, called out to him, 'Are you going to desert me
now, Bjarni?' 'So it must be,' Bjarni answered.

He said, 'That's not what you promised me when I left my father's house in Iceland to follow you.' Bjarni answered, 'I don't see
we've much other choice now. What would you advise?' He said,
'I see the solution – that we change places, you come up here and
I'll take your place there.' 'So be it,' Bjarni answered, 'as I see you
put a high price on life and are very upset about dying.' They then
changed places. The man climbed into the boat and Bjarni aboard
the ship. People say that Bjarni died there in the Sea of Worms,
along with the others on board his ship. The ship's boat and those
on it went on their way and made land, after which they told this
tale.

14 The following summer Karlsefni sailed for Iceland and Gudrid with him. He came home to his farm at Reynines.

His mother thought his match hardly worthy, and Gudrid did
not stay on the farm the first winter. But when she learned what an
outstanding woman Gudrid was, Gudrid moved to the farm and
the two women got along well.

Karlsefni's son Snorri had a daughter, Hallfrid, who was the mother of Bishop Thorlak Runolfsson.

Karlsefni and Gudrid had a son named Thorbjorn, whose daughter Thorunn was the mother of Bishop Bjorn.

Thorgeir, Snorri Karlsefni's son, was the father of Yngvild, the mother of the first Bishop Brand.

And here ends this saga.

Translated by Keneva Kunz

THE SAGA OF THE GREENLANDERS

1   Herjolf was the son of Bard Herjolfsson and a kinsman of
Ingolf, the settler of Iceland. Ingolf gave to Herjolf the land between Vog and Reykjanes.

At first, Herjolf farmed at Drepstokk. His wife was named
Thorgerd and their son was Bjarni; he was a promising young
man. While still at a youthful age he longed to sail abroad. He soon
earned himself both a good deal of wealth and a good name, and
spent his winters alternately abroad and with his father. Soon
Bjarni had his own ship making trading voyages. During the last
winter Bjarni spent in Norway, Herjolf decided to accompany
Eirik the Red to Greenland and left his farm. One of the men on
Herjolf 's ship was from the Hebrides, a Christian, who composed
the drapa of the Sea Fences (Breakers). It has this refrain: I ask you,
unblemished monks' tester, to be the ward of my travels; may the
lord of the peaks' pane shade my path with his hawk's perch.
Herjolf farmed at Herjolfsnes. He was the most respected of men.

Eirik the Red farmed at Brattahlid. There he was held in the
highest esteem, and everyone deferred to his authority. Eirik's
children were Leif, Thorvald, Thorstein and a daughter, Freydis.
She was married to a man named Thorvard, and they farmed at
Gardar, where the bishop's seat is now. She was a domineering
woman, but Thorvard was a man of no consequence. She had been
married to him mainly for his money.

Heathen were the people of Greenland at that time.

Bjarni steered his ship into Eyrar in the summer of the year that
his father had sailed from Iceland. Bjarni was greatly moved by the
news and would not have his cargo unloaded. His crew then asked
what he was waiting for, and he answered that he intended to follow his custom of spending the winter with his father – 'and I want
to set sail for Greenland, if you will join me'.

All of them said they would follow his counsel.

Bjarni then spoke: 'Our journey will be thought an ill-considered one, since none of us has sailed the Greenland Sea.' Despite this they set sail once they had made ready and sailed for three days, until the land had disappeared below the horizon. Then the wind dropped and they were beset by winds from the north and fog; for many days [*dægur*] they did not know where they were sailing.

After that they saw the sun and could take their bearings. Hoisting the sail, they sailed for the rest of the day before sighting land. They speculated among themselves as to what land this would be, for Bjarni said he suspected this was not Greenland.

They asked whether he wished to sail up close into the shore of this country or not. 'My advice is that we sail in close to the land.' They did so, and soon saw that the land was not mountainous but did have small hills, and was covered with forests. Keeping it on their port side, they turned their sail-end landwards and angled away from the shore.

They sailed for another two days [*dægur*] before sighting land once again.

They asked Bjarni whether he now thought this to be Greenland.

He said he thought this no more likely to be Greenland than the previous land – 'since there are said to be very large glaciers in Greenland'.

They soon approached the land and saw that it was flat and wooded. The wind died and the crew members said they thought it advisable to put ashore, but Bjarni was against it. They claimed they needed both timber and water.

'You've no shortage of those provisions,' Bjarni said, but he was criticized somewhat by his crew for this.

He told them to hoist the sail and they did so, turning the stern towards shore and sailing seawards. For three days [*dægur*] they sailed with the wind from the south-west until they saw a third land. This land had high mountains, capped by a glacier.

They asked whether Bjarni wished to make land here, but he said he did not wish to do so – 'as this land seems to me to offer nothing of use'.

This time they did not lower the sail, but followed the shoreline until they saw that the land was an island. Once more they turned their stern landwards and sailed out to sea with the same breeze. But the wind soon grew and Bjarni told them to lower the sail and not to proceed faster than both their ship and rigging could safely withstand. They sailed for four days [*dægur*]. Upon seeing a fourth land they asked Bjarni whether he thought this was Greenland or not.

Bjarni answered, 'This land is most like what I have been told of Greenland, and we'll head for shore here.' This they did and made land along a headland in the evening of the day, finding a boat there. On this point Herjolf, Bjarni's father, lived, and it was named for him and has since been called Herjolfsnes (Herjolf's point). Bjarni now joined his father and ceased his merchant voyages. He remained on his father's farm as long as Herjolf lived and took over the farm after his death.

2   Following this, Bjarni Herjolfsson sailed from Greenland to Earl Eirik, who received him well. Bjarni told of his voyage, during which he had sighted various lands, and many people thought him short on curiosity, since he had nothing to tell of these lands, and he was criticized somewhat for this.

Bjarni became one of the earl's followers and sailed to Greenland the following summer. There was now much talk of looking for new lands.

Leif, the son of Eirik the Red of Brattahlid, sought out Bjarni and purchased his ship. He hired himself a crew numbering thirty-five men altogether. Leif asked his father Eirik to head the expedition.

Eirik was reluctant to agree, saying he was getting on in years and not as good at bearing the cold and wet as before. Leif said he still commanded the greatest good fortune of all his kinsmen. Eirik gave in to Leif's urgings and, when they were almost ready, set out from his farm on horseback.

When he had but a short distance left to the ship, the horse he was riding stumbled and threw Eirik, injuring his foot. Eirik then spoke: 'I am not intended to find any other land than this one where we now live. This will be the end of our travelling together.'

Eirik returned home to Brattahlid, and Leif boarded his ship, along with his companions, thirty-five men altogether. One of the crew was a man named Tyrkir, from a more southerly country.

Once they had made the ship ready, they put to sea and found first the land which Bjarni and his companions had seen last. They sailed up to the shore and cast anchor, put out a boat and rowed ashore. There they found no grass, but large glaciers covered the highlands, and the land was like a single flat slab of rock from the glaciers to the sea. This land seemed to them of little use.

Leif then spoke: 'As far as this land is concerned it can't be said of us as of Bjarni, that we did not set foot on shore. I am now going to name this land and call it Helluland (Stone-slab land).' They then returned to their ship, put out to sea and found a second land.

Once more they sailed close to the shore and cast anchor, put out a boat and went ashore. This land was flat and forested, sloping gently seaward, and they came across many beaches of white sand.

Leif then spoke: 'This land will be named for what it has to offer and called Markland (Forest Land).' They then returned to the ship without delay.

After this they sailed out to sea and spent two days [dægur] at sea with a north-easterly wind before they saw land. They sailed towards it and came to an island, which lay to the north of the land, where they went ashore. In the fine weather they found dew on the grass, that they collected in their hands and drank, and thought they had never tasted anything as sweet.

Afterwards they returned to their ship and sailed into the sound which lay between the island and the headland that stretched out northwards from the land. They rounded the headland and steered westward. Here there were extensive shallows at low tide and their ship was soon stranded, and the sea looked far away to those aboard ship.

Their curiosity to see the land was so great that they could not be bothered to wait for the tide to come in and float their stranded ship, and they ran aground where a river flowed into the sea from a lake. When the incoming tide floated the ship again, they took the boat and rowed to the ship and moved it up into the river and from there into the lake, where they cast anchor. They carried their sleeping-sacks ashore and built booths. Later they decided to spend the winter there and built large houses.

There was no lack of salmon both in the lake and in the river, and this salmon was larger than they had ever seen before.

It seemed to them the land was so good that livestock would need no fodder during the winter. The temperature never dropped below freezing, and the grass only withered very slightly. The days and nights were much more equal in length than in Greenland or Iceland. In the depth of winter the sun was aloft by mid-morning and still visible at mid-afternoon. When they had finished building their houses, Leif spoke to his companions: 'I want to divide our company into two groups, as I wish to explore the land. One half is to remain at home by the longhouses while the other half explores the land. They are never to go any farther than will enable them to return that same evening and no one is to separate from the group.' This they did for some time. Leif accompanied them sometimes, and at other times remained at home by the houses. Leif was a large, strong man, of very striking appearance and wise, as well as being a man of moderation in all things.

3   One evening it happened that one man, the southerner Tyrkir, was missing from their company. Leif was very upset by this, as Tyrkir had spent many years with him and his father and had treated Leif as a child very affectionately. Leif criticized his companions harshly and prepared to search for Tyrkir, taking twelve men with him.

When they had gone only a short way from the houses, however, Tyrkir came towards him and they welcomed him gladly.

Leif soon realized that the companion of his childhood was pleased about something. Tyrkir had a protruding forehead and darting eyes, with dark wrinkles in his face; he was short in stature and frail-looking, but a master of all types of crafts.

Leif then asked him, 'Why were you so late returning, foster-father, and how did you become separated from the rest?' For a long time Tyrkir only spoke in German, with his eyes darting in all directions and his face contorted. The others understood nothing of what he was saying.

After a while he spoke in Norse: 'I had gone only a bit farther than the rest of you. But I have news to tell you: I found grapevines and grapes.' 'Are you really sure of this, foster-father?' Leif said.

'I'm absolutely sure,' he replied, 'because where I was born there was no lack of grapevines and grapes.' They went to sleep after that, and the following morning Leif spoke to his crew: 'We'll divide our time between two tasks, taking one day for one task and one day for the other, picking grapes or cutting vines and felling the trees to make a load for my ship.' They agreed on this course.

It is said that the boat which was drawn behind the ship was filled with grapes.

Then they cut a load for the ship.

When spring came they made the ship ready and set sail. Leif named the land for its natural features and called it Vinland (Wineland). They headed out to sea and had favourable winds, until they came in sight of Greenland and the mountains under its glaciers.

Then one of the crew spoke up, asking, 'Why do you steer a course so close to the wind?' Leif answered, 'I'm watching my course, but there's more to it than that: do you see anything of note?' The crew said they saw nothing worthy of note.

'I'm not sure,' Leif said, 'whether it's a ship or a skerry that I see.' They then saw it and said it was a skerry. Leif saw so much better than they did, that he could make out men on the skerry.

'I want to steer us close into the wind,' Leif said, 'so that we can reach them; if these men should be in need of our help, we have to try to give it to them. If they should prove to be hostile, we have all the advantages on our side and they have none.' They managed to sail close to the skerry and lowered their sail, cast anchor and put out one of the two extra boats they had taken with them.

Leif then asked who was in charge of the company.

The man who replied said his name was Thorir and that he was of Norwegian origin. 'And what is your name?' Leif told him his name.

'Are you the son of Eirik the Red of Brattahlid?' he asked.

Leif said he was. 'Now I want to invite all of you,' Leif said, 'to come on board my ship, bringing as much of your valuables as the ship can carry.' After they had accepted his offer, the ship sailed to

Eiriksfjord with all this cargo until they reached Brattahlid, where they unloaded the ship. Leif then invited Thorir to spend the winter with him there, along with Thorir's wife Gudrid and three other men, and found places for the other members of both his own and Thorir's crew. Leif rescued fifteen men from the skerry.

After this he was called Leif the Lucky.

Leif had now become very wealthy and was held in much respect.

That winter Thorir's crew were stricken by illness and he himself died, along with most of his company. Eirik the Red also died that winter.

There was great discussion of Leif 's Vinland voyage and his brother Thorvald felt they had not explored enough of the land. Leif then said to Thorvald, 'You go to Vinland, brother, and take my ship if you wish, but before you do so I want the ship to make a trip to the skerry to fetch the wood that Thorir had there.' And so this was done.

4   In consultation with his brother Leif, Thorvald now prepared for this journey with thirty companions. They made their ship ready and put to sea, and nothing is told of their journey until they came to Vinland, to Leif 's camp, where they laid up their ship and settled in for the winter, fishing for their food.

That spring Thorvald said they should make their ship ready and several men were to take the ship's boat and go to the west of the land and explore there during the summer. They thought the land fine and well forested, with white beaches and only a short distance between the forest and the sea. There were many islands and wide stretches of shallow sea.

Nowhere did they see signs of men or animals. On one of the westerly islands they did find a wooden grain cover, but discovered no other work by human hands and headed back, returning to Leif 's camp in the autumn.

The second summer Thorvald explored the country to the east on the large ship, going north around the land [*hið nyrðra fyrir landið*]. They ran into stormy weather around one headland, and they were driven ashore, smashing the keel of the ship. They stayed there a long time, repairing their ship. Thorvald then said to his companions, 'I want us to raise the broken keel up on this point and call it Kjalarnes (Keel point).' This they did.

They then left to sail to the east of the country and entered the mouths of the next fjords until they reached a cape stretching out seawards. It was covered with forest. After they secured their ship in a sheltered cove and put out gangways to the land, Thorvald and all his companions went ashore.

He then spoke: 'This is an attractive spot, and here I would like to build my farm.' As they headed back to the ship they saw three hillocks on the beach inland from the cape. Upon coming closer they saw they were three hide-covered boats, with three men under each of them. They divided their forces and managed to capture all of them except one, who escaped with his boat. They killed the other eight and went back to the cape. On surveying the area they saw a number of hillocks further up the fjord, and assumed them to be settlements. Following this they were stricken by sleep, so that they could no longer keep their eyes open, and all of them fell asleep. Then a voice was heard calling, and they all woke up. 'Wake up, Thorvald, and all your companions,' the voice warned, 'if you wish to save your lives. Get to the ship with all your men and leave this land as quickly as you can.' A vast number of hide-covered boats came down the fjord, heading towards them.

Thorvald then spoke: 'We will set up breastworks along the sides of the ship and defend ourselves as well as possible, but fight back as little as we can.' They did as he said, and after the natives had shot at them for a while, they fled as rapidly as they could.

Thorvald then asked his men if they had been wounded, and they replied that they were unhurt.

'I have been wounded under my arm,' he said. 'An arrow flew between the edge of the ship and the shield into my armpit. Here is the arrow, and this wound will cause my death. I now advise you to prepare for your return journey as quickly as possible, but take me to that cape I thought was such a good farm site. Perhaps the words I spoke will prove true enough and I will dwell there awhile. You will bury me there and mark my grave with crosses at the head and foot, and call the spot Krossanes (Cross point) after that.' Greenland had been converted to Christianity by that time, although Eirik the Red had died before the conversion.

Thorvald then died, and they did everything as he had advised, then left to meet up with their companions. Each group told its news to the other and they spent the winter there loading the ships with grapes and grapevines.

In the spring they made ready for the voyage back to Greenland. They steered the ship into Eiriksfjord and had plenty of news to tell Leif.

5   Among the events taking place meanwhile in Greenland was the marriage of Thorstein Eiriksson to Gudrid Thorbjarnardottir, who had previously been married to Thorir the Norwegian who was spoken of earlier.

Thorstein Eiriksson now wished to sail to Vinland to retrieve his brother Thorvald's body and made the same ship ready once more. He selected his companions for their strength and size, taking with him twenty-five men and his wife, Gudrid. Once they had made ready, they set sail and were out of sight of land. They were tossed about at sea all summer and did not know where they were.

The first week of winter had passed when they made land in Lysufjord, in the western settlement in Greenland. Thorstein managed to find places for all his crew members. But he and his wife had no accommodation and remained alone on the ship for several nights. In those days Christianity was still in its infancy in Greenland.

One day some men came to their tent early in the day. The leader of the group asked what men were in the tent.

Thorstein answered, 'There are two of us,' he said, 'and who is asking?' 'Thorstein is my name, and I am called Thorstein the Black. My reason for coming is to invite you and your wife to stay the winter with me.' Thorstein Eiriksson said he wished to seek his wife's guidance, and when she told him to decide he agreed to the offer.

'Then I'll return with a team of oxen [eyki] to fetch you tomorrow, as I do not lack the means to put you up. But it will be an unexciting stay, as there are only the two of us, my wife and myself, and I prefer my own company. Also I have another faith than you, although I expect yours is the better of the two.' He then came with a team of oxen [eyki] to fetch them the next day, and so they went to stay with Thorstein the Black, and he provided for them generously.

Gudrid was a woman of striking appearance and wise as well, who knew how to behave among strangers.

It was early in the winter when the first of Thorstein Eiriksson's companions were stricken by illness and many of them died there.

Thorstein asked that coffins be made for the bodies of those who had died, and that they be taken to the ship and secured away there – 'as when summer comes I intend to take all the bodies back to Eiriksfjord.'

It was not long until the sickness came to Thorstein's house, and his wife, Grimhild, was the first to fall ill. She was a very large woman, with the strength of a man, yet she bowed to the illness. Soon after that Thorstein Eiriksson was stricken, and both of them lay ill until Grimhild, the wife of Thorstein the Black, died.

After she had died, Thorstein the Black left the main room to seek a plank to place her body on.

Gudrid then spoke: 'Don't be away long, dear Thorstein,' she said.

He promised to do as she asked. Thorstein Eiriksson then spoke: 'Strange are the actions of the mistress of the house now; she's struggling to raise herself up on her elbow, stretching her feet out from the bedboards and feeling for her shoes.' At this Thorstein the Black returned and Grimhild collapsed that same instant, with a cracking sound coming from every timber in the room.

Thorstein then made a coffin for Grimhild's body and took it away and secured it. He was a large, strong man, and needed to call upon all his strength before he managed to remove his wife from the farm.

Thorstein Eiriksson's condition worsened and he died. His wife, Gudrid, was overtaken by grief. All of them were in the main room. Gudrid had been sitting on a stool in front of the bench where her husband, Thorstein, had lain.

Thorstein the farmer then took Gudrid from her stool into his arms and sat with her on the bench across from her husband Thorstein's corpse and said many encouraging things, consoling her and promising her that he would take her to Eiriksfjord with her husband Thorstein's body and those of his companions. 'And we'll invite other people to stay here,' he said 'to provide you with solace and companionship.' She thanked him.

Thorstein Eiriksson then sat up and spoke: 'Where is Gudrid?' Three times he spoke these words, but she remained silent.

Then she spoke to Thorstein the farmer: 'Shall I answer his question or not?' He told her not to answer. Thorstein the farmer then crossed the floor and sat on the chair and Gudrid on his knee.

Then Thorstein the farmer spoke: 'What is it you want, namesake?' he said.

He answered after a short pause: 'I want to tell Gudrid her fate, to make it easier for her to resign herself to my death, for I have gone to a good resting place. I can tell you, Gudrid, that you will be married to an Icelander, and you will live a long life together, and have many descendants, promising, bright and fine, sweet and well-scented. You will leave Greenland to go to Norway and from there to Iceland and set up house in Iceland. There you will live a long time, outliving your husband. You will travel abroad, go south on a pilgrimage and return to Iceland to your farm, where a church will be built. There you will remain and take holy orders and there you will die.' At that Thorstein Eiriksson fell back, and his corpse was made ready and taken to the ship. Thorstein the farmer kept all his promises to Gudrid faithfully. In the spring he sold his farm and livestock and loaded all his possessions aboard the ship with Gudrid. He made the ship ready and hired a crew and sailed to Eiriksfjord. The bodies were then buried in the churchyard.

Gudrid went to stay with Leif at Brattahlid, and Thorstein the Black built a farm in Eiriksfjord where he stayed as long as he lived, and was regarded as a most capable man.

6   That same summer a ship from Norway arrived in Greenland. The skipper of the ship was named Thorfinn Karlsefni. He was the son of Thord Horse-head, the son of Snorri Thordarson of Hofdi.

Thorfinn Karlsefni was a very wealthy man. He spent the winter with Leif Eiriksson in Brattahlid. He was soon attracted by Gudrid and asked her to marry him, but she referred him to Leif for an answer. She was then engaged to him and their wedding took place that winter.

The discussion of a voyage to Vinland continued as before, and people strongly urged Karlsefni to make the journey, Gudrid among them. Once he had decided to make the journey he hired himself a crew of sixty men and five women.

Karlsefni and his crew made an agreement that anything of value they obtained would be divided equally among them. They took all sorts of livestock with them, for they intended to settle in the country if they could.

Karlsefni asked Leif for his houses in Vinland, and Leif said he would lend but not give them to him.

They then put out to sea in their ship and arrived without mishap at Leif's booths, where they unloaded their sleeping-sacks. They soon had plenty of good provisions, since a fine, large rorqual had stranded on the beach. After they had gone and carved up the whale they had no lack of food. The livestock made its way inland, but the male animals soon became irritable and hard to handle. They had brought one bull with them.

Karlsefni had trees felled and hewn to load aboard his ship and had the timber piled on a large rock to dry. They had plenty of supplies from the natural bounty there, including grapes, all sorts of fish and game, and other good things.

After the first winter passed and summer came, they became aware of natives. A large group of men came out of the woods close to where the cattle were pastured. The bull began bellowing and snorting very loudly.

This frightened the natives, who ran off with their burdens, which included fur pelts and sables and all kinds of skins. They headed for Karlsefni's farm and tried to get into the house, but Karlsefni had the door defended. Neither group understood the language of the other.

The natives then set down their packs and opened them, offering their goods, preferably in exchange for weapons, but Karlsefni forbade the men to trade weapons.

He sought a solution by having the women bring out milk and milk products. Once they saw these products the natives wished to purchase them and nothing else. The trading with the natives resulted in them bearing off their purchases in their stomachs, leaving their packs and skins with Karlsefni and his companions. This done, they departed.

Karlsefni next had a sturdy palisade built around his farm, where they prepared to defend themselves. At this time Gudrid, Karlsefni's wife, gave birth to a boy, who was named Snorri. Near the beginning of their second winter the natives visited them again, in much greater numbers than before and with the same goods as before.

Karlsefni then spoke to the women: 'Bring out whatever food was most in demand last time, and nothing else.' When the natives saw this they threw their packs in over the palisade.

Gudrid sat inside in the doorway, with the cradle of her son, Snorri. A shadow fell across the doorway and a woman entered, rather short in stature, wearing a close-fitting tunic, with a shawl over her head and light red-brown hair. She was pale and had eyes so large that eyes of such size had never been seen in a human head.

She came to where Gudrid was sitting and spoke: 'What is your name?' she said.

'My name is Gudrid, and what is yours?' 'My name is Gudrid,' the other woman said.

Gudrid, Karlsefni's wife, then motioned to her with her hand to sit down beside her, but just as she did so a great crash was heard and the woman disappeared. At that moment one of the natives had been killed by one of Karlsefni's servants for trying to take weapons from them, and they quickly ran off, leaving their clothes and trade goods lying behind. No one but Gudrid had seen the woman.

'We have to decide on a plan,' said Karlsefni, 'since I expect they will return for a third time, hostile and in greater numbers. We'll follow this plan: ten men will go out on this headland and let themselves be seen there, while the rest of us go into the forest and cut a clearing for our cattle. When approaching from the forest we will take our bull and let him head our group into battle.' In the place where they planned to take them on there was water on one side and a forest on the other. They followed the proposal Karlsefni had made.

The natives soon came to the place Karlsefni had intended for the battle.

They fought and a large number of the natives were killed.

One of the men in the natives' group was tall and handsome, and Karlsefni thought him likely to be their leader.

One of the natives then picked up an axe, peered at it awhile and then aimed at one of his companions and struck him. The other fellow was killed outright. The tall man then picked up the axe, examined it awhile and then threw it as far out into the sea as he could. After that the natives fled into the woods at top speed, and they had no more dealings with them.

Karlsefni and his companions spent the entire winter there, but in the spring he declared that he wished to remain no longer and wanted to return to Greenland. They made ready for their journey, taking with them plenty of the land's products – grapevines, berries and skins. They set sail and arrived safely in Eiriksfjord where they stayed over the winter.

7   Discussion soon began again of a Vinland voyage, since the trip seemed to bring men both wealth and renown.

The same summer that Karlsefni returned from Vinland a ship arrived in Greenland from Norway. The skippers were two brothers, Helgi and Finnbogi, who spent the winter in Greenland. They were Icelanders, from the East Fjords.

We now turn to Freydis Eiriksdottir, who set out on a journey from Gardar to meet with the two brothers, Helgi and Finnbogi, and to propose that they all make the journey to Vinland on their ship and have a half-share of any profits from it. They agreed to this.

From there she went to her brother Leif and asked him to give her the houses he had built in Vinland. He replied as he had before, that he would lend the houses but not give them to anyone.

According to the agreement between Freydis and the two brothers, each was to have thirty fighting men aboard his ship and women in addition.

Freydis broke the agreement straight away, however, and took five extra men, concealing them so that the brothers were not aware of them until they had reached Vinland. They put to sea, having agreed beforehand to try to stick together if possible on the way, and they almost managed this. The brothers arrived slightly earlier, however, and had unloaded their ship and carried their belongings to Leif's houses when Freydis arrived. Her group unloaded their ship and carried its belongings up to the houses.

Freydis then said, 'Why did you put your belongings here?' 'We thought,' they answered, 'that you intended to keep your word to us.' 'Leif lent me the houses,' she said, 'not you.' Helgi then spoke: 'We brothers will never be a match for your ill-will.' They removed their things and built themselves a longhouse farther from the sea, on the bank of a lake, and settled in well. Freydis had wood cut to make a load for her ship.

When winter came the brothers suggested that they hold games and arrange entertainment. This went on for a while, until disagreements arose.

The ill-feelings split the party so that the games ceased and each group kept to its own houses. This continued for much of the winter.

Early one morning Freydis got up and dressed, but did not put on any footwear. The weather had left a thick dew on the grass. She took her husband's cape and placed it over her shoulders and went to the brothers' longhouse and came to the doorway. A man had gone out a short while earlier and left the door half-open. She opened the door and stood silently in the doorway awhile. Finnbogi lay awake at the inner end of the house.

He spoke: 'What do you want here, Freydis?' She answered, 'I want you to get up and come outside. I have to speak to you.' He did as she said. They went over to a tree trunk lying near the wall of the house and sat down there.

'How do you like it here?' she asked.

'I think the land has much to offer, but I don't like the ill-feeling between us, as I don't think there is reason for it.' 'What you say is true,' she said, 'and I agree. But my purpose in coming to see you was that I want to exchange ships with the two of you, as you have a larger ship than I do and I want to leave this place.' 'I suppose I can agree to that,' he said, 'if that will please you.' After this they parted. She returned home and Finnbogi went back to his bed. When she climbed back into bed her cold feet woke Thorvard, who asked why she was so cold and wet. She answered vehemently, 'I went to the brothers, to ask to purchase their ship, as I wanted a larger ship. They reacted so angrily; they struck me and treated me very badly, but you're such a coward that you will repay neither dishonour done to me nor to yourself. I am now paying the price of being so far from my home in Greenland, and unless you avenge this, I will divorce you!' Not being able to ignore her upbraiding any longer, he told the men to get up as quickly as they could and arm themselves. Having done so, they went at once to the longhouse of the brothers, entered while those inside were still asleep and took them, tied them up and, once bound, led them outside. Freydis, however, had each one of the men who was brought out killed.

Soon all the men had been killed and only the women were left, as no one would kill them.

Freydis then spoke: 'Hand me an axe.' This was done, and she then attacked the five women there and killed them all.

They returned to their house after this wicked deed, and it was clear that Freydis was highly pleased with what she had accomplished. She spoke to her companions: 'If we are fortunate enough to make it back to Greenland,' she said, 'I will have anyone who tells of these events killed. We will say that they remained behind here when we took our leave.' Early in the spring they loaded the ship, which the brothers had owned, with all the produce they could gather and the ship would hold.

They then set sail and had a good voyage, sailing their ship into Eiriksfjord in early summer. Karlsefni was there already, with his ship all set to sail and only waiting for a favourable wind. It was said that no ship sailing from Greenland had been loaded with a more valuable cargo than the one he commanded.

8   Freydis returned to her farm and livestock, which had not suffered from her absence. She made sure all her companions were well rewarded, since she wished to have her misdeeds concealed. She stayed on her farm after that.

Not everyone was so close-mouthed that they could keep silent about these misdeeds or wickedness, and eventually word got out. In time it reached the ears of Leif, her brother, who thought the story a terrible one.

Leif then took three men from Freydis's company and forced them all under torture to tell the truth about the events, and their accounts agreed in every detail.

'I am not the one to deal my sister, Freydis, the punishment she deserves,' Leif said, 'but I predict that their descendants will not get on well in this world.' As things turned out, after that no one expected anything but evil from them.

To return to Karlsefni, he made his ship ready and set sail. They had a good passage and made land in Norway safely. He remained there over the winter, sold his goods, and both he and his wife were treated lavishly by the leading men in Norway. The following spring he made his ship ready to sail to Iceland.

When he was ready to sail and the ship lay at the landing stage awaiting a favourable wind, he was approached by a southerner, from Bremen in Saxony. He asked Karlsefni to sell him the carved decoration on the prow [*húsasnotra*]. 'I don't care to sell it,' he replied.

'I'll give you half a mark of gold for it,' the southerner said.

Karlsefni thought this a good offer and the purchase was concluded. The southerner then took the decoration [*húsasnotra*] and departed. Karlsefni did not know of what wood it was made, but it was of maple [*mösur*]. which had been brought from Vinland.

Karlsefni then put to sea and made land in north Iceland, in Skagafjord, where he had his ship drawn ashore for the winter. In the spring he purchased the land at Glaumbaer and established his farm there, where he lived for the remainder of his days. He was the most respected of men. He and his wife, Gudrid, had a great number of descendants, and a fine clan they were.

After Karlsefni's death Gudrid took over the running of the household, together with her son Snorri who had been born in Vinland.

When Snorri married, Gudrid travelled abroad, made a pilgrimage south and returned to her son Snorri's farm. By then he had had a church built at Glaumbaer. Later Gudrid became a nun and anchoress, staying there for the remainder of her life.

Snorri had a son named Thorgeir, who was the father of Yngveld, the mother of Bishop Brand. Snorri Karlsefnisson's daughter Hallfrid was the wife of Runolf, the father of Bishop Thorlak.

Bjorn, another son of Karlsefni and Gudrid, was the father of Thorunn, the mother of Bishop Bjorn.

There are a great number of people descended from Karlsefni, who founded a prosperous clan. It was Karlsefni who gave the most extensive reports of anyone of all of these voyages, some of which have now been set down in writing.

Translated by Keneva Kunz

SOURCES

Icelandic authors are listed in accord with Icelandic custom, alphabetically by first name. Other authors are listed alphabetically by surname.

Adam of Bremen. *History of the Archbishops of Bremen.* Quoted in G.M. Gathorne-Hardy *The Norse Discoverers of America.* 1921.

Agnar Ingolfsson. Personal communication.

Aiken, S.G. et al. 1988. *Wild Rice in Canada.* N. C. Press Limited. Toronto.

Alexanders saga mikla 1945. Heimskringla. Reykjavík.

Alfræði íslensk 1–3 1908–1918. Ed. K. Kålund and N. Beckman. Copenhagen.

Almanak fyrir Ísland 1996. Háskóli Íslands. Reykjavík.

Arbman, Holger 1961. *The Vikings.* London.

Ari Thorgilsson the Wise 1988. *Book of Icelanders.* In Gwyn Jones, *The Norse Atlantic Saga* 1964.

Arnthor Gardarsson. Personal communication.

Arrow-Odd 1970. Trans. Paul Edwards and Hermann Palsson. New York University Press. New York.

Attenborough, David 1995. *The Private Life of Plants.* Princeton University Press. Princeton.

Arni Björnsson 1990. Tímatal. *Íslensk þjóðmenning* VII. Ed. Frosti F. Jóhannsson. Þjóðsaga. Reykjavík.

Arni Bödvarsson 1963. *Íslenzk orðabók.* Bókaútgáfa Menningarsjóðs. Reykjavík.

Arni O.Thorlacius 1867. Extract from a letter. *Journal of the Scottish Meteorological Society.* Edinburgh.

Asgeir Blöndal Magnusson 1989. *Íslensk orðsifjabók.* Erfingjar Ásgeirs Blöndals Magnússonar og Orðabók Háskólans. Reykjavík.

Asgeir Svanbergsson. Personal communication.

Askell Löve 1951. The Plants of Wineland the Good. *The Icelandic Canadian.*

Babcock, William H. 1913. *Early Norse Visits to North America.* Smithsonian Institution. Washington D. C.

Berglund, Joel 1982. *Hvalsø – kirkeplads og stormandsgård.* Qaqortoq kommune. Qaqortoq.

Björn M. Olsen 1914. Um Stjörnu-Odda og Oddatölu. *Afmælisrit Fræðafjelagsins til dr. phil. Kr. Kålunds.* Copenhagen.

Björn Thorsteinsson 1966. *Ný Íslandssaga – þjóðveldisöld.* Heimskringla. Reykjavík.

Book of Icelanders. In Gwyn Jones, *The Norse Atlantic Saga* 1986.

Book of Settlements. In Gwyn Jones, *The Norse Atlantic Saga* 1986.

Brøgger, A. W. and Shetelig, Haakon 1971. *The Viking Ships, their ancestry and evolution.* Twayne Publishers. New York.

Canadian Climate Normals 1961–1990, 1993. Ottawa.

Champlain, Samuel de 1922. *The Works of Samuel Champlain.* Vol 1. Ed. H. P. Biggar et al. The Champlain Society. Toronto.

Cleasby, Richard and Gudbrandur Vigfusson 1975. *An Icelandic-English Dictionary.* Clarendon. Oxford.

Complete Sagas of Icelanders, 1997. Leifur Eiríksson. Reykjavík.

Crumlin-Pedersen, Ole and Olsen, Olaf 1967. The Skulderlev Ships. *Acta Archaeologica,* XXXVIII. Copenhagen.

Dammann, Werner 1996. *Das Gokstadschiff und seine Boote.* Arbeitskreis historischer Schiffbau e.v. Brilon Gudenhagen.

Denton, Daniel 1966. *A Brief Description of New York.* University Microfilms Inc.

Diplomatarium Islandicum (Íslenzkt Fornbréfasafn) XV 1947–50. Hið íslenzka bókmenntafélag. Reykjavík.

Einar Ingi Siggeirsson. Personal communication.

Encyclopaedia Americana 1986. Grolier Inc. Danbury, Conn.

Encyclopaedia Britannica 1964 and 1989. Encyclopaedia Britannica Inc.

Eysteinn G. Gislason. Personal communication.

Fernald, M. L. 1910. Notes on the Plants of Wineland the Good. Rhodora 12. Boston.

Fernald, M. L. et al.1950. *Gray's Manual of Botany.* American Book Company. New York.

Field, William O. 1975. *Mountain Glaciers of the Northern Hemisphere.* Hannover, N. Hampshire.

Finnur Jonsson 1915. Opdagelserne af og reiserne til Vinland. *Aarbog for Nordisk Oldkyndighed*. Copenhagen.

Fritzner, Johan 1883–1896. *Ordbog over det gamle norske sprog*. Universitetsforlaget. Oslo – Bergen – Tromsø. (4. udg. med rettelser og tillæg 1972).

Gathorne-Hardy, G. M. 1921. *The Norse Discoverers of America. The Wineland Sagas*. Clarendon. Oxford.

Grant, D. R. 1975. Recent Coastal Submergence of the Maritime Provinces. *Proceedings of the Nova Scotian Institute of Science 27*, Supplement 3. Nova Scotian Institute of Science. Halifax.

Gudmund Andresson 1949. *Persíus rímur og Bellerofontis rímur*. Ed. Jakob Benediktsson. Rímnafélagið. Reykjavík.

Gudmundur Olafsson. Personal communication.

Gunnar Marel Eggertsson. Personal communication.

Haasum, Sibylla 1974. Vikingatidens segling och navigation. Manuscript.

Halldor Hermannsson 1966. The Vinland Sagas. *Islandica* Vol. XXX. New York.

Halldor Laxness 1969. *Vínlandspúnktar*. Helgafell. Reykjavík.

Haraldur Agustsson. Personal communication.

Haraldur Olafsson. Personal communication.

Haraldur Sigurdsson 1971. *Kortasaga Íslands frá öndverðu til loka 16. aldar*. Bókaútgáfa Menningarsjóðs og Þjóðvinafélagsins. Reykjavík.

Haugen, Einar I. 1942. *Voyages to Vinland: the First American Saga*. Knopf. New York.

Hermann Palsson and Magnus Magnusson 1965. *The Vinland Sagas. The Norse Discovery of America*. Penguin Books. Harmondsworth.

Heyerdahl, Thor 1999. *Ingen Grenser*. J. M. Stenersens forlag A.S. Oslo.

Historia Norvegiæ 1950. Den eldste Noregs-historia. Norröne bokverk nr. 19. Oslo.

Hogarth, D. D. et al. 1994. Martin Frobisher's Northwest Venture 1576–1581. *Mines, Minerals, Metallurgy*. Canadian Museum of Civilization. Québec.

Hovgaard, William 1914. *The Voyages of the Norsemen to America*. The American-Scandinavian Foundation. New York.

Ingersoll L. K. (ed.) 1977. *The Grand Manan Historian.* The Grand Manan Historical Society. New Brunswick.

Ingstad, Anne-Stine 1985. *The Norse Discovery of America* Vol. One. Excavations of a Norse settlement at L'Anse aux Meadows, Newfoundland 1961–1968. Universitetsforlaget. Oslo.

Ingstad, Helge 1985. *The Norse Discovery of America.* Vol. Two. The historical background and the evidence of the Norse settlement discovered in Newfoundland. Universitetsforlaget. Oslo.

Ingstad, Helge 1969. *Westward to Vinland.* Cape. London.

Jansson, Sven B. F. 1945. *Sagorna om Vinland.* Wahlström & Widstrand. Stockholm.

Johnson, Hugh 1985. *The World Atlas of Wines.* Mitchell Beazley Ltd. London.

Jones, Gwyn 1986. *The Norse Atlantic Saga.* Oxford University Press. Oxford.

Jon Arnason 1739. *Dactylismus ecclesiasticus edur Fíngrarím.* Copenhagen.

Jon Arnason 1965. *Íslenskar þjóðsögur og ævintýri.* Þjóðsaga. Reykjavík.

Jon Johannesson 1956–1958. *Íslendinga saga* I–II. Almenna bókafélagið. Reykjavík.

Jon Johannesson 1956. Aldur Grænlendinga sögu. *Nordæla, Afmæliskveðja til Sigurðar Nordals.* Reykjavík.

Jon Sigmundsson from Einfætingsgil. Personal communication.

Jon Vidar Sigurdsson. Personal communication.

Jon Vidalin 1819. Mæling á ósum Ölfusár og kort eftir Jón Vídalín fyrrum sýslumann. Úr Rentukammerskjölum Isl. Journ. 13, nr. 691.

Jonas Jonasson 1961. *Íslenskir þjóðhættir.* Ísafoldarprentsmiðja. Reykjavík.

Jonas Kristjansson 1978. *Saga Íslands* III. Hið íslenska bókmenntafélag – Sögufélag. Reykjavík.

Kalm, P. 1764. *Reise nach dem nördlichen Amerika*, III.

King's Mirror, 1917. Trans. Laurence M. Larson. American-Scandinavian Foundation. New York.

Kleivan, Helge 1966. *The Eskimos of Northeast Labrador.* Norsk Polarinstitutt. Oslo.

Kristjan Eldjarn 1978. Fjöldagröfin í Brattahlíð. Frásögn af nýrri tilgátu Ólafs Halldórssonar. *Árbók hins íslenzka fornleifafélags* 1977. Reykjavík.

Kristjan Eldjarn 1968. Kumlatíðindi 1966–1967. *Árbók hins íslenzka fornleifafélags* 1967. Reykjavík.

Kristleifur Thorsteinsson of Husafell. Personal communication.

Larsson, Mats G. 1992. The Vinland Sagas and Nova Scotia: A Reappraisal of an Old Theory. In *Scandinavian Studies*, Vol. 64. No 5.

Laws of Early Iceland, Grágás 1980. Trans. Andrew Dennis, Peter Foote, Richard Perkins. University of Manitoba Press. Winnipeg.

Lescarbot, Marc 1911. *The History of New France*, Vol. 2. The Champlain Society. Toronto.

Ludvik Kristjansson 1982. *Íslenskir sjávarhættir* II. Bókaútgáfa Menningarsjóðs. Reykjavík.

MacCrimmon, H.R., and Barry L. Gots, 1979. World distribution of Atlantic salmon, *Salmo salar*. In *J. Fish. Res. Board Can.* 36.

Magnus Mar Larusson 1969. Hafís á fyrri öldum. *Hafísinn.* Almenna bókafélagið. Reykjavík.

Magnus Magnusson and Hermann Palsson 1965. *The Vinland Sagas. The Norse Discovery of America.* Penguin Books. Harmondsworth.

Magnus Stefansson. Personal communication.

Matthias Thordarson 1929. Vínlandsferðirnar. *Safn til sögu Íslands og íslenskra bókmennta* VI. Reykjavík.

Meldgaard, Jørgen 1977. Inuit-Nordbo prosjektet. Archaeological Investigations in the Western Settlement in Greenland. *Fra Nationalmuseets Arbejdsmark.* Copenhagen.

Mjöll Snæsdottir. Personal communication.

Morcken, Roald 1977. Veien mot nord. *Sjøfartshistorisk årbok.* Bergen.

Mowat, Farley 1966. *Westviking: The Ancient Norse in Greenland and N. America.* Secker & Warburg. London.

Müller-Wille, M. 1978. Das Schiffsgrab von der Ile de Groix (Bretagne). *In Das archäologishe Fundmaterial III der Ausgrabung Haithabu.* Karl Wachholz Verlag. Neumünster.

Nansen, Fridtjof 1911. *In Northern Mists. Arctic Exploration in Early Times.* Heinemann. London.

Newfoundland and Labrador Pilot 1978. Hydrographer of the Navy. England.

Norsk Landbruksordbok 1979. Band I. Det Norske Samlaget. Oslo.

Nova Scotia (South-east Coast) and Bay of Fundy Pilot 1971. Hydrographer of the Navy. England.

Nova Scotia Nature Map 1993.

Nowlan, Alden 1983. *Nine Micmac Legends*. Lancelot Press. Hantsport, Nova Scotia.

Næss, Almar 1954. *Hvor lå Vinland? En studie over solobservasjoner i de norrøne sagaer*. Dreyers Forlag. Oslo.

Olafur Halldorsson 1978. *Grænland í miðaldaritum*. Sögufélag. Reykjavík.

Olafur Halldorsson 1982. *Gripla* V. Stofnun Árna Magnússonar. Rit 23. Reykjavík.

Olafur Halldorsson 1985. Viðauki við 4. bindi Íslenskra fornrita. Hið íslenska fornritafélag. Reykjavík.

Oskar Ingimarsson. Personal communication.

Pall Bergthorsson 1987. Veðurfar á Íslandi. *Íslensk þjóðmenning* I. Ed. Frosti F. Johannsson. Þjóðsaga. Reykjavík.

Rafn, C. C. 1837. *Antiquitates Americanae*. Copenhagen.

Ramskou, Thorkild 1969. *Solstenen, primitiv navigation i Norden før kompasset*. Rhodos, Copenhagen.

Reman, Edward 1990. The Norse Discoveries and Explorations in America. Dorset Press. New York.

Rey, Louis 1974. *Grønland – Univers de Cristal*, Flammarion. Paris.

Rousseau, Camille 1974. *Géographie floristique du Québec-Labrador*. Les Presses de l'Université Laval. Québec.

Roussell, Aage 1936. Sandnes and the Neighbouring Farms. *Meddelelser om Grønland*, Vol. 88. Copenhagen.

Roy, Claude. Personal communication.

St. Lawrence Pilot 1969. Hydrographer of the Navy. England.

Schnall, Uwe 1975. *Navigation der Wikinger*. Gerhard Stalling Verlag. Oldenburg/Hamburg.

Schoolcraft, Henry R. 1851. *Historical and Statistical Information Respecting the History, Condition and Prospects of the Indian Tribes of the United States*. Philadelphia.

Scoggan, H. J. 1978–1979. *The Flora of Canada*. National Museum of Natural Science, National Museums of Canada.

Severin, Tim 1978. *The Brendan Voyage*. Hutchinson. London.

Sigfus Blöndal 1920–1924. *Islandsk-Dansk Ordbog*. Íslensk-danskur orðabókarsjóður. Reykjavík.

Sigfus Blöndal 1954. *Væringjasaga*. Ísafoldarprentsmiðja. Reykjavík.

Sigrun Stefansdottir. Personal communication.

Sigurdur Lindal, 1974. Ísland og umheimurinn. *Saga Íslands* I. Hið íslenska bókmenntafélag – Sögufélag. Reykjavík.

Sigurdur Nordal 1968. *Um íslenzkar fornsögur*. Trans. Árni Björnsson. Mál og menning. Reykjavík.

Skaare, Kolbjørn 1979. An Eleventh Century Norwegian Penny Found on the Coast of Maine. *The Norwegian Numismatic Journal*, No. 2. Oslo.

Snorri Sturluson 1991. *Heimskringla. A History of the Kings of Norway*. Trans. Lee M. Hollander. American-Scandinavian Foundation. University of Texas Press. Austin.

Snorri Sturluson 1995. *Edda*. Trans. Anthony Faulkes. Dent. Charles M. Tuttle. London.

Speck, Frank G. 1922. *Beothuk and Micmac*. Museum of American Indians, Heye Foundation. New York.

Speck, Frank G. 1940. *Penobscot Man: The Life and the History of a Forest Tribe in Maine*. Octagon Books. New York.

Stefan Adalsteinsson and Blumenberg, B. 1983. Possible Norse origin for two Northeastern United States cat populations. *Zeitschrift für Tierzuchtung und Zuchtungsbiologie*, Bd. 100.

Stefan Karlsson. Personal communication.

Storm, Gustav 1886. Om betydningen af Eyktarstaðr i Flatøbogens Beretning om Vinlandsreiserne. *Arkiv for Nordisk Filologi*, 3. Lund.

Storm, Gustav 1887. Studier over Vinlandsreiserne, Vinlands geografi og ethnografi. *Aarbøger for nordisk Oldkyndighet og Historie*, 2:2. Copenhagen.

Storm, Gustav 1888. *Islandske Annaler indtil 1578*. Kristiania.

Sturlunga saga 1970–74. Trans. Julia H. McGrew. Twayne Publishers. New York.

Thormodur Torfason 1715. *Historia Vinlandiae antiquae*. Copenhagen.

Thorsteinn Vilhjalmsson 1990. Raunvísindi á miðöldum. *Íslensk þjóðmenning* VII. Ed. Frosti F. Johannsson. Þjóðsaga. Reykjavík.

Thor Magnusson 1967. Bátkumlið í Vatnsdal í Patreksfirði. *Árbók hins íslenzka fornleifafélags* 1966. Reykjavík.

Thordur Tomasson. Personal communication.

Vahl, Bolatta M. Personal communication.

Vandal, Joseph O. 1986. *La culture de la vigne au Québec.*

Vikings: The North Atlantic Saga. Eds. William W. Fitzhugh and Elisabeth I. Ward. Smithsonian Insititution Press. Washington/London.

Wallace, Birgitta 1986. The L'Anse aux Meadows Site. In Gwyn Jones, *The Norse Atlantic Saga.* Oxford University Press. Oxford/New York.

Wallace, Birgitta 1991a. L'Anse aux Meadows. Gateway to Vinland. *Acta Archeologica*, Vol. 61 – 1990. Copenhagen.

Wallace, Birgitta 1991b. The Vikings in North America: Myth and Reality. *Social Approaches to Viking Studies.* Ed. Ross Samson. Cruithne Press. Glasgow.

Wallace, Birgitta 1993. L'Anse aux Meadows, the Western outpost. In *Viking Voyages to North America.* Ed. Birthe L. Clausen. Roskilde.

Westman, G. A. 1757. *Itinera priscorum Scandianorum in Americam.* Aboae.

Willoughby, C. C. New England Homes and Gardens. *American Anthropologist* N.S. Vol VIII.

Wilson, Ian 1991. *The Columbus Myth.* Simon & Schuster. New York.

Winther, Niels 1875. *Færøernes Oldtidshistorie.* Copenhagen.

Wood, John George 1868–1870. *Natural History of Man.* George Routledge & Sons. London.

World Weather Records 1965. U.S. Department of Commerce. Washington.

INDEX

Icelandic personal names are listed by first name in accord with Icelandic custom. Other personal names are listed by surname where applicable. Wineland (*Vínland*) is not listed since it occurs on almost every page of the book. Icelandic personal names and placenames that appear in simplified form in this book are also shown here in their authentic form.